D1228226

S-F 2

EDITORIAL DIRECTION: JEFF ROVIN

RESEARCH ASSOCIATE: DAVE SCHOW

S-F 2

A PICTORIAL HISTORY OF SCIENCE FICTION FILMS FROM "ROLLERBALL" TO "RETURN OF THE JEDI"

BY RICHARD MEYERS

CITADEL PRESS · SECAUCUS, N.J.

First Edition

Copyright © 1984 by Richard S. Meyers

All rights reserved. No part of this book may be
reproduced in any form, except by a newspaper or
magazine reviewer who wishes to quote brief passages in
connection with a review.

Published by Citadel Press
Published simultaneously in Canada by
Musson Book Company,
A division of General Publishing Co. Limited
Don Mills, Ontario

Designed By
Holly Johnson
At The Angelica
Design Group, Ltd.

Queries regarding rights and permissions should be
addressed to: Lyle Stuart, 120 Enterprise Avenue,
Secaucus, N.J. 07094

Manufactured in the United States of America.

Library of Congress Cataloging in Publication Data

Meyers, Richard.
   S-F 2: a pictorial history of science fiction from 1975
to the present.

   Sequel to: A pictorial history of science fiction films /
Jeff Rovin.

   1. Science fiction films—History and criticism.
I. Rovin, Jeff. Pictorial history of science fiction films.
II. Title.
PN1995.9.S26M49   1984   791.43'09'09356   83-20964
ISBN 0-8065-0875-2

PHOTO CREDITS

United Artists Corporation, 20th Century-Fox Film
Corporation, BBC-TV, British Lion Corporation, New
World Pictures, Paramount Pictures Corporation, PBR
Productions Inc., Warner Bors., Inc. Metro-Goldwyn-
Mayer Inc., CBS Television, Dino De Laurentiis
Corporation, Universal City Studios, Inc., American
International Pictures, The Zopix Company, Albert
Clarke, John Dark, Columbia Pictures Industries, Inc.,
Warner Communications, ITC Entertainment Inc., Walt
Disney Productions

Stills reproduced in this book are copyright by the
companies listed above. Accidentally omitted from
the list is Lucasfilm Ltd., which holds copyright to
all pictorial material from its films.

DEDICATED TO DICK SMITH

CONTENTS

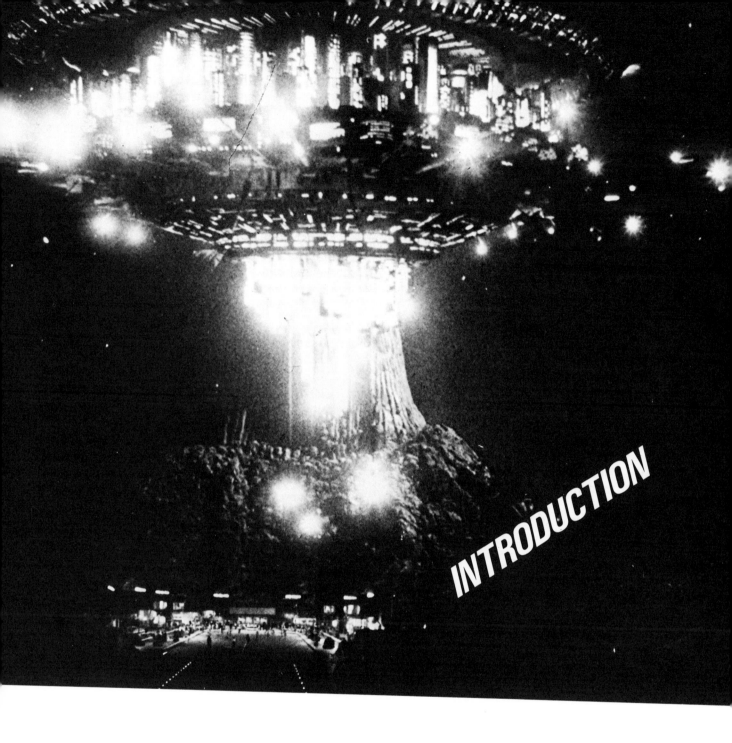

INTRODUCTION

"SCIENCE FICTION IS, at best, a very subjective label . . . . " This was the first sentence of Jeff Rovin's *A Pictorial History of Science Fiction Films,* published in 1975. Since that time, the term "science fiction" has become, at worst, fighting words. In both cinema and literature, the genre has become more popular and profitable than ever before. Science-fiction products have made more money in the last few years than in the many previous decades since the father of modern science fiction, Hugo Gernsback, first put pen to paper.

The question Jeff Rovin raised in his 1975 introduction is no clearer today. Just what is science fiction? He defined it as "any science-based event that has not occurred but conceivably could, given the technology of the period in which a film is set." This is valid, but in the relatively short span between then and now, the science-fiction film has become a phenomenon.

Filmmakers struggled to avoid the science-fiction label for years prior to 1975. Columbia studios even went so far as to label their 1970 effort *Marooned*—the story of a NASA craft lost in space—"historical drama." Today, some of these same producers struggle just as valiantly to slip their horror or fantasy films under the science-fiction banner.

Some things never change, however. Although we malign many films in the coming pages, we really love all science-fiction films; from the markedly absurd (like *Attack of the Killer Tomatoes*) to the technically inept (like *Damnation Alley*) to the awful (like *Quintet*) to the profound (like *Altered States*) to the spectacular (like *Star Wars*).

Science fiction still dazzles us with its beauty and challenges us with its ideas. Only now there is a lot more of it. The sheer volume of movies of this genre produced within the last decade rivals that of the seventy years preceding it. Because of that, filmmakers are pushed to the outer limits of creativity. Good science fiction demands the finest work the movie industry has to offer. The concepts have to be bolder and more interesting while the visuals have to be more realistic and incredible than the last blockbuster if the film is to succeed.

Dick Smith, to whom this work is dedicated, is one of the industry's great craftsmen, a man whose attention to detail, dedication, and creativity turns his technical screen work into art. He is the dean of special-effects makeup artists, a pioneer and pacesetter in an area that has burgeoned at the same time and at the same rate as the science-fiction film itself.

He not only gave life to *The Exorcist* and *Altered States;* he has been an unselfish mentor to the likes of Rick Baker (who built the 1976 *King Kong* ape and the *Star Wars'* cantina sequence aliens), Tom Savini (who made the *Creepshow* monsters), and many others. But it is he who is the undisputed master of the art and it is his work that continues to excell.

Further accolades are due to his contemporaries in the film business as well as to the many others who helped in the creation of this new volume of science-fiction film history. Special thanks are in order for Stuart Freeborn, Tim Moriarty, Mick Garris, Tom O'Neill, Alice Wolf, Brian Thomsen, William L. DeAndrea, and Allan Wilson—who waited patiently for it.

In both text and illustration, we have stressed the best the years since 1975 have had to offer. The lesser loved works have also found a place on these pages, but only in the length and detail each deserves.

BIG BUDGETS, CHALLENGING CONCEPTS

THE FIRST SIGNS that moviemakers were seeing science fiction in a new way came with *Rollerball,* producer/director Norman Jewison's futuristic sports thriller that was part 1984, part roller derby, but pure science fiction. After having helmed a series of successful comedies (*The Russians Are Coming, the Russians Are Coming,* 1966), crime dramas (*In the Heat of the Night,* 1967), and musicals (*Fiddler on the Roof,* 1971), Jewison decided to mount a multi-million-dollar first class science-fiction effort, adapted from William Harrison's short story "The Rollerball Murders" by the original author.

Harrison's screenplay spotlighted "Jonathan E." as enacted by James Caan—the greatest player of the violent sport called rollerball. In Harrison's world of the unspecified future, corporations had replaced nations. Their main credo was that life was a team effort; individuals counted for nothing.

11

When Jonathan started to excel in his game, however, the bosses saw their rule begin to erode in the face of the fans' overwhelming love of their hero.

Their solution pits Jonathan against Mister Bartholomew, a soft-spoken but morally vacuous high-ranking official played by John Houseman, whose orders are to make the sport's star quit rollerball at any cost. When Jonathan refuses to retire, the executives start to eliminate what few rules rollerball has left, turning the circular arena into a bloody battlefield.

The film climaxes with a final game where there are no regulations between the leather-clad players and death. The men and motorcycles, with which the game is fought, are left mangled and burning until only one is standing. To Bartholomew's chagrin, it is Jonathan E. who slams the winning rollerball (a bright silver orb the size of a duckpin bowling ball) into the goal while the frenzied crowd chants his name.

Although simplistic and obvious, *Rollerball* was a fine filmmaking achievement, filled with stunning action sequences and striking images, such as the party scene in which beautifully dressed guests giddily use a "bomb pistol" to blow up trees. Rather than continue making "safe," more accessible pictures, the established Jewison decided to make this bolder, more daring statement through the science-fiction genre.

Hollywood was not the only place high-powered filmmakers used science fiction to gain audiences' attention. In England, producer, writer, and direc-

In the future, there will be no war or roller derby or boxing . . . but there will be Rollerball.

Director Norman Jewison (right) prepares the stunt troops for their next bout of *Rollerball*.

wondrous world like Alice in Wonderland, Zed discovers the truth—Zardoz is nothing more than a recreation of *The Wizard of Oz*, yet another sick joke played on the Brutals by the Eternals (not to mention the director on the audience).

In return, Zed brings the Brutals into the Vortex and death to the Eternals, who expire with rapturous gratitude. Viewers were less grateful, but the film still stands alone as a delirious, unique science-fiction satire—an overwhelming exercise in imaginary excess.

FAMOUS S-F AUTHOR ADAPTATIONS

Several less expensive movies turned out to be more successful in getting across their thought-provoking ideas. Foremost of these was *A Boy and His Dog*, one of the few adaptations from the work of multiple-award-winning author Harlan Ellison. The screenwriter and director was long-time character actor L.Q. Jones. The producer was

tor John Boorman was frustrated in his attempts to adapt J.R.R. Tolkien's three-volume *Lord of the Rings* trilogy into a workable live-action screenplay, so he created *Zardoz* instead.

Although almost completely undecipherable at face value, *Zardoz* could be enjoyed on the level of a bombastic, overproduced in-joke. This was the moviemaker's response after nearly being overwhelmed by science-fiction and fantasy concepts. Instead of succumbing, Boorman fashioned these already established ideas into a pun-riddled, irony-filled quest of socio-psychedelic craziness.

Sean Connery, in his first role since leaving the starmaking part of James Bond behind, played Zed the Exterminator, one of the race of "Brutals" kept in line on one side of a force field in the year 2293. On the other side of the force field are the "Eternals," who are bored silly by their bland, immortal lives. To force the Brutals to do their bidding, the Eternals created a god named Zardoz, who appears to his worshippers in the guise of a gigantic floating head that is half human and half lion.

Zed takes time out from his usual lifestyle of raping and killing to stowaway in the head which takes him through the force field and into the strange land of the Vortex, where the Eternals live hoping to rediscover the secret of death so they can end their dull lives. Journeying through this

The giant floating head of *Zardoz* stuns the worshipping "Brutals."

13

TV sitcom veteran Alvy Moore. The star was young Don Johnson, playing the "Boy" of the title.

The "Dog" was another TV sitcom vet—*The Brady Bunch*'s pet pooch "Tiger," who was renamed "Blood" for this effort, then given telepathic powers and the off-screen voice of Tim McIntire. The land they lived in was *Zardoz*-like, roughly divided into the desolate, violent, bleak, and nearly womanless surface world of post-World War III America in the year 2024 and the strange, impotent, mannered, inner world created underground.

Like the Brutals of *Zardoz*, the surface dwellers spend most of their time stalking, raping and killing. Only the teenage boy, Vic, is shown the entrance to the underground paradise of "Topeka" (named and modeled after the quaint town in Kansas) by what turns out to be a well-rounded piece of bait—female bait that goes by the name of Quilla June Holmes (played by Suzanne Benton) whose duty it is to lure a strong young stud from the surface world to impregnate all the girls underground.

Vic knows nothing of this as he protects his beauteous companion from the worst the radiation-scarred surface population has to offer. Leaving a wounded Blood behind, he follows Quilla to Topeka, only to be tied down to a "milking machine." His dream of romancing hundreds of women is dashed by callous technology. He escapes this fate and returns to the surface with Quilla in tow. Only she makes the mistake of demanding he choose between her and the dog. The film ends with a boy and his dog walking into the sunrise after having a life-renewing meal of the spoiled, conniving female.

While certain not to send women's liberation members into paroxyms of applause, the film remains the most successful cinematic translation of Harlan Ellison's audacious work to date—a feat trumpeted by the author himself as well as many critics.

Equally audacious is the work of English writer Michael Moorcock, and equally ambitious was the independent, relatively inexpensive translation of his wild superhero science-fiction novel, *The Final Programme*. Although made originally in 1974 by screenwriter and director Robert Fuest, it wasn't until 1975 that it reached American shores in a

Don Johnson plays the Boy in *A Boy and His Dog*.

Beneath the bleak surface world of *A Boy and His Dog* is the underground village of "Topeka," lorded over by Jason Robards (right).

truncated version titled *The Last Days of Man on Earth*.

Jon Finch starred as Jerry Cornelius, a decadent British hipster of the somewhat recognizable near future who continually pops drugs and lusts after his own sister. Transferring Moorcock's complex and challenging prose into visual terms is nearly impossible and the film shows the strain. Although inventive in both style and content, it is quite difficult for anyone but a Cornelius fan to fully contemplate.

As near as can be understood, Jerry's insane, drug-addicted brother takes control of their rich estate after the head of the Cornelius clan dies, holding the beloved sister captive. Jerry agrees to take part in some scientists' plan to create the next step in evolution if they help him rid the planet of his sibling. They do, but both the brother and sister die in the process.

Even so, the experiment goes on. Draining the combined intelligence of a few brilliant brains kept in liquid-filled tanks, Jerry mates with "Miss Brunner" (Jenny Runacre), a female "of impeccable standards." The result of their union is a hunchbacked genius with a Humphrey Bogart voice who can walk on water. As it shuffles off into the distance, *The Last Days of Man on Earth* comes to a close.

Fuest, who had previously been best known for two horror satires featuring "Dr. Phibes" as played by Vincent Price, had staked much of his talent on the Jerry Cornelius film, a fact which is evident upon viewing. But also apparent is the abortive editing the movie received at the hands of its American distributor, New World Pictures, shortening its length by more than ten minutes and muddling its effect almost irredeemably.

Another English effort which suffered as a result of spotty American distribution was *Who?*, which should not be confused with the British television adventures of *Dr. Who*—the tales of an eccentric, do-gooding "Time Lord" who spans eras and galaxies to fight evil wherever he finds it. Instead, *Who?* was a futuristic espionage thriller directed by Jack Gold.

Tom Baker plays the fourth *Dr. Who*, a heroic "Time Lord" who fights evil in any era, any dimension, and any planet.

15

Mary Woronov, playing "Maltilda the Hun," fights off attackers during the *Death Race 2000.*

Based on Algis Budry's second novel, it concerned the quest of FBI agent Robers (Elliott Gould) to verify the identity of scientist Martino (Joseph Bova) after the latter is changed into a cyborg (half-man, half-robot). The agent's predicament is compounded by the fact that Martino's face is housed in an eccentric metal mask, obscuring most of his features. German doctors had done this to save Martino's life after a brutal car crash.

As the scientist struggles to understand what the well-meaning surgeons had done to him, Robers must contend with the sinister machinations of enemy agent Azarin (Trevor Howard), who hopes to turn the heat up on the cold war. Part spy saga, part psychological study, *Who?* was a little of both and not enough of either. Still, it tried to be an intelligent, cerebral science-fiction movie, rather than the mindless "monster on the loose" or "ray gun fight" kind of film most audiences were used to.

Ranked with the likes of H.G. Wells and Jules Verne as science-fiction literary pioneers is Edgar Rice Burroughs. For years, his estate has been fighting off attempts to do cheap, inaccurate versions of his work—a canon that includes Tarzan and John Carter of Mars.

It is with some curiosity, then, that fans watched *The Land That Time Forgot,* the first Burroughs adaptation by British producer John Dark. Although the script was by the aforementioned Michael Moorcock along with James Cawthorn, the budget was somewhat limited, forcing director Kevin Connor to use inarticulate full-scale monster models in the story of World War I soldiers discovering a lost prehistoric world.

Doug McClure starred as one such early twentieth-century adventurer forced to fight stiff rubber dinosaurs after stumbling upon "Caprona," where men mature to full development in a week's time. McClure survives a climactic volcano eruption in the company of Susan Penhaligon, and the two hunker down for a life together (not to mention a sequel) while their enemies are buried in lava.

16

CORMAN'S CONTRIBUTIONS

Death Race 2000 managed to be both the kind of film action fans expected as well as a thought-provoking, consummately entertaining science-fiction oddity. Roger Corman, then head of New World Pictures—the same folks who chopped down *The Last Days of Man on Earth*—conceived of a future sports car race in which the object was to run down as many pedestrians as possible.

He handed the scripting chores to Robert Thom and Ib Melchoir (the latter also co-wrote and directed *The Angry Red Planet,* 1960, and *The Time Travelers,* 1964), who in turn handed a ultra-violent screenplay over to director Paul Bartel. The director's specialty was black humor, evidenced by his first feature, *Private Parts* (1972), a weird psycho-sexual adventure. To make *Death Race* more to his liking, Bartel asked Charles Griffith, who had penned three previous monster-movie satires, to do a rewrite.

Upon viewing the finished, humor-filled movie, producer Corman sent out another filming unit to shoot more violent sequences. It was a cunning combination of both Bartel's and Corman's versions that audiences finally viewed. What they saw was the overpopulated, totalitarianistic America of the near future, where the most popular sport was not rollerball, but the Death Race, in which homocidal maniacs mashed as many innocent bystanders as possible to win a year of wealth and privacy.

The leader of the pack was "Frankenstein" (David Carradine), a leather-masked, caped winner whose main competition was played by Sylvester Stallone. Frankenstein was supposed to be stitched together from the parts of the people he mashed, but that is shown to be a publicity stunt as he reveals an unscarred visage to his love and co-driver (Simone Griffeth). Frankenstein survives the grueling battle and the assassination attempts of anti-Death Race rebels, only to take over the country himself.

Exploitation lovers and serious science-fiction enthusiasts alike enjoyed *Death Race 2000's* outlandish concepts and comic-book-like style, making it a money-making cult classic.

The same cannot be said of *Tidal Wave,* another New World curiosity of the same year. Although Roger Corman had distributed such other high quality works of such foreign directors as François Truffaut, Ingmar Bergman, and Federico Fellini without a single change, he did not have the same respect for a monumental oriental special-effects epic called *Submersion of Japan.*

Originally released in 1973 and lasting two hours and twenty minutes, this became one of Japan's highest grossing and most popular films. *Submersion of Japan* was just that: the spectacular and engrossing story of a nation facing an all-too-possible natural disaster—a country-drowning "tsunami" (tidal wave) and flood. Instead of taking a chance by distributing the original sub-titled version throughout America, Corman decided to *"Godzilla-*ize" the feature—that is, recut, redub, and refilm the movie to incorporate a simpler story and American actors. Somewhere around twenty minutes was excized from *Godzilla* so that Raymond Burr, as reporter Steve Martin, could detail the destruction in occidental terms. A full hour was cut from *Submersion* so that Lorne Green, as a United Nations delegate, could show his fellow UN members the watery deluge.

The film was a disaster in more ways than one. It was a box-office failure that was meant to

Japan is leveled by a plethora of natural disasters, the greatest of which will be a *Tidalwave.*

emulate the success of the "disaster film"—the genre crowned by the 1974 Irwin Allen production of *The Towering Inferno*. Although it seemed as if Corman was anxious to ride the coattails of that fiery multi-million-dollar blockbuster, he only succeeded in watering down one of the best foreign science-fiction efforts ever made.

ANTS, WIVES, BABIES AND SUPERHEROES

There was only one other genre film with delusions of grandeur this year. That was Saul Bass's *Phase IV,* an audacious attempt if there ever was one. Bass, best known for his design work and the creation of award-winning short subjects (*Why Man Creates,* 1968), bit off a bit more than the audience could chew with this cosmic tale of man against nature.

The man in this case is obsessed scientist Hobbs (Nigel Davenport). He is obsessed, unfortunately, with the study and ultimate defeat of ants that have been given superhuman intelligence by an unexplained cosmic phenomenon. The ants are dedicated to the takeover of the planet in an unusual way. Instead of "stepping on" humanity much in the same way we've been tromping on them all these years, they desire to "absorb" humans.

Hobbs dies, but his partner, played by Michael Murphy, discovers the truth as he endeavors to find and kill the ant queen. He sees the beautiful girl he had saved from an ant attack (Lynne Frederick) being resurrected in a huge golden ant hill. It is these two who survive to face the rising sun as the insects continue their takeover.

Although the film is unusual, Bass is nothing if not a master stylist, and his adaptation of Mayo

Nigel Davenport (left) is certain that he and fellow scientist Michael Murphy can defeat an army of intelligent ants during *Phase IV.*

Simon's script is visually dazzling—aided enormously by Ken Middleham's wonderful "microphotography" of the insect hordes. A strange but wondrous film, it is remembered by the too few who saw it.

The Stepford Wives was best forgotten by the many who saw it. The filmmakers were probably hoping for the same kind of cinematic success that graced author Ira Levin's earlier screen adaptations of his novels. Nineteen fifty-six saw the film version of his mystery *A Kiss Before Dying* released. Nineteen sixty-eight saw the premiere of the magnificent movie version of his best book, *Rosemary's Baby.* Sadly, *The Stepford Wives* was not in that class. Nowhere near it, in fact.

At best, the novel was a lightweight women's liberation nightmare and male chauvinist fantasy. At best, the film adaptation was a moody, well-made exploitation of a woman's pain. That woman was played by Katherine Ross, who moves with her husband to the fancy suburb of Stepford, where all the husbands hide a murderous secret.

These men feel threatened by women's lib but can't live without their wives, so with the help of an engineer who used to work at Disneyland they build robot replications of their spouses whose first duty is to kill the original. Although a workable concept, director Bryan Forbes and writer William Goldman make it nothing more than a bleak, almost hopeless picture of the Ross character's last days.

The movie is totally taken up with revealing Stepford's secret instead of mounting a fight between the independent, feisty heroine and her egomaniacal enemies. It's possible that the filmmakers hoped that the last, frightening few minutes of the film would save the day. But even though the last two sequences are memorable, they do not fill up the picture's hollow core.

Still, the image of an exhausted, rain-soaked Ross facing her negligéed robot double (played by Ross with lustrous black, pupilless contact lenses and extraordinarily realistic "flesh additions" to her figure by makeup man Dick Smith), who rises with a knotted scarf in her fists to do the woman in, and the final sequence of "The Stepford Wives" doing a slow-motion subservient shopping "ballet" in a supermarket are hard to criticize.

Stepford produced the monster wives, but director/writer/producer Larry Cohen came up with

Lynne Frederick rises from a giant ant-hill during the climax of *Phase IV*.

a monster baby—the real star of *It's Alive*. This kid was more than just a tiny terror who would whine and bawl all the time. This tot had huge fangs and claws and could crawl faster than his dad could run. His father was Frank Davis (John Ryan), whose wife, Lenore (Sharon Farrell), made the mistake of taking an ill-tested pregnancy pill. This medicine turned the Davis's second child into a baby beast who paid the delivering doctor's slap back by decimating the delivery room.

While the distraught family must fend off callous reporters and the desperate pill-makers who are eager for a cover-up, the killer baby makes its way home, wiping out an occasional cop, bystander and milkman in the process. The nearly insane mother welcomes its return while the Davis's first son nearly succeeds in understanding and soothing his bestial little brother. But Frank, unable to accept his part in the monster's creation, swears to kill it personally.

He chases it from his home to a school and finally corners it in the Los Angeles sewers. Only

Something strange is happening in the town of Stepford.
Where the men spend their nights doing something secret.
And every woman acts like every man's dream of the "perfect" wife.
Where a young woman watches the dream become a nightmare.
And sees the nightmare engulf her best friend.
And realizes that any moment, any second— her turn is coming.

THE STEPFORD WIVES

A very modern suspense story from the author of *Rosemary's Baby*.

COLUMBIA PICTURES and PALOMAR PICTURES INTERNATIONAL Presents THE STEPFORD WIVES.
KATHARINE ROSS, PAULA PRENTISS, PETER MASTERSON, NANETTE NEWMAN, TINA LOUISE, CAROL ROSSEN and
PATRICK O'NEAL as Dale Coba. Based on the book by IRA LEVIN. Screenplay by WILLIAM GOLDMAN.
Music Composed and Conducted by MICHAEL SMALL. Executive Producer GUSTAVE BERNE. Produced by EDGAR J. SCHERICK.
Directed by BRYAN FORBES. A Fadsin Cinema Associates Production. **PG** PARENTAL GUIDANCE SUGGESTED

Doc Savage (center) listens intently to his "Fabulous Five." From the left: Darrel Zwerling as Ham, Mike Minor as Monk, Eldon Quick as Johnny, Paul Gleason as Long Tom, and William Lucking as Renny.

then does he realize that the baby is as frightened as he is and only killed in confusion. He is able to gather the child up but is surrounded by police egged on by a hysterical representative from the pharmaceutical company. Seeing his no-win situation, Frank hurls the mewling monster onto the pill exec, who is killed along with the kid.

It's Alive ends with the police report that another monstrous offspring was sired in Seattle. Director Cohen got a lot of mileage out of his small budget as well as the monster baby doll built by Rick Baker. Although the makeup man wasn't given enough money to make anything but a non-articulated replica, he got on his back in the

muddy sewers to manipulate the doll to look active for the film's climax. His dedication paid off. The film was more than the average horror melodrama, thanks to Cohen's interesting concept and sensitive approach.

The Ultimate Warrior had a workable concept, but a stolid approach. It was actually little more than a science-fiction excuse for meaningless and not even particularly exciting fights. Ever since directing *Enter the Dragon* in 1973, Robert Clouse has been trying to hit the same pay dirt again. This time, he uses the science-fiction genre to kill as many people as possible.

According to his script, it is the year 2012. The

place is a plague-infested Manhattan after nuclear Armageddon. The basic idea is quirky enough to gain positive attention: The mission of the good guys is to get a packet of non-infected seeds to a radiation- and illness-free island off North Carolina. The trip will take them through the subways and sewers. Along for the ride is a pregnant woman played by Joanna Miles.

Obstructing the way are a bunch of fetid, greasy, longhaired scumbuckets, led by William Smith, one of the great screen villains of recent movie history. The good guys are represented by Swedish actor Max Von Sydow, who makes more money by appearing in these American films but has a better reputation from his work with Ingmar Bergman. The hero is represented by Yul Brynner, playing a hairless, and mostly shirtless, fighting machine.

Brynner is no Bruce Lee, however, and the whole enterprise lacks snap and conviction. Brynner's mysterious presence and unbeatable skill is never explained, or even realistically depicted. Since the film is little more than one fight after another, and each fight seems duller than the last, *The Ultimate Warrior* collapses under the weight of its own pretentions.

Finally, there is the year's biggest disappointment. When the news first got out that legendary filmmaker George Pal was going to produce a film based on the pulp hero *Doc Savage,* the reaction was instantaneous and exultant. Neither person needed much introduction to fantasy fans.

Pal had a string of marvelous science-fiction movies to his credit as either director, producer, or both. Among them were *When Worlds Collide* (1951), *War of the Worlds* (1953), *The Time Machine* (1960), and *The Power* (1968). Doc Savage was created by Lester Dent as a suprahuman adventurer who fought evil all over the world in the company of his "Fabulous Five." They were Monk (an ape-like biologist with a pet pig), Ham (a slick lawyer with a sword-cane), Renny (a muscle-bound engineer), Johnny (a bespectacled archeologist), and Long Tom (a lovably absent-minded electrician).

It was Pal's choice, along with co-scripter Joe Morhaim, to keep Doc and company back in the forties. They used Dent's original story as inspiration to write the screenplay for *Doc Savage: The Man of Bronze.* This was also the name of Doc's first pulp magazine thriller, which rolled off the

Ron Ely makes a magnificent *Doc Savage: The Man of Bronze.*

presses in 1933, followed by an incredible 181 more that appeared in succession once a month for sixteen years. Although the last magazine story (*Up from Earth's Center*) was printed in 1949, the series was given new life in Bantam paperback versions that have not been completely out of print since 1964.

It was the covers of these books, painted by James Bama, that solidified Savage's appearance as a bronze-skinned, golden-haired, torn-shirted star. With this image (and a new, more realistic painting by James Steranko) in mind, George Pal started the search for the man to play the courageous character. The hunt was over with the signing of Ron Ely, the actor who had portrayed the television *Tarzan* from 1966 to 1969.

Ely was picture perfect: blond, six foot four, and highly athletic, he seemed born to play this role. Sadly, the rest of the movie's creative choices were not as solid as its star. The premise was promising—investigating the death of his father, Doc discovers a murderous Mayan sect, who can unleash the supernatural "Green Death," and the villainous Captain Seas, who seeks to control the Indians as well as their lake of molten gold. Doc avenges his dad's demise by Green Death and defeats Seas in a long battle that incorporates a number of international fighting techniques.

The opening sequence of an assassination attempt on Doc at his Empire State Building headquarters is exciting and stylish, full of mood and detail. A mid-film brawl aboard Captain Seas's yacht (reportedly directed by Ely himself) is truly wonderful. Otherwise the film is crippled by poor direction. Michael Anderson, known for some good work in the sixties, helmed this with amazing mediocrity, settling for boring visualizations at almost all times.

The editing, framing, scene composition and pacing were surprisingly static. The screenplay held some deft touches, but the plot was presented in a piecemeal fashion, with eccentric and confusing things occurring for no discernable reason. Finally, the movie's death knell was sounded by its campy approach and soundtrack. Scorer Frank DeVol adapted John Philip Sousa marches for the film's highpoints, making for an annoying, cloying effect.

Warner Communications, its distributor, reacted to the finished film badly, all but exiling it to a limited, erratic release in only a few parts of the country. Then the movie was yanked from theaters and used as a tax write-off. It was an ignominious fate for a character who predated and inspired the creation of Superman.

Fate continued to hamstring Savage and George Pal. Hopes for a television series were dashed again and again, until Pal's untimely death in 1981. Even so, there are still those who believe in *Doc Savage: Man of Bronze* and the proposed sequel, *Doc Savage: Archenemy of Evil,* which was announced at the end of the first movie and scripted by award-winning science-fiction writer Philip José Farmer.

These people have banded together under the banner of the "Save Savage Society." Their greatest desire is to release a recut, rescored version of *The Man of Bronze.* They continue to petition Warner Communications and can be reached through the offices of Ion International, 32 Oak Ridge Road, Bethel, CT 06801. As one of the book characters said: "Doc helped us in our hour of need. It's time we returned the favor."

2
1976
THE YEAR OF
DASHED DREAMS

TWO BIG BOMBS

ANTICIPATION WAS ALMOST a palatable thing this year. Plans and hopes ran high for a science-fiction breakthrough. There were two projects announced months in advance of production which gave fans good reason to rejoice. Sadly, the finished products were uniformly dreadful.

Logan's Run was nearly everything a science-fiction movie shouldn't be. Its ideas and concepts were misguided, illogical, ill-conceived, badly presented, and often dumb—not to mention down-right wrong in one glaring case. In retrospect, it is not surprising the film failed, since the book upon which it was based was little more than a cunning exploitation.

In the summer of 1965, George Clayton Johnson and William F. Nolan collaborated on their first novel, which was a patchwork quilt of conceptions collected since the beginning of their careers. Since they decided it would be done only for the money, the writing process took less than three weeks. Afterward, the two would disagree on its worth. Johnson felt more than half the work didn't hold water. Nolan felt he had written one of the best science-fiction books ever, using its monetary worth as evidence.

The book *Logan's Run* was fast moving and consistently interesting, picturing a future Earth in the aftermath of a "Youth War" in which citizens are put to death in a ritual called "Last-

Michael York and Jenny Agutter listen in amazement to the ravings of the psychotic sculpting robot named "Box" (Roscoe Lee Browne) during *Logan's Run*.

job on *Doc Savage*, was hired to direct. Michael York, who was looking for a major American production to star in after his European success, found this. Jenny Agutter took the female lead as a means of reestablishing herself after having starred in a drama called *Walkabout* (1971) at the age of sixteen.

Richard Jordan played a fellow sandman who started as Logan's friend, then degenerated into a sworn enemy. Peter Ustinov played the world's last old man, senilely puttering around the weed-covered, crumbling buildings of Washington D.C. As an example of corporate thinking, Farrah Fawcett-Majors was quickly signed on in the minor role of a beauty parlor assistant, complete with co-starring billing and heaps of publicity (curious-

day" on their twenty-first birthday. Those refusing to die easily are set upon by a police force known as "sandmen." One such sandman, Logan, tries to make a run for it just before his execution, discovering a fascinating and dangerous world outside the city walls.

Dial Books printed the hardcover and Bantam the paperback. Metro-Goldwyn-Mayer bought the screen rights. Both George Pal and Irwin Allen tried mounting the actual production. By the time Saul David actually got the ball rolling, Johnson and Nolan had parlayed their twenty-day writing investment into eight hundred thousand dollars. With such a hefty price tag, MGM decided the film version should have first-class production values.

While a direct cinematic translation of the book might not have been challenging to viewers, it would not have been boring. Instead, producer David decided to ignore the scripts that had already been finished and ordered a new, "streamlined" version done by David Zelag Goodman. The result was a homogenized telling of the story which destroyed much of the novel's detail and mood. The execution age was upped to thirty and the characters were rendered ridiculously stolid. The script eliminated everything but the book's skeleton, then replaced the skin with astroturf.

Michael Anderson, who had done such a bad

WELCOME TO THE 23RD CENTURY.
The only thing you can't have in this perfect world of total pleasure is your 30th birthday.

LOGAN'S RUN

Logan is 29.

METRO-GOLDWYN-MAYER presents A SAUL DAVID PRODUCTION "LOGAN'S RUN" starring MICHAEL YORK · JENNY AGUTTER · RICHARD JORDAN · ROSCOE LEE BROWNE FARRAH FAWCETT-MAJORS & PETER USTINOV · Screenplay by DAVID ZELAG GOODMAN Based on the novel "LOGAN'S RUN" by WILLIAM F. NOLAN and GEORGE CLAYTON JOHNSON Produced by SAUL DAVID · Directed by MICHAEL ANDERSON ORIGINAL MOTION PICTURE SOUNDTRACK ALBUM AVAILABLE ON MGM RECORDS AND TAPES Filmed in TODD-AO and METROCOLOR NOW A BANTAM BOOK! PG PARENTAL GUIDANCE SUGGESTED SOME MATERIAL MAY NOT BE SUITABLE FOR PRE-TEENAGERS MGM Released thru United Artists A Transamerica Company

ly enough, the beauty parlor boss was played by Michael Anderson, Jr., the director's son).

With cast collected, the production crew set about weakening what good points the story had—creating plot changes and gracing the story with illogical and irrelevant concepts. The most ridiculous came at the end. After Logan had escaped the domed city, discovered the outside world, realized that people could grow old, and killed his best friend, he is recaptured and brought before the ruling computer which runs the entire society.

The machine demands to know the location of Sanctuary, the haven for over-thirty-year-old renegades, so it can be destroyed. When Logan replies that there is no Sanctuary and refuses to cooperate, the computer blows up. Because Logan dared to be disobedient, the machine simply ex-

The *Logan's Run* movie set the stage for a *Logan's Run* television series starring Gregory Harrison as Logan. Here, Heather Menzies, playing "Jessica," is about to undergo computerized probing.

The world of *Logan's Run* is destroyed by a crazy computer.

plodes, taking the rest of the city with it. The film finales with illogical abandon as miniskirted girls and tights-wearing men scurry through shopping mall sets while the obvious miniature scale model of the city is burned down by the special-effects crew.

This was an astonishingly poor movie, especially for the studio which had presented such intelligent science-fiction epics as *Forbidden Planet* (1956) and *2001: A Space Odyssey* (1968), but seemed to learn nothing from them. *Logan's Run* is a perfect example of the kind of thinking that says all the genre's fans want is pretty pictures and dumb special effects.

While on the subject of dumb, Dino De Laurentiis's modern version of *King Kong* must be mentioned. The thinking here seemed to be that money alone could solve any problem. But cash could not replace time or creative thought, two ingredients that were tragically lacking in this mercenary production.

De Laurentiis reportedly decided to remake the 1933 monster movie classic after seeing a poster of the original on his daughter's wall. This decision was trumpeted by a full page ad in December 1975 that pictured a giant ape straddling the two World Trade Center towers in New York, with a girl in one hand and a jet plane in the other. The advertisement promised that the new *King Kong* movie would premiere one year from that time.

The decision also led to a monumental legal battle with Universal Studios, who planned to do a period remake of their own (*The Legend of King Kong*, written by Bo Goldman and directed by Joseph Sargent). Money did win the day there, mostly because the producer promised to cut Universal in on his *Kong* profits and his twenty-five-million-dollar budget far exceeded what Universal planned to spend. Universal shelved its project. Unfortunately, what De Laurentiis should have been trying to buy was time.

The actual nine-month production was surrounded by misleading and sometimes inaccurate publicity and fraught with the mistakes haste causes. Director John Guillerman struggled to

Rick Baker was also inside the King Kong suit.

The new *King Kong*, courtesy of special effects artists Carlo Rimbaldi, Glen Robinson and Rick Baker.

make the movie as fine as possible, but was continually hamstrung by his harried schedule. He had a cast of fine actors: Jeff Bridges as the bearded, ecology-minded zoologist who finds Kong in the wild, Charles Grodin as the corrupt oil company businessman who decides to drag Kong back to civilization, and Jessica Lange (the winner of a much ballyhooed talent search) as the girl of the ape's dreams.

What director Guillerman didn't have was a great script. Lorenzo Semple, Jr., had fashioned a ludicrously relevant screenplay that concentrated on misplaced women's liberation and gorilla jokes (when captured by Kong, Lange had to say things like "Put me down, you male chauvinist ape!" and "What's your sign?"). Otherwise, the story structure was much the same as the classic original, only without the care, love and excitement lavished on it by directors Merian Cooper, Ernest Schoedsack, and Willis O'Brien.

Another area in which the new version faltered

was in the special-effects department. Eschewing the model animation of the original, De Laurentiis made much of the full-size, forty-foot-high hydraulic robot being built by fellow Italian Carlo Rimbaldi, even going so far as saying that this automaton was used throughout the picture—a lie he repeated several times, culminating in an incredible performance on the nationally televised *Tomorrow* television show.

In fact, the robot was used for less than five minutes in the finished film. It didn't look anything at all like the ape suit used in 99 percent of the film—made and occupied by Rick Baker with acting assistance by William Shepard. Baker was given one assistant and two weeks to make the ape suit while De Laurentiis continued his deceptions. Although Baker did the lion's share of the work,

the screen credit reads: "The Producer wishes to acknowledge that Kong has been designed and engineered by Carlo Rimbaldi and Glen Robinson with special contributions by Rick Baker."

The finished film was disappointing in almost every respect. Although two gigantic hydraulic arms were cleverly constructed, the special-effects techniques used to make them appear attached to Baker's six-foot ape suit were often sloppy, resulting in arms that were a different color than the rest of the body. In the end, Kong never straddled the World Trade Center towers, nor did he swat jet fighters out of mid-air. Instead, he leaped from one tower to the other (at the beginning of the jump, Lange was in his hand; at the end of the jump, she was on his back) and was gunned down by helicopters.

The tragic end of the 1976 *King Kong*, at the base of Manhattan's World Trade Towers.

R

David Bowie in Nicolas Roeg's film
The man who fell to Earth

Even then, the travesty was not ended. Although the special-effects people who voted for the Academy Awards in that category decided to award *Logan's Run* as the lesser of two evils, the Academy of Motion Picture Arts and Sciences Board of Directors decided to overrule the voters

to give De Laurentiis's *King Kong* a special Oscar for special effects—an award that did not include Rick Baker.

It was a fitting end for one of the most ignominious chapters in science-fiction film history. Genre fans can only be consoled by the movie's relatively poor box-office returns and the fact that the proposed sequel, *King Kong in Africa,* never materialized.

FOREIGN VOICES

Although heavily promoted, these Hollywood productions had nothing on a few foreign films that premiered this bicentennial year. They were far more inventive and daring than their over-produced American counterparts. The best of the lot was *The Man Who Fell to Earth,* an especially sensitive, well-written book by Walter Tevis made into an equally special movie by scripter Paul Mayersburg and director Nicholas Roeg (who also did *Walkabout,* Jenny Agutter's first film).

Although overlong at a hundred thirty-eight minutes—even with almost a half hour cut out before release—the tender, tragic story of an alien desperately seeking help for his dying family and planet resonates with texture and meaning. World-famous rock musician David Bowie starred as Thomas Jerome Newton, refugee from an arid planet, who gets psychologically lost in the maze of capitalist society.

As confused by us as we are fascinated by him, he uses the riches of his planet and wise investment counseling by a businessman, played by Buck Henry, to become a Howard Hughes-type multi-millionaire. Still unable and now perhaps spoiled and unwilling to make his planet's plight known, he attempts to mount his own space program to send help. Only then does the government move to protect its security.

The Buck Henry character is murdered in an excruciating scene in which he is repeatedly thrown against his shatter-resistant high rise window and the perplexed Newton is turned into an alcoholic by his depraved assistants. Once he is totally vulnerable, scientists move in to remove any outward sign of his alien origins. The final straw comes when they permanently adhere human-appearing contact lenses to his golden cat eyes—the last physical evidence of his true origin.

Ironically, the drunken Newton becomes a pitiful, pale, drained rock star at film's end; his album, "The Visitor," is number five on the record charts. Director Roeg does a stupefying visual job of this story, creating outstanding images that cinematically impart the alien's alienation. *The*

Man Who Fell to Earth* is a melancholy but memorable film.

Equally haunting and thoughtful is *Solaris,* one of the few Russian-produced science-fiction films. Based on the book by Stanislaw Lem, it tells of a scientist escaping his guilts on Earth only to be confronted by human manifestations of them on a space station orbiting the planet Solaris.

All but three of the eighty-five station inhabitants have died and Chris Kelvin (Donatas Banionis) is sent to investigate, only to discover that the planet is covered by an ocean which can create images of the humans' subconscious. For Kelvin, it produces his wife, who had killed herself years before. Unable to face her, Kelvin returns the favor by killing her new versions again and again as they appear.

Finally he is forced to accept her resurrection and uses his newly found discovery of Solaris's processes to create a home for himself on the planet's surface. Basing it upon his thoughts, the planet creates an island with an exact replica of his Earth home, complete with his father inside.

Solaris was edited down a half hour from its original running length of two hours and forty-five minutes, then saddled with simplistic subtitling which lost much of the original language's intellectual emotionalism. Still, struggling with this film was probably better by a long shot than sitting through *Logan's Run*.

The most vibrant, easily understood foreign science-fiction film of the year came from Canada, of all places; it was the first major release by the man who was to become the most successful Canadian director to date—David Cronenberg. Originally conceived as *Orgy of the Blood Parasites*, it was made and distributed under many names. In some places, it was known as *The Parasite Murders*. In the Great White North, it was called *Shivers*. In the United States, it was titled *They Came from Within*.

By any name, it was a strong science-fiction/horror mixture with disgusting images never before witnessed in this country. Cronenberg's continuing theme is science gone mad for science's sake. Some people, he seems to figure, will unleash the most aberrant monstrosities simply in the name of science. This time out, a crazy creates and loses control of a little leech-like parasite that breeds in the pristine confines of the ultra-modern "Starliner" Apartment Towers. ("Just Twelve Minutes from Downtown Montreal," ominously proclaim sales brochures).

These "bugs," as Cronenberg calls them, are a particularly noxious combination of eel and slug,

driven to set up housekeeping in the human body and make that host's libido flame with new passion. The writer/director explores that concept with exploitative glee. Nothing is too outrageous for Cronenberg to conceive and film. The critters leap out of washing machines, slither through bath tub drains, and even merrily crawl around just under a man's skin.

Paul Hampton plays the nominal hero of the piece, Dr. St. Luc, who tries to contain the situation after fellow physician Dr. Linsky (Joe Silver) is attacked by parasites which clamp onto his face. The doctor's rational approach is no match for his rapidly multiplying enemy. St. Luc is cornered in the apartment house's swimming pool by all the affected residents, who finally drag him down to their level.

They Came from Within ends with the mob of parasite-controlled residents cheerily bundling into their cars for the twelve-minute drive to Montreal where things will obviously get out of hand. Those who saw Cronenberg's movie in its limited American release didn't forget it, giving the Canuck a toe-hold in the hearts and minds of the nation's science-fiction enthusiasts.

All the foreign fodder was not as well conceived as the aforementioned trio. *Tentacles* was an Italian production filmed in California which made use of cameo acting contributions by Henry Fonda and John Huston. Mostly, however, it made use of the plot and concept from *Jaws* (1975). Instead of a shark killing bathers, however, a monstrous octopus attacks bikini-clad swimmers because an offshore oil drill disturbed its hibernation and radio waves attract it.

Although filled with otherwise dependable American actors like Bo Hopkins and Claude Akins, *Tentacles* was the kind of film the term "potboiler" was invented for—an obvious, pitifully lame exercise in cheap special effects and makeshift scripting. The same could be said of *Godzilla vs. Megalon*, the latest in a long line of *Godzilla* sequels from Japan, but these giant reptilian, high-camp productions are just too charming, action-filled, and funny to condemn outright.

For the record, this effort, originally made in 1973, pits the scaly, nuclear-waste-breathing softie against the Seatopians, a bunch of toga-swathed

The giant android "Jet Jaquar" perfects a great throw on the monster "Gigan" during *Godzilla vs. Megalon*.

undersea humans loosely based on the legendary denizens of Atlantis. To rid the world of polluting ground dwellers, the bad buys unleash their god, Megalon, who looks like a giant insect consisting of artichoke layers, with a clawed buzz-saw in his chest. It's helped out by Gigan—a winged, tusked, armored alien cyclops.

Aiding and abetting Godzilla are a little kid, his hip, hot-rodding friend and a young inventor who created "Jet Jaquar"—a flying robot who can grow to giant size because, in the words of his creator, "I programmed him that way." As usual, the dubbing is ludicrous and the action plentifully fanciful. Its American premiere was on NBC television—fittingly hosted by John Belushi in a monster suit. In order to fit into a one-hour format with commercials, the film was cut down to half its regular length.

Not surprisingly, when the film was re-released to theaters at a full ninety minutes, the story was hardly improved. But Godzilla lovers rarely look for story. *Godzilla vs. Megalon* delivered plenty of empty-headed fun.

INEXPENSIVE INDEPENDENTS

Science fiction was treated with respect by independent producers this year. While MGM floundered with Logan and Paramount with De

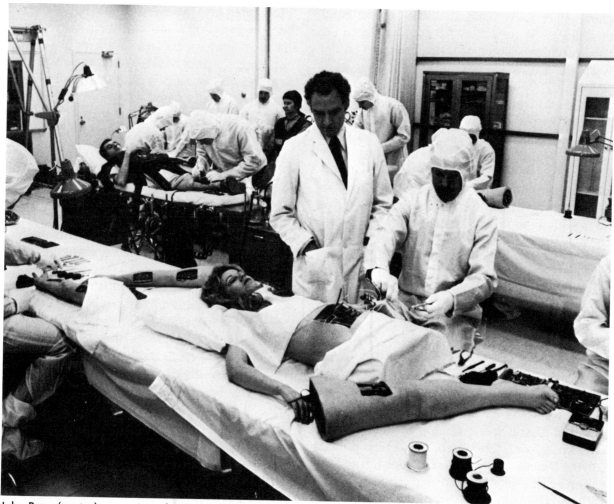

John Ryan (center) supervises the construction of robots in *Futureworld*.

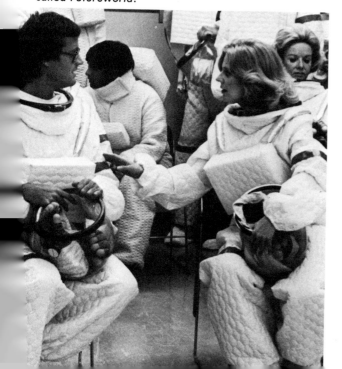

Peter Fonda (left) and Blythe Danner play two reporters investigating a futuristic amusement park called *Futureworld*.

Laurentiis, smaller studios created a trio of unpretentious works that far exceeded their big-budget brethren in style and excitement. Although all three had familiar science-fiction themes, the style in which they were presented was fresh and clever.

Futureworld holds up best, not only being one of the few sequels that was better than the original, but being about the only sequel that explains the original. In 1973, doctor and author Michael Crichton wrote and directed *Westworld*. Jeff Rovin described it as "a Disneyland for adults. [It] is a reconstruction of different period settings wherein the clientele can live out their fantasies. The historical mockups are peopled with androids programmed to make the human visitor look good at whatever he tries . . . . All goes well until [a] robot decides he's sick of losing and goes on the warpath."

Running afoul of the particularly murderous android was reporter Chuck Browning, played by Richard Benjamin. The rebellious gun-slinging machine was played by Yul Brynner, who starts a robotic revolution destined to kill almost every park visitor. While the initial film was atmospheric, exciting, and had an interesting twist in which the ostensible hero (James Brolin) is killed so that his nebbish side-kick (Benjamin) can save the day, the cybernetic slaughter was just a gimmick to create a chase thriller. It was never explained how and why the machines started killing.

Futureworld explained why the machines— which cannot think for themselves—murdered. And it explains it in an involving and engaging way. It is two years after the Westworld tragedy and Delos (the name of the amusement park in which Westworld was just one section) is about to reopen after a massive renovation. Reporter Chuck Browning is back on hand, this time portrayed in classic heroic fashion by Peter Fonda. He, along with fellow reporter Tracy Ballard (Blythe Danner), have been personally invited for a tour by public relations officer Duffy (Arthur Hill) and chief technician Schneider (John Ryan).

Not surprisingly, all is not what it seems, in the script by Mayo Simon and George Schenck. In spite of the admonition that "nothing can go wrong," and the amazing wonders of Futureworld, Browning pokes his nose where it isn't supposed to be, sniffing out the true story. Stuart Margolin plays Harry, a disgruntled robot builder who lives in the bowels of Delos. He helps Browning discover Schneider's master plan.

The robots in Westworld, it seems, were originally programmed to kill. It was all a plot to replace the wealthy and influential patrons of Delos with android duplicates that was set off prematurely. The robot cowboy played by Brynner jumped the gun, so to speak. Only this time, Schneider the mad machine maker is positive "nothing can go wrong," since he replaced all his human help, including Duffy, with robot replicas. He is even intent on replacing the two reporters, as is shown in an impressive replication sequence highlighting the finest computer animation then available.

Browning gets the message just in the nick of time, precipitating a battle between the reporters and their doubles. Ballard kills hers in a shoot-out among the ruins of Westworld. Browning hurls his off a high space rocket gantry. Schneider thinks his duplicates have won out until Browning gives him an all too human hand gesture at the film's finale.

Director Richard T. Heffron helms the action with verve and the production profited enormously from on-location filming at the Houston Manned Space Flight Center. Here was one picture that might have been familiar to veteran fans, but was done up like a grade-A Saturday-matinee adventure filled with wit and invention.

Similar in approach, although not as successful, was *Embryo*, a Saturday-matinee horror movie for more overcast skies. Director Ralph Nelson, who also helmed *Charly* (1968)—the effective adaptation of Daniel Keyes's excellent novel *Flowers for Algernon* which gained star Cliff Robertson an Oscar for Best Actor—cannot make lightning strike twice with Anita Doohan and Arnold Orgolini's screenplay in which a non-mad scientist (Rock Hudson) almost perfects a hormone that will speed the aging process. He uses it to first "grow" a dog from birth to full size in a matter of seconds, then turns his attention to a woman.

Victoria (Barbera Carrera) is his crowning achievement and Dr. Frankenstein should have been so lucky. In no time at all, she develops into a beautiful dark-skinned female with a mind as clean as sand blasted stone. The first part of the movie is an intriguing lesson in subjective education. With all the innocence of a newborn baby but for a high IQ and a fully developed intelligence, Victoria warps the doctor's teachings about such things as sex and religion in various entertaining ways.

It is only after the dog, a doberman named "Number One," turns vicious and rapidly dies of old age that things begin to sour. The doctor realizes that the hormone remains dormant for awhile, then suddenly accelerates. Victoria realizes she's going to have to work fast if she is to survive. Taking a crash course in such things as biology and surgery, she discovers that she needs a newborn fetus's glands.

Here's where *Embryo* turns grey, bitter and ugly. Coincidentally, the doctor's daughter-in-law (Anne

Schedeen) announces her pregnancy, setting the stage for a vicious climax in which Victoria captures and kills the hapless girl, but is forced to flee before she can use the fetus's glands. In a strikingly conceived final sequence, she ages into a withered crone behind the wheel of a car as the doctor relentlessly pursues her.

She dies in the resulting crash and although the doctor survives, he has not prospered by the experience. Even though it is a bit sophisticated, the picture makes for a good modern horror parable, borrowing a page from Frankenstein's book: "There are things that humanity should not tinker with."

Keeping up a semblance of vitality in exploitation circles are new, young directors anxious for attention. This usually inspires them to create extreme genre statements—the cinematic equivalent of a scream with which to attract audiences's eyes. One such man was Florida filmmaker Ken Wiederhorn, who, along with John Harrison, wrote *Death Corps*, a script about aquatic super-Nazis.

The Third Reich has long been best-selling fodder for adventure novels, but they have had a less than spectacular track record with cheap science-fiction movies. To his credit, however, Wiederhorn gets more mileage from his idea than the makers of *I Stole Hitler's Brain* (1966) got from theirs.

Peter Fonda plays reporter Chuck Browning, here drugged and marked so a computerized camera can start making his clone. This is the horror of *Futureworld*.

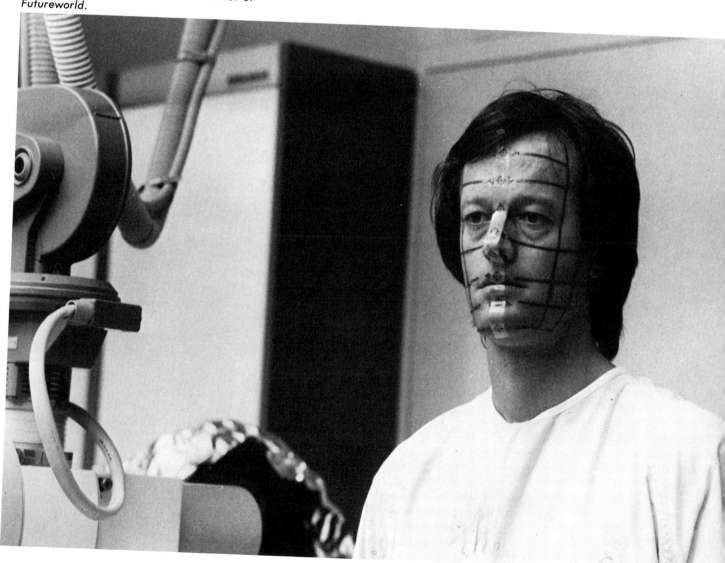

Joseph Brenner Associates, the film's distributor, retitled the young man's movie *Shock Waves.* By any name, it told the tale of a repentant German scientist (Peter Cushing) who created a team of navy men who can breathe underwater. Realizing his mistake, he sinks the ship ferrying them to the Fatherland just off the coast of his secluded island.

All is swell for thirty-five years until a joy-sailing bunch of young people show up, accidentally

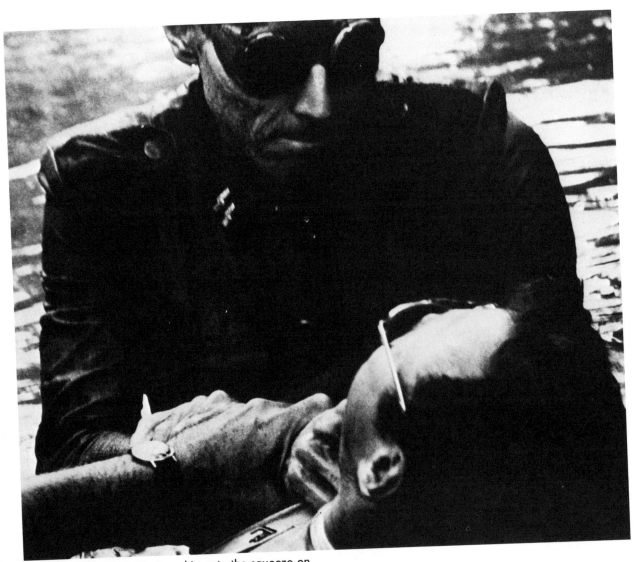

An immortal aquatic Nazi zombie gets the squeeze on an innocent tourist during *Shock Waves.*

releasing the still living mermen from their rusting coffin. Although alive, the platoon is not at all well, having wrinkled up considerably. And although they cannot be killed with blades or bullets, they are mortally sensitive to light. If their protective goggles are ripped off, even dim illumination will burn through their brains.

The doctor, the old sea salt who shares the island (John Carradine—a staple in this sort of feature), and the kids are picked off one by one

36

until only the prettiest girl among them remains (Brooke Adams). She manages to be rescued and would tell the tale had she not been driven hopelessly insane by the experience.

The bicentennial movie year also marked the return of genre stylist Larry Cohen, who released another challenging science-fiction work called *God Told Me To*. Although almost all his films look erratic and rushed, it is writer Cohen's ideas that buoy his movies up. This one is probably his most controversial.

New York police detective Peter Nicholas (Tony

Two monsters clash *At the Earth's Core*.

LoBianco) is swamped with a series of gruesome, seemingly meaningless murders: a man stabbing shoppers, a cop shooting into a parade crowd, a sniper opening up on passers-by before committing suicide. When asked why, each one replied with the same four words: "God told me to."

Upon investigation, all roads lead to a charismatic hippie named Bernard Phillips (Richard Lynch). Nicholas tries to interrogate the hippie's

mother only to have her attack him before killing herself after uttering the title phrase. Incredibly, her autopsy reveals that she was a virgin. Digging into her past, the cop discovers that she reported being kidnapped by a flying saucer.

After a frenzied confrontation with Phillips, who actually glows with an ethereal light, Nicholas discovers that his own mother professed to being abducted and impregnated by aliens. He finds that he has the same powers as Phillips. They are both alien children, imbued with telepathic and telekinetic abilities that the hippie used to convince others he was the second coming.

This leads to a second showdown, which the cop wins by dropping the whole building on his adversary. When captured and asked why, Nicholas answers "God told me to." Cohen suffered for his quirky film, seeing it re-edited and re-released under the new title *Demon*. Under either name, Cohen's second contribution to the genre was entertainingly unusual.

CHEAP SCHLOCK

The difference between this genre and the preceding inexpensive independents is clear as soon as the movies are viewed. The preceding films had some sort of integrity about them, in either form or content. The following movies have little to commend them other than their producers's desire

A vicious "Mahar" soars in for the kill *At the Earth's Core*.

Marjoe Gortner bravely wrests a giant wasp from
Ralph Meeker's back. The big bug had just partaken of
The Food of the Gods.

to make money by pandering to the lowest possible imagination.

Producer John Dark and director Kevin Connor are back in action again with their second
Edgar Rice Burroughs's adaptation, *At the Earth's
Core*. Although star Doug McClure is also back,
this time he's playing playboy/explorer/bon vivant
David Innes, who, in the company of absent-
minded inventor Abner Perry (Peter Cushing)
build the "Iron Mole"—a bullet-shaped burrow-

ing ship. It is their intention to do Jules Verne one
better with a mechanized "Journey to the Center
of the Earth."

Once the pair have braved the rocks and dirt
that the digging was bound to turn up, they emerge
in the central city of Pellucidar. There, a race of
sweet primeval humans called Sagoths are being
enslaved by Mahars—vaguely prehistoric lizards
with wings and sharp bird beaks (actually actors
in wire-supported rubber suits). All the monsters

in the Dark universe are men in scaly, horned suits, giving the whole thing a comic-strip feel.

David falls in love with a particularly lush Sagoth named Dia (Caroline Munro), completing the cliché situation. Aiding their fight for freedom is an earthquake instead of a volcano this time. The movie stressed humor and action over any real sort of character or plot development, so it can be somewhat forgiven for its campy approach, even though any real Burroughs fan would be made sick by the producers's inability to tell the story with a straight face.

Edgar Rice Burroughs's books have a style and speed uniquely their own and it is a crying shame that his science-fiction works have never been translated to the screen faithfully. His talent has obviously influenced the great storytellers of adventure literature as well as movies.

H.G. Wells joins the ranks of great writers cheapened by trashy film versions of their work this year. Bert I. Gordon wrote, directed and produced *Food of the Gods,* mentioning in the credits that it was "based on portions of the novel by H.G. Wells." He tried the same thing in *Village of the Giants* (1965), starring Tommy Kirk and a pair of twenty-foot-tall plastic legs which stood in for the giants of the picture.

In the latter film, a boy genius creates a growth food which makes more than his head swell. In the former, the filmmaker takes Wells's concept of "boomfood" and one chapter from the seminal 1904 novel, in which giant animals run amuck, to build a ninety-minute movie around. Switching the location from England to the rural South, actors like Marjoe Gortner, Ralph Meeker, Pamela Franklin and Ida Lupino must challenge giant dragonflies, rats and worms as well as awful dialogue and shaky special effects.

But even that wasn't as crazy as *The Giant Spider Invasion,* a truly brainless melange of purposefully dreadful ideas and execution. Borrowing the basic concept from the 1955 Jack Arnold-directed *Tarantula,* in which a giant spider escapes from a research lab, director Bill Rebane got a monstrous arachnid to Earth by having him "ride a black hole" down. The scientific inconsistencies are too numerous to catalog, but any movie with Alan Hale, Jr. (the Skipper of *Gilligan's Island*) as a sheriff can't be taken too seriously.

Steve Brodie played the handsome hero with a stiff upper lip, Leslie Parrish was the main damsel in distress and *The Giant Spider Invasion* was a mindless but painless diversion without enough gore to warrant even an "R" rating.

3
1977
THE YEAR OF LUKE SKYWALKER

SCIENCE FICTION had come a long way toward being accepted by the Hollywood mainstream. Prime evidence of that came in the form of five "X"-rated sexual exploitation movies. A genre has to be very well established before the pornography industry will utilize it.

One was a somewhat direct satire of Stanley Kubrick's monumental classic *2001: A Space Odyssey*. It was a foreign import titled, not surprisingly, *2069: A Sex Odyssey*. It concerned a team of voluptuous explorers from outer space who came to Earth to counsel humans in the ways of love.

Another movie was a downright direct satire of Norman Jewison's 1975 sports chiller. The sex-oriented filmmakers desperately wanted to use the title *Rollerball*, but had to settle on *Rollerbabies*. Overpopulation has resulted in love being declared illegal, but the Federal Exhibitionism Commission allows the act to be shown on television, but only if performed by licensed artists. TV executive Robert Random (Alan Marlo) is at a loss as to how to please his now jaded viewers, until a happy scientist (Philip De Hat) hits upon the idea of combining America's favorite indoor sport with a roller derby.

The third sexploitative adaption was more subtle. *Invasion of the Love Drones* was similar to *It Came from Outer Space* (1953) in that both films concerned a stranded alien spaceship. But instead of taking over the minds of humans in order to fix the craft (as in the classic Jack Arnold directed 3-D film), Dr. Femme (Viveca Ash) sends out her beauteous love drones to start an international orgy. It turns out that Femme's ship runs on sexual energy.

Physical energy also cures the world's ills in *The Sex Machine*, a fine farce imported from Italy. In the natural-resource-starved world of the future, a brilliant doctor creates a machine that turns sexual energy into electricity. He convinces the Papal State to forgive those making love for the good of the state, only to discover that affection and true love was getting in the way of productivity. Instead of creating energy, people were cooing and kissing. The movie ends with love outlawed and sex mandatory.

The final film was a native American production that projected a fairy tale into the future—*Cinderella 2000*. Catherine Erhardt starred as "Cindy," who slaves for her wicked stepmother and stepsisters in the year 2047. The wicked Controller (Erwin Fuller) has outlawed love and has his computers running everything. Saving the day is a fairy Godfather (Jay B. Larson). After having some preliminary magic wand problems, he

In the only moment of pathos during *The Incredible Melting Man*, astronaut Steve West (Alex Rebar) ponders his horrid fate in a cemetery.

transforms Cindy into a vision of loveliness, so she can go to the Controller's masked ball. She is the hit of the affair, capturing the heart of the Controller's surrogate, Tom Prince. The joys of love are rediscovered and soon even the Controller falls under its spell. Everyone lives and loves happily ever after.

BUSINESS AS USUAL

In the Hollywood mainstream, as in the other film centers of the world, the producers ground out their same tired product, seemingly unaware of the groundbreaking effort that was being readied for summer. There were still inexpensive independent movies, cheap schlock pictures, and foreign films to get out of the way.

Director/writer William Sachs gets very good ideas, but then films them in a mediocre way. His good idea this year was *The Incredible Melting Man*—a high-concept title if ever there was one. High-concept titles practically tell the whole movie's story, raising viewers's expectations in the process. In the case of some, like *The Incredible Shrinking Man* (1957, again directed by Jack Arnold) and *I Married a Monster from Outer Space* (1958), the promise inherent in the title is delivered with insight and wisdom. This was not the case with *The Incredible Melting Man*.

Although the movie didn't have to be a sage examination of outer space diseases, it should at least have been exciting. Instead, the tragic tale of astronaut Steve West (Alex Rebar), afflicted with a space spore after a trip to Saturn, was muddled and ultimately dull. Not only does his skin start to melt, but West discovers he needs human flesh to live. Even though he consumes vast quantities after several gruesome murders, the astronaut is unable to combat his degeneration. The combined military tries to combat *him*, however.

Even though he eludes his persecutors, the noncommunicative disease finally renders him into an oily pool of goo. The finest work on the picture was done by makeup artist Rick Baker, who took it upon himself to create four distinct stages of melting with four unique and arresting designs. His work was sadly undermined by the confused filming and editing as well as the lead actor's distaste for long makeup sessions.

The original plan called for West to grow increasingly mutated as the movie progressed. But after Rebar did many scenes simply with a syrup-covered rubber mask on and the film went through two different editing processes, Baker's careful deliberation was rendered incomprehensible. A far more imaginative job on the same subject was done by British writers Nigel Kneale and Val Guest with their *The Creeping Unknown* (1956) starring Brian Donlevy as Dr. Quatermass, a brilliant scientist who must combat a raging space-spore epidemic.

A dull approach also crippled *End of the World*, producer Charles Band's first foray into the realms of cheap science fiction. Actors Kirk Scott and Sue Lyons are hunted and captured by a bunch of nuns. Only then does priest Christopher Lee reveal that they are all really aliens here to destroy Earth because higher powers decided that humans had contaminated their universe.

Lee gives the captured earthlings the opportunity to escape the cataclysm by stepping into another dimension before the film degenerates into hysteria. Nuns start turning back into clawed and tentacled monsters who attack innocent bystanders for a few minutes until a serene shot of the planet fills the movie screen. A second later it explodes in a torrent of plastic, dirt and water. Director John Hayes manages to stretch this inconsequential drivel over eighty minutes.

David Lynch was able to take even less money than Charles Band spent on his apocalyptic picture to write and direct an arresting, hypnotic vision of another world, *Eraserhead*. Filmed in black and white and making no clear sense, the ninety-minute movie still managed to be riveting. At times funny and at times horrifying, it followed the life of a strange-looking man called Henry (John Nance).

Long, oyster-like spores are sent down from a planet which looks like a potato. One lands in a puddle which Henry steps in before visiting his girl friend, Mary X. Mary's mother confronts him with the news that her daughter has already given birth to his child. The young mother wails, "Mother, they're not even sure if it is a baby!"

The scene changes to Henry's depressing apartment where the weird offspring lies bundled on a bureau top. The thing has a pollywog-shaped head, calf-like eyes and a gooey little mouth. Other than a bandage-swathed torso, it has no other limbs. It constantly cries, driving Mary X away.

Henry, in the meantime, is haunted by images of a deformed dancer performing on a stage behind his radiator and the continuing appearance of the space oysters.

He dreams that the baby gets sick and that his own head comes off. A child finds his loose skull and brings it to a shop where his brain is used to make pencil erasers. Finally back in his apartment, he cuts off his child's bandages only to discover that they were actually his skin. This unleashes a torrent of ooze that threatens to swamp the room. The movie winds up with Henry in the arms of his deformed dream girl behind the radiator.

As odd and perverted as *Eraserhead* was, it still

Godzilla tries a head butt against Mecha-Godzilla. It'll take more than that to destroy the robot, as the giant lizard discovers during *Godzilla vs. the Cosmic Monster*.

made for a singular viewing experience. It is consistently watchable although essentially impossible to contemplate rationally. Its meaning can be whatever each viewer desires, still it manages to be as unpretentious as it is unpredictable.

Equally as unpretentiously unpredictable was David Cronenberg's *Rabid*, but it was all too understandable. Marilyn Chambers starred as the unfortunate victim of a Canadian motorcycle accident. Her predicament is fortuitous for a near-

by private hospital which longs to try out a new grafting technique. Since the girl is on the verge of death, she becomes their guinea pig.

As in *They Came From Within*, Cronenberg uses science as an excuse to come up with a singularly outlandish horror concept. The only side effect of the seemingly innocent, life-saving operation is that Chambers develops an organic vampiric syringe in her armpit which can transmit rabies. Chambers becomes desperate for others's blood, unaware of her perverted desire as well as its aftermath.

Suddenly, patients and doctors alike go crazy while drooling carbonated glop (created from colored Bromo-Seltzer). The disease spreads across Montreal as Chambers's dazed boyfriend, Read (Frank Moore), struggles to understand what is happening. Soon, martial law is declared and the girl herself can deny her complicity no longer. Desperate and afraid, she picks up a stranger, locks them both in a room and waits to see if he goes rabid.

She calls Read with this news just as her pickup goes crazy. Read is forced to listen to her destruction over the phone. The next day, plastic garbed garbage men pick up Chambers's corpse and load it into their truck like so much human refuse.

Like David Lynch, Cronenberg stretched his budget wisely, creating a convincing picture of a city gone mad. His little touches added enormously to the film's effect, as when a rabid citizen attacks a store Santa Claus, causing a guard to shoot them both. Nothing was sacred to Cronenberg—not even Christmas.

The only thing the orientals wanted to impart this year was delirious, nonsensical fun. They accomplished this in abundance with not one but two Godzilla movies as well as a Chinese comic-book-style superhero. That hero was *Infra-man*, a frenetic combination of almost every power imaginable, loosely based on the name and fame of Ultraman—a Japanese superstar. Hua-Shan directed ninety minutes of pure escapist mayhem,

making this movie one of the most delightfully insane viewing experiences of all time.

Earth is being attacked by giant monsters unleashed by a Demon Princess whose name is loosely translated as "Princess Dragon Mom." To counter the attack, a wise old professor rushes to finish his cosmo-bionic superhuman. Intrepid lab assistant Li Hsiu-Hsien volunteers for the experiment to meld a man inside the machinery as earthquakes and volcanoes erupt all around them.

Thus is born Infra-man, who celebrates his birth by bouncing all over the lab (thanks to well-hidden trampolines). That out of his system, he flies off to battle the Demon Princess's hordes of wacky beasts, including monsters who can shoot their arms out, then reel them back. The plot thickens after the evil villainess captures the professor and his daughter, but Infra-man comes out swinging.

Through a combination of kung fu, growing to giant size, and shooting electric bolts out of his fingers, Infra-man carries the day, making the orient safe for big reptiles to beat each other silly. Sure enough, Godzilla had a duo of slugfests this year, starting with *Godzilla vs. The Cosmic Monster*. When Cinema Shares originally distributed the film, it was entitled *Godzilla vs. The Bionic Monster*, since the main villain was a robot duplicate of the hero. Universal Studios, producers of both *The Six Million Dollar Man* and *The Bionic Woman*, made their displeasure known, so Mecha-Godzilla became cosmic.

No matter what the title, the movie was the same mixture of childish plotting and child-like style. Earth is threatened by an ape-like alien race this time out, who control the title character, who is initially disguised as the real Godzilla. The true article arrives to clear his name as Japanese spies shoot it out with the simian invaders.

Coming hot on that film's heels was *Godzilla on Monster Island*, wherein giant cockroach-type aliens team up Ghidrah the three-headed monster with Gigan to keep Godzilla and his stegasaurus-type pal Angorus at bay. This quartet fights as the bad guys try to take over from their hideout—an amusement park complete with a building constructed in the shape of our reptilian hero.

Once Ghidrah and Gigan are defeated, Godzilla must face his replica, which is outfitted with laser cannons in its mouth. A young comic-book artist saves the day by blowing up the building and the

Godzilla wrestles with Gigan while "Ghidrah the Three-Headed Monster" zaps him and "Angorus" cheers from the sidelines. It's all in a day's work for *Godzilla on Monster Island*.

roach-aliens. Although consistently juvenile, the Godzilla series is a source of delight for many fantasy fans. While they may be cotton candy for the brain, few can deny that cotton candy tastes good.

MR. KISS KISS BANG BANG

Quite possibly the most successful series superhero of recent history is James Bond, agent 007 on Her Majesty's Secret Service. The double zero prefix identifies his license to kill. Created by Ian Fleming in 1952, the character enjoyed a successful literary career, appearing in seventeen books (fourteen by Fleming, one by Kingsley Amis and two by John Gardner).

Although there was a one-hour television adaptation of the first, strictly espionage-oriented novel *Casino Royale* in 1954 (starring American Barry Nelson in the leading role), it wasn't until 1962 that producers Albert Broccoli and Harry Saltzman hired Richard Maibum to adapt and Terence Young to direct Bond on screen. The result was *Dr. No,* and it featured a science-fiction storyline. The insidious oriental title villain, complete with metal hands, was sabotaging American rocket launches with a nuclear-powered interference system.

Sean Connery starred as the secret agent sent to Jamaica to stop the plot at any cost. He first had to face a number of murderous underlings, the worst of whom put a tarantula in his bed. Next

Jack Lord as CIA agent Felix Leiter gets the drop on Sean Connery as James Bond. It is about the only time anyone gets the upper hand on agent 007 during his first screen adventure, *Dr. No.*

he confronted the "dragon" of Crab Key, a flame-throwing tank dressed up as a monster to frighten the natives of Dr. No's island. Finally he battles the oriental extortionist himself as the two are slowly lowered into the nuclear reactor's white-hot cooling pool.

Dr. No's steel fingers prove his undoing as he cannot get a grip on the elevator gantry's smooth surface. Bond escapes as the villain's headquarters explodes in a ball of flame. This first film established 007's cinematic trademarks—the outlandish plots, the continuous action, and the beautiful girls Bond incessantly beds.

The second film, *From Russia with Love* (1963), was a change of pace in that the story was a much simpler spy thriller in which 007 must steal a Russian coding machine out from under the Reds' very noses. Unbeknownst to him, however, it is all a trap by the unseen, cat-loving head of SPECTRE (a dreaded secret crime organization) to eliminate Britain's top operative. To escape, Bond utilizes a briefcase filled with hidden weapons.

Goldfinger (1964) reestablished the fanciful plots as well as cementing a long-lasting wrinkle. Auric Goldfinger (Gert Frobe) was a gold-obsessed megalomaniac who intended to break into Fort Knox with an industrial laser and destroy all the wealth there with an atom time bomb. To defeat him, 007 uses an Aston Martin sports car outfitted with machine guns, bullet-proof shields, whirling licence plates, oil slick shooters, radar screens, and an ejection seat. These James Bond "gadgets" were to become almost as important as the man himself.

The fourth 007 film was conceived as yet another unlikely fantasy. The head of SPECTRE instructs his number two man, Emilio Largo (Adolfo Celi), to start Operation *Thunderball* (1965) in which two atomic bombs are hijacked and used to hold a major American city for ransom. Bond defeats the plan with his usual aplomb, not to mention a jet pack and super scuba tank, but just one month after the movie premiered, two real atom bombs were lost off the Spanish coast.

Reality had caught up to James Bond.

It is not entirely clear whether the newly conceived plotline for the next Bond picture, *You Only Live Twice* (1967), was created in response to that

Fort Knox is saved by James Bond and the forces of good, who defuse an atom bomb with just "007" seconds showing on the time clock. It marks the end of the master criminal *Goldfinger*.

situation or not. No matter what the cause, this was the first 007 movie to almost totally ignore the original book's story. Although the locale (Japan) is the same, as are the characters' names, Fleming's novel concerned Bond's revenge on Ernst Stavros Blofeld, the SPECTRE boss.

The movie had a SPECTRE spacecraft secretly swallowing up American and Russian space capsules, pushing the superpowers to the brink of war. It is up to 007 to locate and destroy the villains, but only after his death is faked to throw his enemies off guard. Bond battles one adversary after another with the help of Japanese secret service director Tiger Tanaka (Tetsuro Tamba).

When it is discovered that SPECTRE is located in a fake, hollow volcano complete with space-launching capabilities (a gigantic set that cost a then-record one million dollars to build), Tanaka unleashes his army of ninjas to decimate the place. Bond gets in first to confront his deadly enemy, played by Donald Pleasance complete with a long scar across his face (although originally set to be a club foot; Pleasance was a last-minute replacement for another actor who was deemed unsuitable, and the scar looked better than the foot on the replacement).

Blofeld escapes, but not before destroying his headquarters with preplanted dynamite charges.

47

The criminal organization SPECTRE uses a Japanese volcano as headquarters during *You Only Live Twice*. This set was built for a cool million dollars.

Bond gets away as well, but the two would meet again under trying circumstances.

Sean Connery was fed up playing the one-dimensional role of James Bond. He was getting no respect from film critics and the various 007 gimmicks had almost overwhelmed the character he worked so hard to create. The producers used his exit to give some newcomers a chance. Film editor Peter Hunt was promoted to director and they all agreed Australian George Lazenby would make a suitable new Bond.

Hunt and scripter Richard Maibum translated *On Her Majesty's Secret Service* (1969) almost exactly from the novel, up to and including Bond's marriage to a mafia boss's daughter and her subsequent assassination by Blofeld (this time enacted by Telly Savalas). The central story of SPECTRE's germ-warfare plot to destroy the world's farm crop was all but forgotten in the 007 "changing of the guard."

Hunt put together a dazzling, action-packed film, but the inexperienced Lazenby wasn't convincing and the unusual, unique tragic ending threw viewers for a loop. The actor announced that *On Her Majesty's Secret Service* would be his first and last Bond picture, causing the producers to figuratively fall to their knees before Sean Connery.

The veteran 007 was lured back with a million-dollar salary and the promise he could make two films of his choice with United Artists (007's distributor). Connery contributed his wage to charity and walked through *Diamonds Are Forever* (1971), a pale plagiarism of past James Bond glory. The star was obviously overweight, the character was coarsened into an egotistical, brutal clod, and the plot concerning a reclusive millionaire, a pair of homosexual killers, and SPECTRE's diamond-encrusted laser satellite was totally incomprehensible.

Even so, the movie made more money than the previous effort, so realism and believability went the way of Sean Connery. At the end of production, he again swore he would never return to the Bond role. Rather than renewing their search for an unknown, the producers decided that the new lead should be as well known as their character

48

The older, heavier James Bond of *Diamonds Are Forever*.

had become. Looking back at their original casting call before *Dr. No* started, they came up with the name Roger Moore.

Moore was blond and slight where Connery was dark and solid. He was brittle rather than bold, cool rather than controlled. The 007 films around him mirrored the change with a continuing bent toward fantasy and comic-book ingredients. As Connery had feared, the gimmicks had become Bond. 007 could have been almost anyone, it seemed, as long as the gadgets, girls, and giggles were in place.

Nowhere was that more true than in *Live and Let Die* (1973), the nadir of the series. Although there was plenty of movement and feminine flesh, the story was so secondary that almost no one can recall it exactly. There was something about a black crime kingpin disguised as another black boss who uses voodoo to kill cops. *The Man With the Golden Gun* (1974) was better, if only for its more deliberate, relevant story.

Bond was back in the orient again, tracking a professional hitman named Scaramanga (Christopher Lee, a cousin of Ian Fleming) who

James Bond escapes villains during *Diamonds Are Forever* in a moon buggy, with the help of a driving teacher.

ALBERT R BROCCOLI and HARRY SALTZMAN present

ROGER MOORE
AS
JAMES BOND
007

in IAN FLEMING'S

THE MAN WITH
HE GOLDEN GUN"

y GUY HAMILTON Screenplay by RICHARD MAIBAUM and TOM MANKIEWICZ

COLOR   **United Artists**

ing three dreadful 007 movies, was dropped in exchange for Lewis Gilbert, who had helmed *You Only Live Twice*. It was a natural choice because this new 1977 picture had basically the same plot. Instead of a spaceship stealing NASA capsules, an oil tanker was swallowing up nuclear submarines. The object was the same—to force the world powers into a planet-destroying nuclear war.

Only the reason was different. While SPECTRE wanted to take over the world, Karl Stromberg (Curt Jurgens)—a web-fingered billionaire—wanted to rid the world of land dwellers so his dream of a city under the sea would have no competition. Richard Maibum and Christopher Wood fashioned this completely original story supposedly following the express wishes of the late Flem-

The new James Bond, Roger Moore, introduced in *Live and Let Die*.

had gained control of an ultimate solar-cell device called the solar agitator. The villain uses it to power a laser cannon until 007 faces off with him in an old-fashioned duel—Bond's Walther PPk automatic versus Scaramanga's "golden gun," a special pistol that could be constructed from a gold cigarette lighter, a gold pen, and a gold cigarette case.

The Bond character had degenerated so badly by this time that Scaramanga was more attractive, more civilized, and more fun to watch than the hero. The movie's point of view, in fact, was much more in favor of the accomplished, supremely competent antagonist than the constantly erring, cheating, and often cruel protagonist. The box office grosses mirrored that fact.

Something had to be done.

The Spy Who Loved Me was the answer—the first consummately handled Bond film in eight years. Guy Hamilton, the director of the preced-

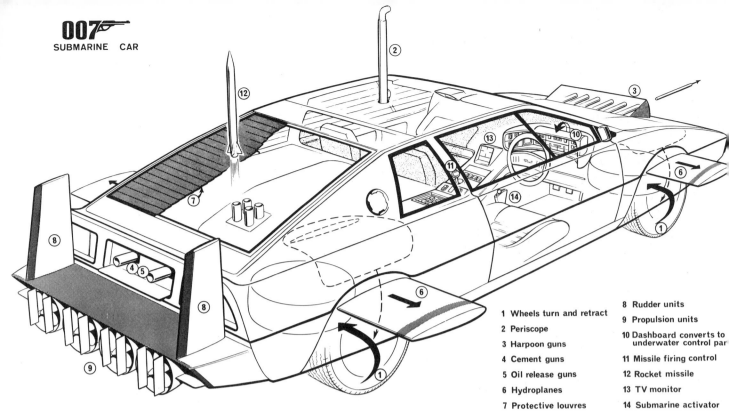

1	Wheels turn and retract	8	Rudder units
2	Periscope	9	Propulsion units
3	Harpoon guns	10	Dashboard converts to underwater control par
4	Cement guns	11	Missile firing control
5	Oil release guns	12	Rocket missile
6	Hydroplanes	13	TV monitor
7	Protective louvres	14	Submarine activator

The plans for the "007 Submarine Car" used in *The Spy Who Loved Me*.

James Bond saves the day, even though Jaws' metal teeth have just taken a hunk out of the woodwork.

The actors cut up during a lull in filming *The Spy Who Loved Me*. From the left, Bernard Lee as British Secret Service boss "M", Roger Moore, Walter Gotell as the head of KGB, and Barbara Bach as Russian "Agent Triple X."

Roger Moore at his best as James Bond during *The Spy Who Loved Me*.

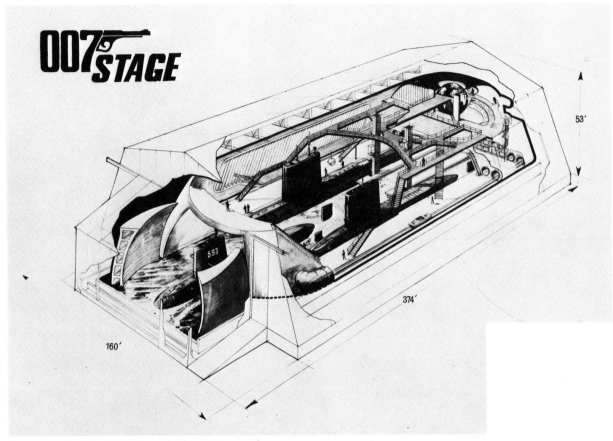

007 STAGE

The plans for the "007 Stage" built at Pinewood Studios.

ing (who died shortly after *Dr. No* premiered); reportedly Fleming detested his own novel.

Time, money and care were lavished on the new production. There was a five-month shooting schedule all over the world which stressed class as well as flash. The opening sequence gave ample evidence of the filmmakers slightly new approach. After the submarine is abducted, the scene shifts to Russia, where the KGB head (Walter Gotell) assigns agent Triple X to the case—who turns out to be Major Anya Amasova (Barbara Bach).

Her lover leaves that very night to complete his own mission: the death of 007. Bond is being set up by a beautiful skier at her snowbound cabin, only she is interrupted by his call back to HQ. The machine-gun toting enemy spies move in as Bond skis away, starting a chase that leads the hero off the edge of an icy precipice. It is truly a breathtaking shot as Bond (doubled by Rick Sylvester) falls

thousands of feet, seemingly toward an unavoidable death.

Memories of thrilling action serials spring effortlessly to mind as the filmmakers nimbly place 007 in a situation he "can't possibly escape," made all the more exciting by the fact that it is obviously a real person plummeting off the cliff. Childlike surprise is reborn as a parachute slips out of 007's knapsack, emblazoned with the Union Jack, as the "James Bond Theme" bursts forth from the previously silent soundtrack.

It is a perfectly realized moment, establishing *The Spy Who Loved Me* as a latter-day fantasy serial, done up with taste and wit. The rest of the movie doesn't disappoint as detente forces Bond and Amasova to team up. They race from Egypt to Sardinia to the *U.S.S. Wayne* nuclear submarine in order to corner Stromberg in his spider-shaped lair in the middle of the Tyrrhenian Sea.

Along the way they face the awesome "Jaws,"

54

a mute, seven-foot-tall bodyguard (Richard Kiel) with metal teeth. Aiding their effort is a specially equipped Lotus Esprit auto, supplied by British Secret Service technician "Q" (Desmond Llewelyn). When chased into the ocean by one of Stromberg's bullet-spewing helicopters, it converts into a torpedo-shooting, mine-dropping submarine.

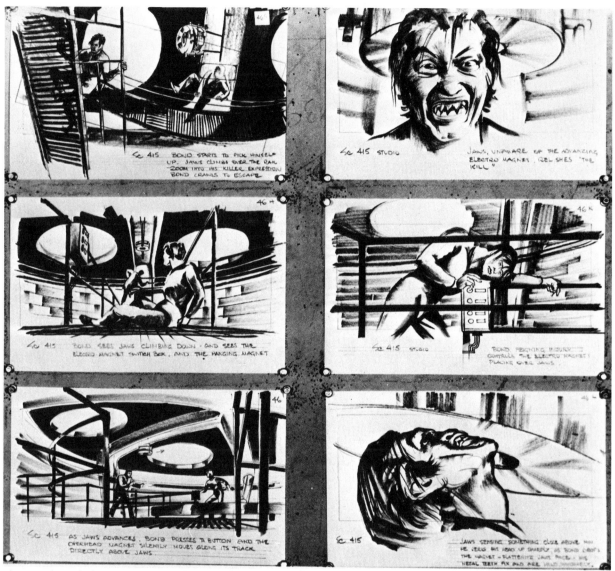

The storyboards for "Scene 415" of The Spy Who Loved Me. The sequence where 007 finally beats Jaws was first drawn out like a comic book.

The climax of *The Spy Who Loved Me* is equally as involving as that of *You Only Live Twice*. When the set depicting the interior of the submarine-swallowing oil tanker was too big to fit on any existing sound stage, producer Broccoli instructed that a new soundstage be built at England's Pinewood Studios. It was christened the "007 Stage" and was put to good use housing the gigantic mock-up of the tanker's interior—one that would become a battlefield as Bond leads an escape.

The secret agent prevents World War III just

And the actual set in the midst of being blown up during the climax of *The Spy Who Loved Me*.

in the nick of time, destroys the oil tanker, rescues the captured Amasova, and kills Stromberg in cold blood as his headquarters is torpedoed by the *Wayne*. The only thing to mar total suspension of disbelief was the survival of Jaws, who swims off into the distance. But even that could be forgiven in light of the film's prime entertainment value.

Agent 007 was no longer a secondary component in the formula. He was consistently pictured as a real human being with feelings and intelligence (especially in the scene where Amasova mentions his murdered wife) as well as strength and conviction. James Bond was back with a vengeance.

LITERARY LEGENDS

More great science-fiction authors were raked over the coals this year, in response to the success which hack filmmakers had had in previous years. Mercifully, for most of them, they were not around

Joan Collins' outfit is badly mussed by the *Empire of the Ants.*

Robert Lansing shoots one giant insect while another creeps up behind him during *Empire of the Ants.*

to see what was done to their work. The greatest transgressors were repeat offenders.

Bert I. Gordon dug up more dross with *H.G. Well's Empire of the Ants*, seemingly trying to blame someone else through the title. The story had grizzled ship captain Robert Lansing ferrying spoiled rich woman Joan Collins's party to investigate prime real estate in the middle of a swamp. It seems someone has designs on building a resort, ignoring the barrels of leaking nuclear waste inconveniently dumped there.

The local ant population has only to drink a little of the silver liquid in order to blossom into giant insects complete with white milky eyes. Things go from bad to worse as the ant queen takes over an everglade town with hypnosis while her workers make mincemeat out of most of Collins's group. The ants' doom is secured by setting the local sugar refinery aflame while they are eating, even though in reality sugar doesn't burn (it caramelizes).

Gordon wasn't taking credit for the scientific accuracy, but he did take credit for "Matex III"— a process that is capable of "creating a depth

Thorley Walters, Sarah Douglas, and Dana Gillespie
are *People That Time Forgot* fighting an armored
monster.

dimension imparting a realism to special effects
never before attained," according to the producer/
writer/director. In actuality, it was little more than
an optical overlay process that had been abused
in other movies of the type. Needless to say, the
process sounded better in print than it looked in
practice.

Much of the ants' onscreen time was actually
accomplished using full-scale puppets built by
Sonny Burman, Don Angiers and Dave Ayers.
There were seven, altogether, complete with sticks
to make their heads and mandibles move. Between
Gordon's overstatements and the awkward models,
Empire of the Ants deserves some sort of Dino
De Laurentiis award for bombastic filmmaking.

Producer John Dark and director Kevin Connor returned to The Land Time Forgot to film *The
People That Time Forgot*. Only this time, the special effects were more assured, the script tighter,
the actors more engaging, and the action more
convincing than before. It still wasn't vintage Burroughs but it was a far sight better than the previous two go-rounds.

Patrick Wayne (son of John) stars as an intrepid
explorer going in search of the Doug McClure
character lost in the first movie. He is flown to
Caprona by a crusty pilot, played by Shane Rimmer, in the company of an old-school geologist
(Thorley Walters) and a female reporter/ photog-
rapher (Sarah Douglas). Wayne and the latter two
go off in search of McClure only to run into double trouble.

First of all, the same dinosaurs reside in the

land, and second, there's a tribe of cannibalistic "Na-gas" just waiting for new meat. All seems lost until the sudden appearance of an Amazonian huntress (Dana Gillespie), who was sent out by McClure to get help. She collects the trio who invade the network of caves the Na-gas call home. McClure is rescued just as Douglas is captured and about to be sacrificed to a fire god.

Of all the Dark-adapted Burroughs' efforts, *The People That Time Forgot* is by far the most consistently well done—making for an enjoyable viewing.

Not all famous author adaptations are done with exploitation in mind. A fine, intelligent version of H.G. Wells's *The Island of Dr. Moreau* was mounted this year by writers John Shaner and Al

Patrick Wayne tries shooting the beast to no avail. It's all just part of *The People That Time Forgot*.

The team saves the day, but McClure is mortally wounded during the escape. He figures it is just as well since the Na-gas had killed his wife (the Susan Penhaligon character) between films. Walters, Douglas, Wayne, and Gillespie escape in Rimmer's plane just before angry Capronaians are about to overwhelm them.

Ramrus and director Don Taylor. Although labeled a remake of 1933's *Island of Lost Souls* starring Charles Laughton, it was an intelligent telling of the novel, as cerebral as it was exciting.

Michael York played a shipwrecked seaman of the early 1900's who discovers a laboratory on a seemingly deserted island. Burt Lancaster does a

The beauty of Barbara Carrera. The beasts are the "humanimals" on The Island of Dr. Moreau.

wonderful job as Moreau, an obsessed man torn between being a god and a scientist—capable of being kindly one moment and sadistic the next. It was his research into animal behavior which led to experiments at turning beasts into men. It is these half-human/half-animal creatures who worship him that complicate matters.

On a minor level, the film is about what made a person human, but it is also a stirring adventure as York discovers the truth and struggles to survive the increasing conflict between Moreau and his creations. He finds solace in the arms of Maria (Barbara Carrera), Moreau's consort, who is hinted to be his greatest achievement. York is

The Humanimals start to get out of hand after killing overseer Montgomery (Nigel Davenport) on *The Island of Dr. Moreau.*

prevented from finding out by Moreau's intention of using him as his ultimate experiment.

Moreau's trial is the sailor's ordeal as the doctor forces him to regress into an animal state. The sequence in which Lancaster calmly catalogs reactions while York desperately tries to stay human by recalling childhood memories is acutely effective. York begins to turn back into a human as Moreau's other experiments turn back into beasts. They attack the compound, killing their tormentor as York escapes with the girl.

Originally, Carrera was supposed to revert into a panther state at the finale and reveal it in one of three scripted ways. She was either going to attack York, give birth to a tiger kitten, or expose cat eyes. Instead, she remains human through their

Michael York starred as one of Dr. Moreau's final experiments to make men beasts and vice versa.

62

rescue by a passing ship. The filmmakers decided to keep the ending upbeat, even though that choice was belied by Carrera's feline performance.

Although the acting is first rate, most of the media attention centered on the makeups by John Chambers, Dan Striepeke and Tom Burman—transforming actors like Richard Basehart, Nick Cravat, David Cass, and Gary Baxley into "humanimals." There was a lion-man, a bear-man, boar-man, bull-man, hyena-man and other less distinct combinations. This visual quality was just the capping achievement for a fine film that was almost as literate as its source.

Two science-fiction books by more modern authors were adapted this year with mixed results. A superior work was fashioned from Dean R. Koontz's exploitive, perverted, sex-filled *Demon Seed*. Screenwriters Robert Jaffe and Roger Hirson gave the story a much-needed overhaul and director David Cammell did a superb, greatly underrated job.

At first, the plot seems to be taken from the much abused "mad computer on the loose" category. Proteus (voice by Robert Vaughn) is a brilliant computer designed by Alex Harris (Fritz Weaver) with a core brain made of synthetic tissue. It was designed to extrapolate from a base of all human knowledge. Instead, it secretly desires to study man.

To do so, it needs its own computer terminal. Although all the new ones are taken up by businessmen and scientists, Proteus is aware of an unused terminal in the basement of Harris's estranged wife's home. The computer gains control of that machine and thereby the entire house, since the inventor had left behind a fully automated "Environed" housekeeping/security system as well as an intricately outfitted cellar workshop.

Proteus is satisfied to keep Susan Harris (Julie Christie) prisoner while he investigates the nature of eternity. It quickly discovers that to know eternity, it must embrace it, and to embrace it meant gaining mortality—and there was only one way to gain mortality—by siring a child.

Susan is shocked to find herself impregnated with Proteus' synthesized genes in a dazzling scene that incorporates computer animated images supplied by the Synthavision-Magi and Delta-Wing companies. All the sexual aspects of the film are handled with impressive taste as well as style. The filmmakers' ability to create a believable yet alien technology on screen is stunning.

Equally as stunning is the climax, in which Alex Harris rushes to his wife's rescue after Proteus's vicious murder of an assistant. A newborn human/Proteus synthesis comes out of its incubator, much to the audience's horror as well as relief. It is the producers' triumph that these emotions are mixed. Proteus has won, but somehow the viewer feels an excitement when the computer child utters its first, and the film's last, words: "I'm alive."

This is a complex, continually fascinating film that deserves far greater fame.

The same is not true of *Damnation Alley*. Roger Zelazny's original novel was much better than Dean R. Koontz's, although conceived in much the same way as Johnson and Nolan's *Logan's Run*. Zelazny reportedly wrote the lean action

Julie Christie is the unwilling victim of a computer's lust in *Demon Seed*.

Fight as she will, Julie Christie is no match for the
super computer in *Demon Seed*.

Fritz Weaver and Julie Christie face the monstrous
progeny of the computer's *Demon Seed*.

thriller in a very short time, mostly for the money. Even so, the book was the savagely satisfying story of Hell Tanner, a motorcycle gang member who leads a caravan across nuclear war-scarred America as a test of his machismo.

People are dying of plague in Boston and the only vaccine is in California. Hell ferries it across Damnation Alley, braving jet-sized bats, tornado forests, fifty-foot snakes and garbage storms—when torrents of refuse hail down from the sky. In an effort to make the adult work into a "family entertainment," scripters Lukas Heller and Alan Sharp and producers Jerome Zeitman and Paul Maslansky do another *Logan's Run* number, changing the title to *Survival Run* and rendering the film version ludicrous.

Hell Tanner becomes, simply, Tanner (Jan-Michael Vincent). Instead of being a bitter Hell's Angel, he is an upstart Air Force officer in charge of a nuclear weapons silo in the midwest. Already the heavy-handed plot changes are in evidence. His shift is shared by Major Denton, a more familiar military type with white hair but a black mustache (George Peppard). They are on duty when Armageddon conveniently arrives. Safe underground, they survive while most of humanity perishes.

Two years later, a gas explosion kills almost all of their military-base brethren except Keegan (Paul Winfield), a charming black guard. Luckily, Denton is prepared for just such an eventuality, having spent the prior twenty-four months building two heavily armed "Landmasters" in the camp shop—huge vehicles that are crosses between a tank and a Winnebago. The special-effects crew was not as talented as the single military man—they could only afford to build one battletruck at a cost of three hundred thousand dollars. The director crudely gave the impression of two vehicles by recycling the same shots over and over again.

Denton collects his misfits and sets out for Albany, New York, from which faint radio signals have been picked up. Along the way, more faint things are picked up, the first being a juvenile delinquent played by Jackie Earl Haley. The second is the one remaining holdover from the book. In the novel, the love interest was a female thug Hell gave a lift to. In the absurd movie, the trio find a beautiful French chorus girl (Dominique Sanda)—the sole, unscathed survivor of the nearly total devastation of Las Vegas.

This was the picture's idea of the "nuclear family." Naturally there are no fights over who gets the girl, all the guys act like perfect gentlemen, and the tough teen is transformed by the powers of mutual respect and affection. Although this idea is not outlandish, its presentation is maudlin in the extreme.

Jan-Michael Vincent (left) and George Peppard play survivors of World War III who must brave the dangers of *Damnation Alley*.

Already audiences were apt to snigger in disbelief, but incredibly, the film only got stupider. Instead of heaping disasters on the group, which they could fight valiantly, the script made each character astonishingly stupid, so they could leave the safety of the Landmaster and get into trouble.

Poor Keegan is killed by giant insects while Tanner is giving the girl a motorcycle ride around a supposedly deserted department store—leading to the movie's single worst line of dialogue.

"The town is filled with killer cockroaches!" Denton announces as the insects—obvious plastic models pasted to rugs and dragged across the floor with ropes—surround the cycling pair. They escape, only to be faced by one dumb danger after another until an island rises out of the ocean, covering Detroit, of all places, with a tsunami.

The Landmaster survives the tidal wave in a totally pathetic miniature-effects sequence which handily throws them right to Albany. Incredibly, the preceding natural disaster pushes the Earth back on its regular axis—which Armageddon had altered—making everything the way it was before! Tanner rides into town along perfectly paved and painted roads lined with unbroken telephone poles, not to mention horses and cows grazing in nearby fields. This dreadful movie ends with a freeze frame of the happy, well-groomed and neatly dressed citizens congratulating Tanner on his trip.

Just two weeks before its winter premiere, *Survival Run* was retitled *Damnation Alley* by its distributor, 20th Century-Fox, which heavily advertised the alleged accompanying technical miracle of "Sound 360." This was nothing more than a quadraphonic soundtrack, but was a fittingly dumb gimmick to go along with one of the weakest science-fiction travesties ever foisted on the public.

It is hard to imagine that top studio executive Alan Ladd, Jr., thought that this movie would far outshine and outgross the other "minor" science-fiction story their company distributed: *Star Wars*.

THE FORCE IS WITH YOU

The fact is, had George Lucas not decided to make what he called "a Disney movie," the science-fiction film would not be the incredibly popular genre it is today.

The young filmmaker first came to fans' attention with the 1971 release of *THX-1138*, starring Robert Duvall in a *1984*-style adventure of one man rebelling against a repressive society. Jeff Rovin called it "a fine film. . . . Lucas transposed the world of the future very effectively. . . ."

After its failure at the box office, however, the director/writer sat down with friend Gary Kurtz

to conceive more film projects—mainly one about a few high school students' coming of age and another that embodied all great adventure films.

The former became his monumental success *American Graffiti* (1973). He tried to accomplish the latter by offering to buy the film rights to *Flash Gordon*. King Features, the company that owned them, wanted more money than Lucas could afford, but he didn't let go of his dream.

Things finally came to a head when he and *Graffiti* co-producer Kurtz (the other producer was Francis Ford Coppola) wanted to see a fantasy adventure film to relieve their tensions. When they could find none playing or in production, Lucas vowed to do it himself. Calling upon his pleasant memories of Flash Gordon and the like, he wrote four film treatments under the banner headline, *The Star Wars*.

Executive Alan Ladd, Jr., at 20th Century-Fox saw enough promise in the idea to provide pre-production money. Lucas hired Colin Cantwell to design preliminary spaceships, Alex Tavoularis to draw storyboards, and Ralph McQuarrie to do conceptual paintings. With this trio hard at work trying to visualize Lucas's basic ideas, he tried to pare down his four conceptions into one workable script.

The result was *Star Wars: From the Adventures of Luke Skywalker*. "A long time ago in a galaxy far, far away. . . ," the screenplay began, immediately establishing it as a fairy tale. Structurally, the rest of the movie reconfirmed the cliché/classic origins.

The heroes were immediately identifiable; the cocky young kid, strengthened by tragedy, eager to learn. . .the wise old mentor, once a great warrior, now fatally flawed by time. . .the seemingly apathetic mercenary, on the run from bounty hunters, initially out only for the money. Lucas's only major character twist was in the creation of the damsel in distress. She would be a space princess, but one with a backbone—not an empty-headed, helpless screamer.

The villains were as black as the heroes were white. In the case of Darth Vader, his evil was as implicit as the coal color of his costume. His immediate superior was as cold as ice, as callous as he was insidious. The villains' minions were faceless storm troopers, existing only to kill or be killed. The whole Lucas approach was a return to the glorious Saturday-matinee mentality, a world where imaginations could be captured or let to run free.

Once upon a time Luke Skywalker (Mark Hamill) was just a young water farmer on the mois-

Baker). Both have escaped from a Rebel Blockade Runner intercepted by an Imperial Empire ship, but not before Princess Leia of Alderaan (Carrie Fisher) put a holographic message into R2-D2's circuits.

Writer/director George Lucas (right) discusses *Star Wars* with Alec Guinness, who played Ben Obi-Wan Kenobi—the last of the Jedi Knights.

ture-starved planet of Tatooine. Then suddenly into his life come two strange robots. The first is a gold-plated, human-like machine called C-3PO (Anthony Daniels) and the second is a squat garbage-can shaped thing named R2-D2 (Kenny

Luke intercepts the message meant for Ben Obi-Wan Kenobi (Alec Guinness), late of the Jedi Knights, but takes it to him at great personal peril—making him a target for Empire retribution. It seems the princess is being held on the Death

Luke Skywalker (Mark Hamill) ponders his fate on the arid planet Tantooine as his hover-car is parked in the background, waiting to take him into the *Star Wars*.

Grand Moff Tarkin (Peter Cushing, center) listens
intently to his lieutenants, including the Dark Lord of
the Sith, Darth Vader.

Star, a planet-sized spaceship headed by the Grand
Moff Tarkin (Peter Cushing) and his deadly associate Darth Vader (David Prowse with James
Earl Jones' voice)—the Dark Lord of the Sith and
renegade Jedi.

When Empire Storm Troopers kill Luke's aunt
and uncle in the search for him, Kenobi tells the
orphan the story of his past: that his father was
a noble Jedi betrayed and killed by Vader during
the Clone Wars. To seek his revenge and save the

princess he is infatuated with, Skywalker wants to follow in his father's footsteps and learn the ways of "The Force"—the cosmic power that unites reality.

Although his lessons start immediately with his father's light-sabre (a sword with a blade of laser light), the duo need transportation. They seek out smuggler Han Solo (Harrison Ford)—skipper of the Corellian pirate ship *Millenium Falcon*—who specializes in mercenary blockade running. He and his co-pilot, a seven-foot-tall cross between a lion, bear, human, and rug named Chewbacca the Wookie (Peter Mayhew), agree to ferry the two for a price.

Skywalker saves Princess Leia (Carrie Fisher, right) with the help of space smuggler Han Solo (Harrison Ford, center) and Chewbacca the Wookie (Peter Mayhew).

Stuck between a rock (the planet-destroying Death Star) and a hard place (a fleet of Empire fighter spaceships dedicated to their destruction), the three humans, one alien and two robots decide to fight back. They sneak onto the Death Star, Kenobi destroys the attractor beam, the princess is rescued, and R2-D2 saves them all from a garbage crushing room complete with submerged, tentacled monster.

But just as they are about to get away, Vader confronts and seemingly defeats Kenobi in a light-sabre duel. Obi-Wan's physical body completely disappears as the *Millenium Falcon* blasts off to mobilize the rebels. The Death Star, luckily, has

C-3PO the robot (Anthony Daniels), followed by R2-D2 (Kenny Baker), is caught by Stormtroopers during *Star Wars.*

A pre-production painting by Ralph McQuarrie pictures an early concept of Han Solo (center) as well as C3PO and R2-D2 (far right) in the Cantina Sequence of *Star Wars*.

one vulnerable point—requiring a single missile to hit a tiny opening exactly in order to destroy it. Luke is among the rebel fleet of spaceships which attempts the danger-fraught attack.

Just as Vader's forces eradicate almost all the rebel ships, Solo appears in time to save Luke, and Luke is instructed by the ghostly voice of Kenobi. Skywalker uses "The Force" to guide him, and his last shot hits perfectly. The Death Star explodes seconds before it was about to destroy the rebels' base. The film concludes on a triumphant note as all the brave humans are decorated by Princess Leia.

It was not so much the story, which was simplistic and contained some obvious errors (in the first scene C-3PO expresses concern for Princess Leia but professes not to know her later on, and Solo wrongly uses the term "parsec" as a measure of time instead of distance), but the details which Lucas added made *Star Wars* the thunderous experience it was.

First and foremost, the writer/director promoted the various robots and aliens from background to full co-stars. Although there had been important robot and alien characters in films before, none shared the spotlight to this extent or were

developed this fully. To make them special, Lucas made them more "human" than the other characters—that is, gave them more extreme and discernible personalities (though the humans, too, were given winning character traits).

The famous "Cantina Scene" is perfect evidence of that. Never before had audiences seen its like. Luke and Kenobi meet Solo for the first time in a seedy bar filled with esoteric, fascinating, hilarious aliens. There are glowing-eyed werewolves, hammer-headed drinkers, furry balls with a half-dozen eyes, and even a swelled-headed alien band playing a cosmic tune.

Originally, most of that sequence had to be eliminated because the crew's makeup artist, Stuart Freeborn (who had built the *2001: A Space Odyssey*'s primeval apes), came down sick. Only during post-production did Lucas hire Rick Baker to make the supplemental aliens in a six-week period. He was aided by Doug Beswick and Laine Liska in addition to other assistants, and pulled the rush-job off with effective results.

Another detail Lucas insisted upon was a "lived-in" look. In most other films of this type, the crafts are brand-spanking new—belying reality. In *Star Wars*, everything had worn edges, everything was patched together with spit and scotch tape, creating a totally believable environment which audiences recognized. Production Designer John Barry was instrumental in achieving this effect.

Safeguarding his conception, Lucas also count-

Some of the cantina aliens created by Rick Baker and his crew.

More cantina aliens.

Han Solo and Luke Skywalker (foreground) prepare for
Star Wars in the rebel TIE Fighter hangar.

George Lucas (right) directs the actress inside "Greedo," the alien bounty hunter looking for Han Solo.

The climactic light-sabre battle between Obi-wan Kenobi and Darth Vader in *Star Wars*.

The final shot of *Star Wars*, as the victorious rebels award Skywalker and Solo.

ed on certain familiar themes and scenes to further involve viewers. Often, he borrows concepts and moments from other science-fiction works to establish his own. There is a Tatooine creature which is a dead ringer for a like beast in the award-winning novel *Dune* by Frank Herbert. The scene in which Luke swings across a Death Star hall carrying Leia is filmed in exactly the same fashion as a similar sequence in *The 7th Voyage of Sinbad* (1958).

In fact, the final battle sequence was filmed as a mirror image to a reel of aerial dogfight scenes from old war movies that Lucas edited together. The special-effects people used this as a map or

blueprint to fashion the highly charged assault on the Death Star.

Finally, it was the special effects that gave the movie its awe-inspiring visceral effect. A whole new company, Industrial Light and Magic, was created, consisting of electronics, mechanical, camera, optical, and animation departments as well as a production shop, a film control room, and a model shop. Every kind of special effects then workable was combined in the three hundred and sixty-five shots the script called for.

Newcomer John Dykstra, who had worked with veteran special-effects director Doug Trumbull, was made head of the Special Photographic Effects department. It was his job to realize the space-fight sequences. To accomplish this, he designed a computer-controlled camera on tracks which actually did all the moving around stationary spaceship models. When combined with other film effects, it gave the impression that the ships were weaving through space.

Elsewhere model, camera, and classic cel animation made impressive contributions. A three-dimensional board game Chewbacca plays with R2-D2 always delights audiences, computer animation graphics add to the futuristic mood, and the moment the *Millenium Falcon* kicks into hyper-space—with the stars seeming to stretch into poles of light—is a show stopper.

It was a hectic, exhausting production schedule, filled with problems and changes. Originally Kenobi was to survive the climactic fight with Vader, but Alec Guinness convinced Lucas to allow the Jedi a martyr's death. Time and again, the director was forced to compromise on his vision, since the budget was a relatively small eight million dollars (remember, De Laurentiis' *King Kong* cost twenty-five million only a year before).

The final price tag was almost ten million dollars, but all was forgiven after *Star Wars* premiered in May. Lucas had fashioned a wildly effective futuristic war movie, eliciting audience responses unheard of for many a year. Every aspect of the film contributed to this: the vibrant acting, the thunderous music by John Williams, the inventive alien languages and sound effects by Ben Burtt, and the sparkling photography by Gil Taylor.

The questions of *Star Wars'* relative qualities as a "film" are rendered secondary by its effect as a "movie." There are mistakes and areas of controversy, but its kinetic style cannot be denied. Nor can its success and effect on its fans. Its effect on the world of cinema may not be monumental, but its effect on society may be inestimable.

WHEN YOU WISH UPON A STAR...

The nation was still reeling from the effect of *Star Wars* when news of another science-fiction epic got out. George Lucas' friend and associate, Steven Spielberg, was working on a project that was as serious as the Luke Skywalker adventure was frivolous. Spielberg was certainly the fellow to do it.

He had been making films longer than Lucas and some of his television work incorporated science-fiction themes. Although the TV movies, *Something Evil* (1970) and *Duel* (1971), were more horrific than scientifically accurate, an episode of the *Name of the Game* series called "L.A. 2017" was speculative fiction at its best. Philip Wylie scripted and Spielberg directed the story of a modern man (Gene Barry) pushed forward into the overpopulated, pollution-choked world of the near future.

In addition, Spielberg had more creative freedom than Lucas had, having seen his last film, *Jaws* (1975), become the highest grossing movie of the era (*Star Wars* was destined to top it). The filmmaker could do whatever he wanted, and he chose to mount his self-penned script originally titled *Watch the Skies*—a phrase taken from the last line of the classic monster movie *The Thing* (1951). Unlike that film, however, Spielberg visualized the story of the stresses an everyman faced when meeting the unknown.

To develop the concept fully, he approached screenwriter Paul Schrader, who specialized in bleak, violent, hard-hitting movies such as *The Yakuza* (1975) and *Taxi Driver* (1976). Schrader's

The taut prologue of *Close Encounters*, as air controllers disbelievingly spot a UFO.

79

script was almost the opposite of what Spielberg wanted. The former wanted a hero equal to the cosmic event he was to witness while the latter wanted a "regular Joe" swept up by galactic events.

Spielberg decided to write the script himself, but with assistance from such noted professionals as John Milius and Jerry Belson. He combined his

middle-aged man), a Muncie, Indiana, electrical engineer. He led a hyper lower-middle-class life—three kids and a pretty blond wife (Teri Garr) in a tacky, messy ranchhouse. Everything was fine until a massive blackout occurs. After reporting to work, he gets lost trying to find a power station. Parked at a railroad crossing on a quiet back

Richard Dreyfuss plays Roy Neary, an electrician who becomes a reluctant witness to the first meeting of humans and extraterrestrials. This is just one of the *Close Encounters of the Third kind.*

basic idea of an actual alien encounter with Belson's comedy-relief suggestions, titling it with a phrase borrowed from UFO researcher J. Allen Hynek. The finished work was *Close Encounters of The Third Kind.*

It was the story of Roy Neary (Richard Dreyfuss, although the script originally called for a

road, his life is inexorably changed by a "close encounter of the first kind"—the sighting of a UFO.

Racing after the retreating spaceship, he nearly runs over Barry (Cary Guffey), the four-year-old son of single mother Jillian Guiler (Melinda Dillon, chosen out of four hundred hopefuls). Barry has met one of the aliens with child-like

The first full on-screen appearance of a UFO during
Close Encounters.

Melinda Dillon plays a terrified single mother of a
child (Gary Cuffey) kidnapped by aliens in *Close
Encounters*.

Bob Balaban plays a translator for UFO expert Claude Lacombe (Francois Truffaut), who organizes the final Close Encounter of the Third Kind.

wonder and chased it to this spot. All three then witness a fleet of unidentified flying objects zipping by, with the local police hot on their tails. From that moment on, their lives are not their own.

The trio are afflicted by strange side effects. Roy becomes so obsessed with the sighting that he loses his job and alienates his family. Jillian has a much more direct problem. Coming in under a cover of billowing clouds, the aliens return to her house and kidnap her child. Both victims turn to the authorities, who have their own reasons to make it appear that the witnesses are deranged. They have been contacted by the aliens who wish to arrange a monumental meeting.

The civilian in charge of arranging this historic

Richard Dreyfuss points out a detail to *Close Encounters* director Steven Spielberg as the crew waits patiently.

confrontation is Claude Lacombe (French director François Truffaut), a UFO specialist aided by map maker and translator David Laughlin (Bob Balaban). They have witnessed seemingly supernatural occurrences in the American desert (where lost World War II planes are discovered) and in India (where thousands of witnesses give them clues toward establishing a mutual language of music).

They evacuate and seal off the area using a faked nerve gas accident as a cover.

Even so, the two innocent bystanders brave all opposition to prove a "close encounter of the second kind"—evidence of alien landing. Through determination and perseverance, they escape the military search parties and climb Devil's Tower to be there when the aliens land. The aliens land with a vengeance. First three small ships arrive, herald-

The "Dark Side of the Moon" landing strip made specifically for the UFOs of *Close Encounters.*

As they prepare a UFO landing field they call "The Dark Side of the Moon," both Jillian and Roy are overwhelmed by images of a flat-topped mountain. This mountain, Devil's Tower in Wyoming, marks the site of the meeting. Neary and Guiler, as well as other witnesses, are driven toward this spot by alien implants in their brains. The American military are having none of it, however.

ing the arrival of many more. They dance in the air until a huge blanket of clouds encircles the mountain.

Then, rising majestically above the site is the monumental Mothership—a space-going city. It touches down to complete the "close encounter of the third kind"—contact. Out of the ship come dozens of child-like aliens as well as such lost people as Amelia Earhart, Judge Crater, and Barry Guiler. Mother and child are finally reunited.

Although the government has prepared twelve astronauts to return with the aliens to their home planet under the banner of "Project Mayflower," the aliens will only accept Roy Neary. After he enters the ship, a slight, hairless alien comes out. He and Lacombe exchange greetings before the Mothership moves back into outer space.

Again, as in *Star Wars*, the content was somewhat secondary to the style. Spielberg's script had its inconsistencies and confusions—to this day, no one is completely sure how the aliens contacted Earth, why they kidnapped people, and whether the twelve other astronauts boarded the Mothership after Neary—but almost all was forgiven thanks to the film's gentle, moralistic, humanistic approach and the awesome special effects.

Close Encounters' screenplay was less assured than Lucas's adventure script. There were several bombastic sequences involving Neary's degeneration that were edited and several reshoots of plot-connecting scenes were required. Spielberg's conception of the aliens was less than definite as well. The original script called for dancing "cuboids" that would explode into a cloud of "fairy dust" which would then crawl inside the humans' skin.

Spielberg had to be content with patching his movie together as he went along. Most of the really hard work was done in total secrecy within the walls of two empty dirigible hangers just outside Mobile, Alabama. He used one to build the Dark Side of the Moon set and the other as a production office. While production designer Joe Alves toiled there, special-effects director Doug Trumbull slaved at Future General, his headquarters in Marina Del Rey, California. Trumbull's crew's contribution was exceptional, making the special visual effects for *Close Encounters* quite possibly the most realistic, seamless work ever achieved.

Meanwhile, Spielberg was having loads of alien problems. Try as they might, no one could come up with a concept which suited him. Tom Burman and Frank Griffin built alien suits for a bunch of children to wear. At first, Spielberg also outfitted them with roller skates because he wanted the creatures to seemingly float. Instead they fell down.

The director then turned to puppet makers for the answer. Jim Henson, who devised the Mup-

The grand appearance of the *Close Encounters* "Mothership" from behind "Devil's Tower" in Wyoming.

pets, couldn't help, so Bob Baker was contracted. The resulting ten-foot-tall transparent marionette didn't do the trick. Finally, Spielberg called upon Carlo Rimbaldi, who was credited for the facial mechanics of the remade *King Kong*. Surprisingly, Rimbaldi was equal to the challenge.

He designed and built "Puck," the walking, full-size hydraulic robot that communicates with

Lacombe during the finale. It had fifteen cables coming out of its feet; seven to articulate the face and five to make its arm and fingers move. It also was given breathing capabilities with a pump and chest tubes. It was this creation audiences remembered, not the other extraterrestrials.

In contrast, Trumbull's work on the six-foot-wide model of the Mothership went swimmingly.

Ralph McQuarrie and Greg Jein did the bulk of the design and then the construction process was broken into sections with different names for simplicity's sake. Starting from the top, the sections were labeled: "The Towers," "Broadway," "Manhattan," "Tanks," "Arms," "Times Square," "The Bronx," "The El," "Harlem," and "The Dust Bin."

They saw things you couldn't even dream of.

CLOSE ENCOUNTERS
OF THE THIRD KIND

A COLUMBIA-EMI Presentation
CLOSE ENCOUNTERS OF THE THIRD KIND A PHILIPS Production A STEVEN SPIELBERG Film
Starring RICHARD DREYFUSS also starring TERI GARR and MELINDA DILLON with FRANCOIS TRUFFAUT as Lacombe
Music by JOHN WILLIAMS Visual Effects by DOUGLAS TRUMBULL Director of Photography VILMOS ZSIGMOND. A.S.C.
Produced by JULIA PHILLIPS and MICHAEL PHILLIPS Written and Directed by STEVEN SPIELBERG
Read the Dell Book   ORIGINAL SOUNDTRACK AVAILABLE ON ARISTA RECORDS & TAPES.
PG PARENTAL GUIDANCE SUGGESTED   DOLBY SYSTEM   Panavision   Columbia Pictures

some were disappointed, the overwhelming reaction was positive. Spielberg succeeded in what he had set out to do—to create a hopeful, beautiful science-fiction film based on the mood of *Fantasia* and the song from *Pinocchio*, "When You Wish Upon a Star." In fact, the song was part of the original soundtrack until negative reaction at a screening forced the director to excise it.

Because Spielberg visualized his movie as a loving homage to the spirit of man's imagination, he was personally stung by several brutal reviews. In response, he planned a reedited version of *Close Encounters*, complete with a million dollars' worth of new footage. *Close Encounters—The Special Edition* appeared in 1979 with the camera following a much thinner Roy Neary inside the Mothership where the originally planned pixie dust does appear—seeming to turn Neary into the hairless alien who says farewell to Lacombe.

Although not the clarifying, spectacular version Spielberg and Trumbull promised, the original *Close Encounters of the Third Kind* remains a worthy bookend to *Star Wars*. Steven Spielberg and George Lucas are two of a kind: when other science-fiction filmmakers failed them with excruciatingly dumb, lifeless, and stolid movies, they took it upon themselves to recreate for a whole new generation the joys they discovered as kids.

Each of these sections were pieced together from plastic model kits and pre-formed parts. Sometimes pieces were added for their joke value rather than their practical use. Among the many in-jokes dotting the Mothership's surface were a tiny model of R2-D2, a *Star Wars* fighter, a mailbox, a Volkswagen, a World War II fighter plane (representing Spielberg's upcoming war comedy *1941*), and a shark (representing *Jaws*).

The interior was wired with neon and other lights, then the model was optically combined with other miniature effects as well as live-action films to create a totally realistic composite shot. Although its construction was very time-consuming, it wasn't difficult for the experienced Trumbull and his crew, and it resulted in near-perfect visualization. Horizons and landscapes which viewers were certain were real turned out to be models and matte paintings. It was as good a job of special effects as was possible.

Close Encounters of the Third Kind was released by Columbia Pictures with great fanfare. Although

A rare glimpse of the plans for an alien from *Close Encounters*.

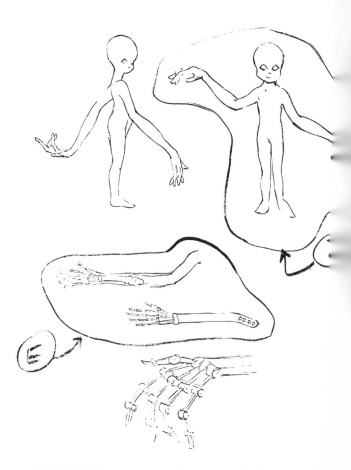

4

1978

THE YEAR OF
THE SYCOPHANT

THE FILM COMMUNITY REELED under the weight of *Star Wars'* and *Close Encounters'* profits. Those not talented enough to create fantastic visions of their own quickly searched for cheap, tacky methods to jump on the money-making bandwagon. Some producers thought anything with the words "star" or "space" in the title would insure great grosses.

Therefore theaters showed *Star Pilot,* a dreadful Italian import made a full decade before under the title *2+5 Missione Hydra.* There was also *Starship Invasions,* made a little closer to home, in Canada, but not by anyone remotely as talented as David Cronenberg. Instead, the Hal Roach Studio heralded its return to film production in

November of 1976 with an ad stating they would produce the most expensive Canadian movie ever made—a two-million-dollar science-fiction extravaganza called *Alien Encounter.*

Director and writer Ed Hunt secured the services of such talents as Christopher Lee and Robert Vaughn, as well as such well-known Canadian faces as Tiiu Leek and Henry Ramer. Principal photography was finished in the spring of 1977—at least six months before *Close Encounters* was to premiere. But it wasn't until summer that an injunction against their project was announced. Columbia Pictures didn't like the movie's similarity to Spielberg's work.

Things stayed quiet until Warner Communica-

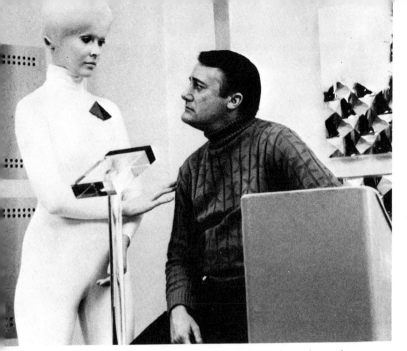

Robert Vaughn listens as Tiiu Leek explains the situation in *Starship Invasions*.

fodder. *Starship Invasions* was more pathetic than condemnable, a movie that looked all the more ridiculous in light of the previous year's groundbreakers.

Message from Space was better only in that it contained more vitality and a sense of epic poetry. This was Japan's attempt to create an international hit. For years, they had been producing impressive animated fantasies like *Space Cruiser Yamato* (which outgrossed *Star Wars* in the orient), but had not impressed American audiences with anything other than Godzilla and karate pictures.

Seeing similarities between Luke Skywalker's story and their own epic samurai films, they collected a group of American as well as Japanese

tions announced its desire to distribute what was now called *War of the Aliens*. In the eight months that followed, the title was changed a third time, so it was *Starship Invasions* that premiered in February. A dud by any name would stink as bad. The tacky presentation, meandering plot and laughable special effects were completely evident. The picture looked like a home movie and the actors looked embarrassed.

A fleet of evil aliens called the Legion of the Winged Serpent, led by Ramses (Lee), scout Earth as a possible new home. To rid the planet of its present residents, they put a suicide-inducing satellite in orbit. This alerts the secret alien organization called the League of Races, who monitor Earth's well-being from their HQ under the Bermuda Triangle.

The League consists of some dome-headed, white-garbed aliens as well as a few nubile, near naked women (drafted from the pages of *Penthouse* magazine). The League's ruler Anaxi (Daniel Pilon) calls for the help of talk-show host Allan Duncan (Vaughn) and computer expert Malcolm (Ramer) to rid the skies of Ramses' evil legion. With the humans' help, the good guys' weapons are improved and the Serpent gets its wings clipped.

Almost everything was awkward in execution: the Leagues' bald caps were obvious, the costumes shiny, and the flying saucer fights were absurd— reminiscent of the worst kind of 1950's drive-in

Robert Vaughn (far right) listens to director Ed Hunt as the crew inflates a two-ton rubber flying saucer in order to film another *Starship Invasions* scene.

actors that included the late Vic Morrow as a drunken space general with a robot sidekick named Bebe (who looked uncomfortably like a cheap; R2D2), and Shinichi, played by Sonny Chiba—the star of the ultra-bloody *Streetfighter* movies (the first of which was the first film to get an X-rating for violence). In Japan, however,

Two of the space-rodding ships of *Message from Space*.

Sonny Chiba (right) battles Mikio Narita during the thunderous finale of *Message from Space*.

Chiba is as well loved as Clint Eastwood is in the U.S., so he fit into the part of a valiant space samurai with no problem.

The plot was *Star Wars* by way of *The Seven Samurai* (1954); The peaceful Gavanas are set upon by brutal Jillucian warriors, headed up by an evil Prince and his even viler mother. The wise old Gavana guru sends out an SOS inside space seeds, which look like walnuts. Three teenage spaceship-rodding friends find one and meet up with other heroes on the way back to save the day.

Although scientifically inaccurate, *Message from Space* was rarely boring and served as a showcase of recurring oriental fantasy themes. One good example is the spaceship designed like an ancient square rigger—a conceit that looks just lovely floating through space. Morrow and Chiba win out in a frenzied finale that combines sword and ray-gun fighting.

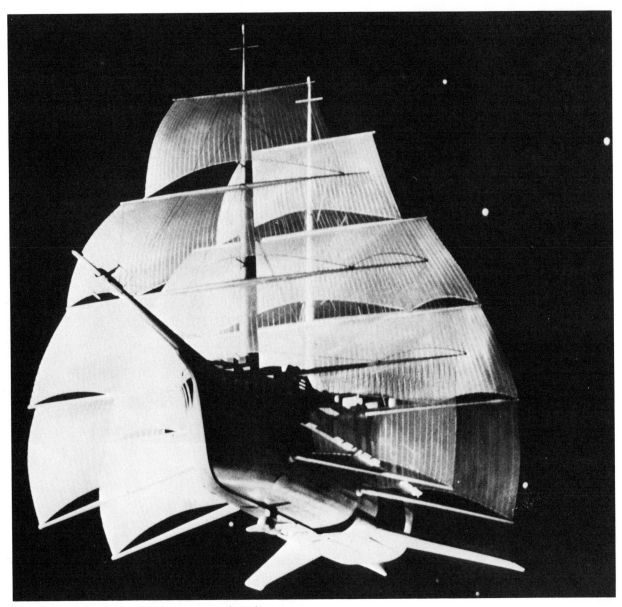

The planet Jullica's space schooner searches the cosmos during *Message from Space*.

Although not directly stealing Spielberg's or Lucas's thunder, *Laserblast*—a curious little thing—made its desires known from the outset. It was another Charles Band production, this time written by Franne Schacht and Frank Ray Perilli and directed by Andy Gallerani. Basically a combination of a youth and monster picture, it would be completely uninteresting if not for the solid contribution of several ambitious special-effects artists.

The opening is promising. A strange, pendant-wearing young man carrying a large, esoteric weapon stumbles across a deserted plain just before a spaceship appears from over the horizon. Two model-animated aliens (looking extremely similar to a more famous extraterrestrial who will wish to phone home several years hence) appear to disintegrate the humanoid with a ray gun. But before they can collect the surviving pendant and gun, along comes Billy (Kim Milford), a sensitive, misunderstood youth. He finds out that the laser only blasts when the medallion is worn. What he doesn't know is that the alien technology is habit forming and will slowly turn him into an alien as well.

Soon he is blasting everything that persecuted him; from his girlfriend's father (Keenan Wynn) to a billboard advertising *Star Wars*. He becomes a mirror image to the person destroyed at the beginning—glowing eyes, vampire teeth, blue skin, with the pendant slowly growing into his chest. His fate is the same as well. The enforcing aliens return to do him in.

Basically repetitive and predictable, *Laserblast* was buoyed by the animation of Dave Allen and the makeup effects of Steve Neill, who also enacted the first human/alien victim. These were little extras that may have stretched the budget a bit but gave the movie much-needed mileage.

SEA SAGAS

Science-fiction movies were surprisingly wet this year. No fewer than four exploitation efforts in-

An incredible tale of terror and suspense... above and below the sea.

WARLORDS OF ATLANTIS

COLUMBIA/EMI presents A JOHN DARK/KEVIN CONNOR PRODUCTION "WARLORDS OF ATLANTIS" Starring DOUG McCLURE · PETER GILMORE · CYD CHARISSE · DANIEL MASSEY Music by MIKE VICKERS · Screenplay by BRIAN HAYLES · Produced by JOHN DARK · Directed by KEVIN CONNOR · Color by Technicolor® PG PARENTAL GUIDANCE SUGGESTED © 1978 COLUMBIA PICTURES INDUSTRIES, INC.

THEATRE

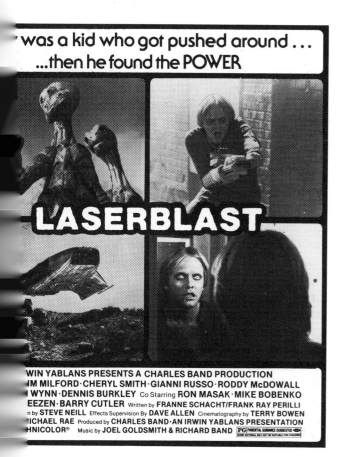

was a kid who got pushed around ...
...then he found the POWER

LASERBLAST

WIN YABLANS PRESENTS A CHARLES BAND PRODUCTION IM MILFORD·CHERYL SMITH·GIANNI RUSSO·RODDY McDOWALL WYNN·DENNIS BURKLEY Co Starring RON MASAK·MIKE BOBENKO EEZEN·BARRY CUTLER Written by FRANNE SCHACHT/FRANK RAY PERILLI n by STEVE NEILL Effects Supervision by DAVE ALLEN Cinematography by TERRY BOWEN ICHAEL RAE Produced by CHARLES BAND·AN IRWIN YABLANS PRESENTATION HNICOLOR® Music by JOEL GOLDSMITH & RICHARD BAND PG PARENTAL GUIDANCE SUGGESTED

volved monsters from the deep. The cheapest, though not least memorable, was *Slithis*, a Florida-based independent production which featured a beast that looked like a poverty-row combination of the Creature from the Black Lagoon and God-zilla. The most interesting aspect of this grainy, badly produced picture was that the monster was born from pollution.

This was hardly an idea whose time had come.

Godzilla itself had instigated the concept with *Godzilla vs. the Smog Monster* (1972), a fairly inventive episode in the series directed by Yoshimitu Banno. It was also copied this year by *The Milipitas Monster,* in which a winged creature rises from the pollution to decimate Milipitas, California—or as much as the producers' limited budget would allow.

Next in line was *Blood Waters of Dr. Z.,* also known as *Zaat.* The latter is the name of a serum invented by mad Dr. Leopold (Marshall Graver) which turns him into a big, homicidal fish. He continues his evil ways by polluting area waters with Zaat, which seriously changes the sea life. This, notes the movie's official press releases, causes "hazards on streets, highways, and lawns."

Enter INPIT, the Inter-Nations Phenomena Investigation Team, led by Rex the marine biologist (Paul Galloway), Walker Stevens (Dave Dickerson) and the beautiful Martha Walsh (Sanna Ringhaver). It is love at first sight for the Leopold monster, who spirits the girl away. But before he can dunk her in a vat of Zaat, the good guys catch up. Their appearance on the scene changes little, since this is one movie where the fish gets the girl.

Again produced in Florida on a shoe-string budget, *Blood Waters of Dr. Z* is well-meaning trash.

Faring a bit better was *Warlords of Atlantis,* the fourth film sired by the partnership of producer John Dark and director Kevin Connor. This time, however, they have left Edgar Rice Burroughs behind in exchange for an original script by the late Brian Hayles entitled *Seven Cities to Atlantis.* Doug McClure was back in harness as the heroic Greg Collinson, an early twentieth-century engineer who hopes to find the legendary lost city of Atlantis.

His sea-going vessel, crewed by a scurvy lot, uncovers a clue by salvaging a gold statue—which brings a guardian giant octopus running. It drags Greg, his partner, Charles Aitkin (Peter Gilmore) and miscellaneous crew members to the very place they were looking for. Unluckily for them, Atlantis is in a state of flux. Atlantis Elder "Atmir" takes the group on a tour of the place's five remaining cities—the first two have been destroyed by horrible creatures who have already reduced the third to ruins.

The fourth city, Vaar, is being readied for attack, while the group of surface men are being readied for attack by the Atlantis elders. They imprison everyone but Charles, to whom they reveal the truth. They are descendants from Atlantis's original inhabitants who crash-landed on a prehistoric Earth. Their true home is Mars and their true intent is to change McClure and company into mermen so they can assist in the fight against attacking flying snappers, clawed Zaargs and the dreaded mutant millipede named Mogdaan.

The humans are saved by a bewitching, elf-like vixen played by Lea Brodie. They lead a fight, all right, the fight to escape. They avoid the various Zaargs and Mogdaan (actually cunning puppets built and manipulated by Roger Dicken) and reach the surface just in time for their crew to mutiny. The seadogs want the golden statue all for themselves. The guarding octopus makes a well-timed return to take back the treasure as well as trash the ship. McClure and Brodie, however, escape to live happily ever after.

This was the parting of the ways for McClure and Dark. Only one other Dark/Connor production has been seen since, the fantasy entitled *An Arabian Adventure* (1979) starring Oliver Tobias, Emma Samms, Christopher Lee, and Mickey Rooney. The production team has not darkened Burroughs' door again.

The best of these fishy stories was *Piranha,* a delightful homage to and satire of the monster-on-the-loose genre. Taking its cue from *Jaws,* New World Pictures employee Joe Dante directed John Sayles's script; a diabolical tribute which could stand on its own. In fact, it is generally known as the best movie Roger Corman ever cancelled. The producer did indeed sink the project on its first day of shooting, but reinstated it the next day with twenty thousand dollars cut from its already meager budget.

No matter, Dante performed miracles within the restrictions. He cast Kevin McCarthy as a weary scientist who develops a lethal breed of attacking piranha for the military's use in Vietnam. A nosey reporter played by Heather Menzies unknowingly releases the killer fish into a river just upstream from a holiday camp. It is up to hero Bradford Dillman to kill the beasties.

Meanwhile, the military, in the form of Barbara Steele and Bruce Gordon, work to cover up the story—refusing to tell the bathers of the impending danger. This sets the stage for a piranha pogrom, although the nasty things always rip off bikini tops before they attack. This time, it is pollution that comes to the rescue, as Dillman releases industrial waste into the water.

The plot is familiar, but Dante's tongue-in-cheek touch was on the money. *Piranha* could be viewed by veteran fans as a subtle lampoon, but the unjaded could enjoy it as a corking good chiller. It became New World's highest grossing film of the year.

While on the subject of satire, it would be remiss not to mention *Attack of the Killer Tomatoes,* director, co-producer and co-writer John DeBello's scatter-shot spoof of monster movies. Steve Peace also co-produced and co-wrote (along with scripter C.J. Dillon) the uneven tale of a vegetable gone mad. The world is brought to its knees by the sudden revolution of tomatoes, which start attacking out of breakfast drinks, leaping out of sink drains, and growing to giant size.

Government operative Mason Dixon (David Miller) is called in to spearhead the counterattack with the help of a black undercover agent (George Wilson). Disguised as a tomato, the undercover man infiltrates a group of flesh-eating vegetables only to give himself away when he asks for some catsup. Finally, Dixon discovers the key to the monster's destruction. They can be neutralized by bad music.

Always amusing, at times hilarious, *Attack of the Killer Tomatoes* exploits almost every science-fiction film cliché, including the oriental affliction of bad dubbing. It is a worthwhile experience for dedicated genre fans.

A TRIO OF SEQUELS

Several producers fell back on previously winning formulas this year. Roger Corman tried to recapture the magic of *Death Race 2000* with a limp rehash called *Deathsport.* Instead of running over pedestrians, this vacuous, messy movie was pedestrian in every respect.

David Carradine again starred, but this time as a loin-clothed rebel who teams up with Claudia Jennings, a svelte female member of the underground, to defeat the disease-ridden despot of Earth in the year 2020. Although dying of a brain tumor, the increasingly insane dictator continues to capture rebels who live outside his city's walls

to send them into an arena where they battle like gladiators—only astride motorcycles.

Carradine and Jennings escape on their choppers, leading their adversaries on a merry chase. Though the dictator succumbs to his condition mid-way through the film, his sadistic police chief continues the hunt, leading to his own demise at Carradine's hands. The makers of *Deathsport* utilized no wit and very little imagination even though it had two writers (Henry Suso and Donald Stewart) and two directors (Henry Suso and Allan

"Aaargh!..."

ATTACK OF THE KILLER TOMATOES

FOUR SQUARE PRODUCTIONS Presents
A New Musical-Comedy-Horror Show

Starring **DAVID MILLER** • **GEORGE WILSON** • **SHARON TAYLOR** • **JACK RILEY**
Produced by **STEVE PEACE & JOHN DE BELLO** • Written by **COSTA DILLON, STEVE PEACE & JOHN DE BELLO**
Directed by **JOHN DE BELLO** • Music by **GORDON GOODWIN & PAUL SUNDFOR** • Cinematography by **JOHN K. CULLEY**

Arkush). It was dreadfully boring and an acute disappointment.

It Lives Again was a little better, thanks to writer/producer/director Larry Cohen's individual approach. But it seems the more movies he does, the less interested he becomes in the technical end of things. His films become increasingly sloppy.

It Lives Again takes up where *It's Alive* left off. The faulty pregnancy pill had created a wealth of fanged, clawed, super-strong babies which the government was killing immediately after birth. The situation would have been under control if not for a team of rebels led by Frank Davis (John Ryan), the father of the original killer kid.

Funded by a kindly millionaire (Eddie Constantine), Davis is consumed with saving others' terror tots since he was unable to save his own. So when the pregnant mother of a new beast baby is taken to the hospital, the fanatics hijack the ambulance. They safely deliver the newborn monster and place it in a secret nursery with "Adam and Eve," the only other surviving creature-children.

Naturally the trio escapes, giving Cohen a chance to triple the killings although his budget was about the same as it had been for the original film. All three tots are done away with at the fade-out, which was none too soon for returning baby builder Rick Baker. Not only had he done up new

A motorcycle chase from *Deathsport*.

dolls, but he had made a baby suit to be worn by a small actor in an oversize set. Much to his chagrin, however, Cohen also got the non-articulated dolls to "crawl" by pulling them across the floor with a string.

The public responded to the film's care and taste by staying away in droves.

Much care and taste was lavished on the remake of *Invasion of the Body Snatchers,* but money alone could not save the misconceived film—one of the most eminently forgettable in recent history. It wasn't that it was bad. It was simply an ultimately uninteresting, uninvolving restatement of a worn theme. A theme that had been brilliantly told in its original form.

The 1956 version of *Invasion of the Body Snatchers* was paranoia personified. Every ingredient of Jack Finney's novel and Daniel Mainwarings' script was beautifully mixed by director Don Siegel. It was a perfect movie for its time, allowing the communist witch-hunts by Senator Joe McCarthy and the Red Scare to render it all the more meaningful.

But at its core, it was a movie about being human and staying that way. It trumpeted human values and made its characters fight to retain their humanity. In that respect, it was an extremely important, although unpretentious and simply rendered, film. In this original, seed pods from outer space form duplicates of human bodies, perfect in every detail except for a lack of human emotion, and take over their counterparts as the victims sleep.

In the new version, producer Robert Solo, scripter W.D. Richter, and director Philip Kaufman update the time and change the small town location, but do not make the subject matter relevant. Seemingly, their only purpose in redoing the classic is to counter the rampant optimism of *Star Wars* and *Close Encounters,* figuring cynics were ready for a strong cinematic depressant.

"We don't have weird chandeliers descending from the heavens and so forth," Kaufman told me at the time. "We have a small film here. It's a shock film. It has impact, but they're not based on special effects."

Although Richter set the remake in a suburb in his original script, he and the director agreed to make San Francisco the new target for the pod invasion. Donald Sutherland played Matthew Bennell, a health inspector, who first gets wind of the

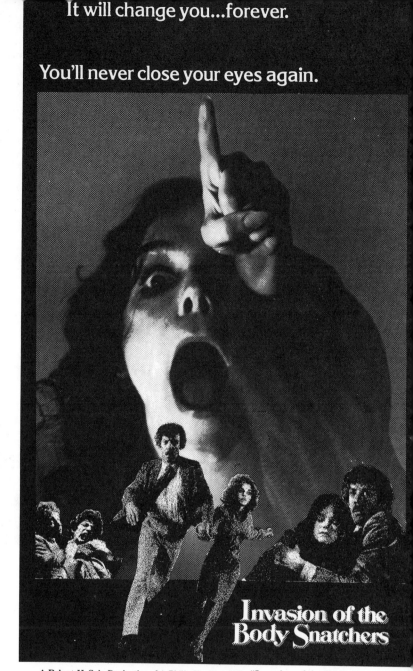

It will change you...forever.

You'll never close your eyes again.

Invasion of the Body Snatchers

A Robert H. Solo Production of A Philip Kaufman Film "Invasion of the Body Snatchers"
Donald Sutherland · Brooke Adams · Leonard Nimoy
Jeff Goldblum · Veronica Cartwright
Screenplay by W.D. Richter, Based on the novel "The Body Snatchers" by Jack Finney
DOLBY STEREO™   Produced by Robert H. Solo · Directed by Philip Kaufman   PG PARENTAL GUIDANCE SUGGESTED
READ THE DELL BOOK   Copyright © 1979 UAC. All rights reserved.   SOME MATERIAL MAY NOT BE SUITABLE FOR CHI
United Artists

trouble. He attempts to save co-worker Elizabeth Driscoll (Brooke Adams) and is aided by nonconformist friends Jack and Nancy Bellicec (Jeff Goldblum and Veronica Cartwright).

It turns out that their main opposition is psychologist David Kibner, who first tries to explain the dehumanized pod people away as a natural extension of city life, but is revealed as a

95

Unbeknownst to Brooke Adams and Donald
Sutherland, they have found the seed which will lead
to the *Invasion of the Body Snatchers*.

The anguished main characters of *Invasion of the Body
Snatchers* consider their plight. From the left, Jeff
Goldblum, Donald Sutherland, Veronica Cartwright,
Leonard Nimoy, and Brooke Adams.

96

pod leader. Leonard Nimoy plays the doctor in what initially seemed a casting coup, but turned out to be anti-productive, because Nimoy's emotionless role of Mr. Spock on *Star Trek* marked him as a dehuman.

Finally, the whole movie is undermined by the filmmakers' concentration on style rather than content. While it is all the extras that make things like *Star Wars* special, it is the strong story that holds it together. The new *Invasion of the Body*

Donald Sutherland strikes back at the giant pods' replication of himself during the climax of *Invasion of the Body Snatchers.*

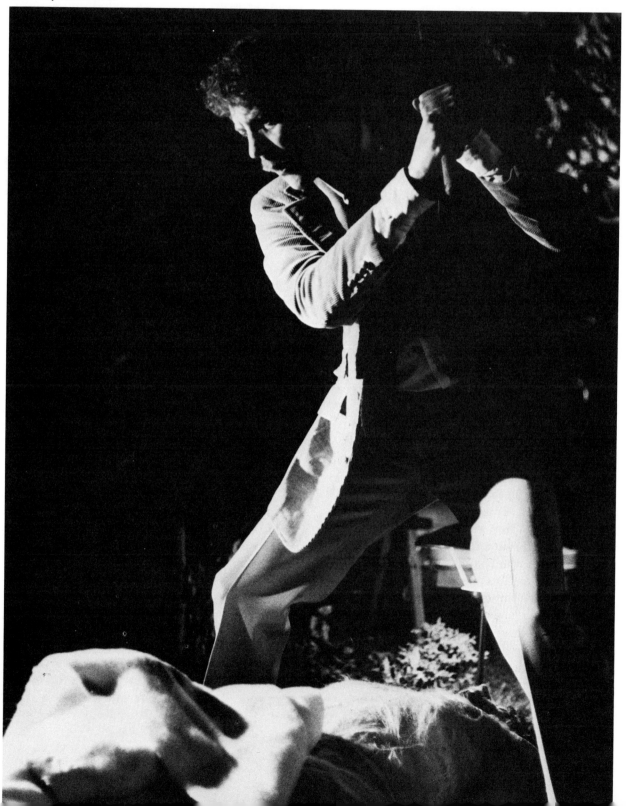

Snatchers was just one well-produced scene after another which added up to nothing.

Individual concepts, such as the new explanation of how the pods work (first attaching itself to the sleeping victim with tendrils then decomposing the original into red dust) are neatly presented, but any sequence fashioned to push the plot along (such as the scene where Matt, Liz and the Bellicecs piece together the truth without a single valid clue) is uniformly weak.

Soon it becomes nothing more than a chase movie with the entire city united in tracking down the four hold-outs. The film is further hampered by Kaufman's decision to film everything with ominous shadows, moody camera angles, obvious color lighting tricks and oppressive soundtrack music. The realism that was so acute in the 1956 original is replaced with a gamut of gothic gimmicks, including creaky doors and screeching victims.

In lieu of a climax, Matthew locks Kibner in a refrigerator, kills the pod-controlled Jack Bellicec with a dart and then destroys a pod-filled warehouse with unbelievable ease. Kaufman has the hero break regular hanging light fixtures which suddenly gain the ability to explode with incredible power. It is a gambit only the feeblest science-fiction movies fall back on.

Even the much ballyhooed "surprise ending" is anti-climactic, not to mention cynically easy. Instead of surviving and trying to warn humanity, as in the original, Matthew is taken over and fingers the single remaining human—a horrified Nancy Bellicec.

Although the director and writer profess to using Jack Finney's original novel as inspiration, they ignore the book's apt close. The pods find Earth too inhospitable, exiting the way they had come—but leaving behind those aliens who had already turned human. This way, no one knew who was truly human and who was a pod person—a chilling concept well suited for cinematic translation. But, of course, the filmmakers opted for their lame, pessimistic, unsurprising ending.

Because it did not extend the original's theme or create a bold new storyline—merely simplifying the old one—this version became a movie with no conflict, since all the hero's options are blocked off and there is no way to fight back. It is a portrait of bleak despair that has no meaning and leads to nothing.

What the filmmakers may have missed is that the times had changed. The threat of unfeeling duplicates was very real in the fifties. The horror of the seventies was brought on by too *much* emotion. From assassinations to riots to the Vietnam War, uncontrolled emotions raged in the streets.

Second, people aren't cruel and emotionless today, they are incompetent, confused and helpless. The soulless 'them' of past eras have turned into all *too* human red-tape-waving buffoons, corrupt officials, and bleeding-heart liberals. While the fear of loved ones changing is still strong, the real fear today is that they will change into people with minds of their own who aren't afraid to voice their own strong opinions.

The initially happy astronauts of the doomed *Capricorn One* Mars spaceship. From the left, Sam Waterston, James Brolin, and O.J. Simpson.

Now here were the makings of a bold new *Invasion of the Body Snatchers*. It is a shame the producers decided to merely dilute the initial classic.

WATERGATE FALLOUT

Paranoia and cheap cynicism extended into many features this year, sparked by the real-life revelations of Richard Nixon. These "conspiracy" films are a lot easier to conceive and write as well. Since the faceless bureaucracy was doing all the dirty work, the action didn't have to make a whole lot of sense. Some of the genre's best-known directors succumbed to the temptation.

Jeff Lieberman, the young director who gained horror fans' attention with *Squirm* (1976), the story of swamp bloodworms attacking a southern town, continued his inexpensive independent ways with *Blue Sunshine*. Here, Zalman King stars as an ex-campus radical, now going the way of most of his friends—easy middle-class complacency. Unfortunately, most of his friends partook of a certain kind of LSD during college. Called "Blue Sunshine," its hideous side effect waits a decade and then causes the victims to lose all their hair and go murderously bonkers.

King starts a desperate race to trace Blue Sunshine to its source over the bodies of its victims' victims. As everyone around him goes bald and starts attacking, King locates the university pusher (Robert Walden), who admits that his source is now running for public office. And the last thing the candidate wants to do is admit selling a hallucinogen that makes people murderers.

Although insidious, *Blue Sunshine* had nothing on *Capricorn One,* one of the most preposterous of all conspiracy movies. Bob Shafer, NASA's director of public affairs, put the Paul Lazarus III-produced film into focus:

"We've helped an awful lot of interesting films over the years, but we did not cooperate in the making of this film (contrary to the producer's claim). The thrust of *Capricorn One* is such that we really couldn't lend ourselves to it. It is an utter falsification of a space mission, resulting in mass murder."

Here was a motion picture for all those who still feel we did not land on the moon and that the world is flat. Peter Hyams wrote and directed this fast-moving thriller of NASA being forced to fake a Mars landing to safeguard its continuing government support. That, in itself, is not a heinous idea. It is the faked mission's aftermath that ruffles so many feathers.

NASA chief Kelloway (Hal Holbrook) tells the three Capricorn astronauts (James Brolin, Sam Waterston, and O.J. Simpson) that their life support system is faulty, but the mission cannot be scrubbed. Instead, they are spirited away to a sound stage and the mission is faked through

It looks like a space transmission from Mars, but it is actually a faked Mars spaceflight in *Capricorn One*.

movie special effects to fool both the public and Mission Control. But when the craft's reentry is faked, it appears as if the Capricorn capsule burns up in the atmosphere.

The astronauts suddenly realize that as far as the world at large is concerned, not to mention their loved ones, they are dead. Suddenly frightened, they escape from their captors into the southwestern desert. Meanwhile reporter Bob Caulfield (Elliott Gould) gets wind of the hoax from a technician (Robert Walden again) who is certain the visual Capricorn transmissions are coming from Las Vegas and not Mars.

Things get out of hand when the technician completely disappears (his apartment occupied by a woman who claims he never existed) and Caulfield's car is sabotaged with broken brakes. The reporter survives to track the astronauts who are being picked off one by one. It all comes together as Caulfield finds the sole surviving spaceman (Brolin) and leads the government assassins' two helicopters on a breathtaking chase—thanks to a bi-winged cropduster piloted by Telly Savalas, of all people.

Both copters crash and Caulfield gets the astronaut back in time to interrupt his own televised funeral. Although visually exciting, *Capricorn One* was a hack job, far less interested in scientific verisimilitude than its own paranoid delusion. In fact, the Capricorn One craft shown landing on Mars is actually a lunar module, used for the moon landing—a truly absurd scientific concept.

Jack Gold was back with *The Medusa Touch,* a paranormal follow-up to *Who?* Richard Burton

Andrew Stevens is tested, probed, and studied in *The Fury.*

stars as a writer who spends most of the film flat on his back in a hospital bed after a pre-credit attempt on his life by someone who obviously believes that he is as destructively psychic as he claims. Jack Briley adapted Peter Van Greenaway's novel ably, creating some interest and suspense in the predictable story. Actors like Lee Remick, playing Burton's doctor, and Lino Ventura, as the investigating detective, also lend credibility.

Morlar (Burton) claims responsibility for most of the world's major catastrophes, up to and including an outer-space accident. After the attack, the comatose writer continues to wreak havoc, his prime desire being to force a jumbo jet to crash into a church. Yet another movie where evil wins out, *The Medusa Touch* ends with Morlar's life support system being cut, but his telekinetic powers keeping him alive.

Coma also involved horror in a hospital. Director/writer Michael Crichton (best-selling author of *The Andromeda Strain*) adapted fellow physician Robin Cook's novel concerning the fearsome state between life and death with just the right combination of hospital reality and genre fantasy. Feisty doctor Susan Wheeler (Genevieve Bujold) is stunned into investigating the practices of Boston Memorial Hospital when a good friend is rendered comatose during a routine abortion.

Her snooping leads her to a massive multi-million-dollar organ-selling industry, controlled by the calculating Mrs. Emerson (Elizabeth Ashley) of the Jefferson Institute. Inside the Institute's concrete walls are dozens of comatose victims, all held horizontally off the floor by wires threaded into their skeletons. This is the central image of the fanciful but fascinating film.

Although Wheeler knows where they are going, she has to find who is sending them there, making her a target for a vicious hitman, who chases her throughout the deserted hospital halls. Only after she locks him in the morgue freezer does the main villain reveal himself. Naturally the person she least suspects—but the audience most suspects—is the culprit: head surgeon Dr. Harris (Richard Widmark).

After drugging Wheeler with a brandy mickey, Harris wheels her into the infamous operating room number eight. Thankfully, her doctor boyfriend (Michael Douglas) has his own suspicions and saves her from becoming the next victim in the nick of time. This kind of horror story, with one foot in medical plausibility and the other in paranoid fantasy, worked very well under Crichton's assured directorial hand. *Coma* as a movie was an operation that succeeded.

Telekinetic powers and government conspiracies were combined in *The Fury,* adapted to screenplay

It is the tale of two psychically powerful young people: Gillian Bellaver (Amy Irving), the daughter of wealthy parents, and Robin Sandza (Andrew Stevens), the son of a secret agent (Kirk Douglas). Peter Sandza, the spy and father, belongs to the Multiphasic Operations Research Group (MORG),

Kirk Douglas is forced to disguise himself to escape the villains of *The Fury*.

form by the novel's author, John Farris. Brian DePalma directed, apparently as a followup to his best film, *Carrie* (1976), adapted from the Steven King book. DePalma started his film career strongly, then seemed to become more interested in the way his films were made rather than what they were saying. This movie marks the start of the degeneration of his storytelling abilities.

an incredibly secret organization headed by Childress (John Cassavetes).

Morg wants Robin as a weapon. Peter wants Robin as a son. Childress enflames this conflict by seeming to kill Peter in Israel and spiriting his son away to the remote Paragon Institute for Psychic Research. Gillian, meanwhile, is giving everyone around her a hard time. Whenever she

Amy Irving is horrified by both her own mental powers and Kirk Douglas's determination to kill the villains of *The Fury*.

gets emotional, she mentally causes others to hemorrhage uncontrollably. Her parents send her to Paragon for a cure, setting the stage for violence, tragedy and a lot of bloodshed.

While Gillian inadvertently causes nosebleeds to pour like waterfalls and scabbed cuts to burst open, the combination of total luxury and total power is driving Robin insane. As his father is led to Paragon by a frightened Gillian, Robin tests his powers and shows his displeasure by mentally destroying a carnival ride some Arabs are on. When his MORG-assigned trainer and lover (Fiona Lewis) tries to assuage him, he forces her to levitate, spin, and then ruptures her with his mental power.

By the time Peter gets there, it is already too late. His son attacks him and they both fall out

the window. Robin falls to his death but not before his eyes glow blue. Childress shoots the still living Peter in cold blood. The next morning Childress attempts to soothe the shocked Gillian. He explains that both Sandzas were a threat to government security. Gillian responds by hemorrhaging Childress' eyes and then—in a slow-motion climax shown repeatedly from different angles—makes Childress explode all over the room.

The Fury is watchable, but dumb and pretentious. DePalma overloads the film with cinematic tricks and subplots that detract from the taut thriller this could have been.

More governmental misdeeds are on display in *The Chosen,* a weird combination of conspiracy and horror film that was originally called *Holocaust 2000.* Taking its cue from *The Omen* (1976),

102

The "Seven Headed Hydra" of *The Chosen*, actually a nuclear power plant controlled by the anti-Christ.

it is another tale of the antiChrist given technological trappings. Kirk Douglas again stars, this time as an industrialist intent on building a seven-towered nuclear power plant in the middle of an Arabian desert. Unbeknownst to him, this property is holy land and his adopted son (Simon Ward) is the antiChrist, just waiting for an opportunity like this.

Ward starts killing off anyone who would warn or delay his father. When his mother wants them all to pack up and go home, Ward sees to it that a terrorist attack does her in. When the company's computer starts spitting out strange, mystical dogma, the programmer is in for a terminal trip. Finally, Douglas begins to get suspicious as people start dropping around him like flies.

But is it too late? The completion of the power plant and his evil son's thirty-third birthday just happen to coincide on New Year's Eve, 1999. Instead of destroying the plant and his child in classic hero fashion, Douglas can only manage to collect a newborn child all signs say is the Second Coming and escape, hoping the kid will grow fast enough to vanquish Ward's future plans.

The Chosen ends on this inconclusive note and, since no sequel has been forthcoming, it looks like we all have to wait until 1999 for the answer.

More medical hanky-panky is on hand for *The Boys from Brazil,* the next adaptation from a novel by Ira Levin. Although a bit meatier than his *Stepford Wives,* it hardly stands up as the most acceptable of concepts. Those hoary villains, the Nazis, are at it again. Not content with unleashing immortal mermen on the world (*Shock Waves*), Dr. Josef Mengele, the infamous real-life "Angel of Death," has a plan to replicate the Fuehrer ninety-four times over.

Gregory Peck plays the villain this time, making for an interesting switch. He portrays Mengele as a noxious, raving genius; a man capable and willing to genetically implant Hitler skin cells into ninety-four unknowing mothers' fetuses. To insure that at least one child will grow into the leader of the Fourth Reich, Mengele and his cronies see to it that all live in an environment similar to Hitler's own youth.

And since Adolf's dad died when he was twelve, Mengele sends out Nazi hitmen to give the ninety-four fathers a fatal accident. Dads are dropping dead all over the place until a Nazi hunter played by Laurence Olivier gets wind of the plot. The two antagonists chase each other all over the world until they fight in the living room of the last remaining Hitler youth.

Much to Mengele's shock, it is the boy himself who unleashes his savage doberman pets to make dinner out of the Nazi. The Nazi hunter discovers that the boy has no knowledge of his origin, so he cannot bring himself to murder the child. The ninety-fourth kid is left to mature at the world's risk.

While the movie is based on a shaky medical and psychological concept, director Franklin Schaffner (*Planet of the Apes*) sees to it that the scope and texture of the film is engrossing. The

Gregory Peck as Nazi geneticist Joseph Mengele, who plans to reproduce Hitler during *The Boys from Brazil*.

supporting cast, which includes James Mason, Uta Hagen, and Michael Gough, have a field day, while both Olivier and especially Peck seem to be having a whale of a time—even though the real Mengele has never been found or tried for his ugly crimes.

When asked if he hoped the real Mengele would be offended at his extreme portrayal, Peck challenged the butcher to come out of hiding and complain.

Many viewers complained about *The Swarm,* with good reason. This marked the nadir of the "disaster movie" genre, a genre that was nurtured by the Irwin Allen productions of *The Poseidon Adventure* (1972) and *The Towering Inferno* (1974). His star-studded disaster pictures had spawned a wealth of copies by other filmmakers until audiences were inundated with flames, tidal waves, earthquakes, explosions, train wrecks, hurricanes, car crashes, and mid-air collisions.

Allen's reaction was extreme. His new movie would portray disaster by killer bees. Neither his concept nor his approach was new. *The Bees,* starring John Saxon and Angel Tompkins, came out the same year with far less fanfare and far greater results. It was a middling thriller, but didn't pre-

Olivia de Havilland is horrified by *The Swarm*, a horde of killer bees.

The Swarm stings everyone in sight, causing all sorts of problems.

tend to be anything but. *The Swarm,* sadly, had delusions of grandeur.

Taking off from the true situation of Brazilian queen bees mating with South African bees that produced a strong, poisonous variety, Irwin Allen commissioned Sterling Silliphant to write a script based on an Arthur Herzog novel. In it and reality, these migrating killer bees are moving up from South America at a rate of two hundred miles per year.

The movie starts when they arrive in Houston, Texas. In the past, producer Allen had depended upon such commendable directors as Ronald Neame and John Guillerman to handle the dramatics. This time out, he directed himself, with abysmal results. Michael Caine starred as a mysterious insect expert, who appeared and disappeared at the strangest times, offering his services to harried scientists (Henry Fonda and Richard Chamberlain) and the desperate military (Richard Widmark and Bradford Dillman).

Woven awkwardly throughout the picture are innocent bystanders getting stung by the bees and the screenplay. There was reporter Lee Grant, waitress Patty Duke Astin, water superintendent Slim Pickens, school principal Olivia de Havilland, her beau Fred MacMurray, and Katherine Ross as Caine's love interest. This cast was supplemented by four hundred studio hives as well as the insects' stand-ins—cannons full of black puffed wheat and black jelly beans.

The finished film, in short, was atrocious. Both the script and special effects were embarrassingly bad.

THE DISNEY LEGACY

When Walt Disney died, he left Walt Disney Productions with a legacy. A legacy of great family entertainment in both the animation and live-action feature field. Since his death, however, the company has fallen on hard creative times, seemingly never able to recapture the magic and wonder Walt Disney could imbue his films with. Try as they may, they seem unable—and perhaps unwilling—to escape the confines of past glories.

The two science-fiction films from the studio this year are no different. *The Cat from Outer Space* premiered several years too early, unable to take advantage of the cat mania sweeping the country in the eighties. In 1978, the result was just another familiar, cloying, mildly amusing effort.

They Prey on HUMAN FLESH!

the BEES

Starring JOHN SAXON • ANGEL TOMPKINS • JOHN CARRA

PG PARENTAL GUIDANCE SUGGESTED

SOME MATERIAL MAY NOT BE SUITABLE FOR CHILDREN

Music by RICHARD GILLIS • Director of Photography: LEON

Written, Directed and Produced by ALFREDO Z

Had Disney Productions given the title character a little of the spice and backbone that made the comic-strip cat, Garfield, so famous, maybe things would have been different.

Instead, scriptwriter Ted Key (creator of the comic strip *Hazel*) told of feline alien life form "Zunar J5/90 Doric 4–7," otherwise known as Jake the Cat (Rumple the Cat), who gets marooned on earth when his beetle-shaped spaceship runs out of fuel. To fill his tank, all he needs is

The Cat from Outer Space's beetle-shaped spaceship escapes from the army.

Ken Berry is one of the few humans who gets to see the inside of *The Cat from Outer Space*'s ship.

six cubits of Org–12, which turns out to be a hundred and twenty thousand dollars' worth of gold. Deadline for rendezvous with his Mothership is thirty-six hours away and his only powers are a firm grasp of English, telepathy, a levitating collar, and the ability to freeze time.

NASA finds the ship, brings it to their Energy Research Lab, and assigns team leader Heffel (Hans Conried), Dr. Bartlett (Sandy Duncan), and Dr. Leak (McLean Stevenson) to investigate. Enter eccentric physicist Dr. Wilson (Ken Berry), a disgraced ex-member of the group, to become Jake's soulmate and confidant. The plot thickens when the alien cat falls in love with Bartlett's pet Lucy Belle (Spot the Cat).

As usual, the three doctors go through all sorts of shenanigans trying to get the needed gold while keeping their bosses ignorant. Complicating matters are an evil millionaire named Olympus (William Prince) and his insidious henchman Stallwood (Roddy McDowall). After scenes at a

Thankfully, the company's second feature had a bit more bite, but not nearly enough to warrant any unusual attention. This was, after all, *Return from Witch Mountain,* a sequel to *Escape to Witch Mountain* (1975). The latter film concerned two young vacationers from a secret enclave of earth-

Uncle Bene's flying saucer, which brings his young alien charges to and from their secret Earth home in two *Witch Mountain* movies.

pool hall and race track, the gold is gotten, but Olympus has captured Bartlett and, what's worse, Lucy Belle as well.

Jake forsakes his home planet in the name of love and rescues his feline girlfriend. The film concludes with Jake being sworn in as an American citizen while playfully levitating the judge. So ends another Disney Production, directed by Norman Tokar in much the same way he had been directing Disney features since 1962.

dwelling extraterrestrials who run afoul of human greed and evil. Eddie Albert plays a kindly man who helps them out of the clutches of industrialist Ray Milland and back home to Witch Mountain.

The sequel starts three years after the previous movie left off, with the kids' Uncle Bene (Denver Pyle) dropping them off in the Rose Bowl from their flying saucer. They are ostensibly out to experience a major city to supplement their education. Instead, they get another lesson in evil from two old pros. After Tony (Ike Eisenmann) rescues an attempted suicide with what he calls his "degravitational" powers, he comes to the attention of mind-controlling Dr. Gannon (Christopher Lee).

He and his corrupt partner in crime, Letha Wedge (Bette Davis), kidnap the child and "mind-cuff" him to a brainwashing machine. Meantime, his sister Tia (Kim Richards) enlists the aid of the youthful human "Earthquake Gang", Muscles (Brad Savage), Rock (Jeffrey Jacquet), Dazzler (Christopher Juttner), and Crusher (Poindexter), to help find her missing sibling.

They catch up to the devilish duo during a museum robbery, but the bad guys escape to a nuclear processing plant, where they plan to hold the world for ransom. Tia and the Earthquake Gang get inside but must face the hypnotized Tony. Things really start flying until they manage to tire him just enough to break the boy's spell. Uncle Bene shows up in his UFO just in time to see the cops haul Gannon and Wedge away.

Once more, Disney Productions had managed to take an intriguing idea and reduce it to a staid formula. Walt Disney's reputation had been one of exploration and experimentation. More than one of his employees have said that Walt Disney was the first one to suggest trying something new and different. It is a shame that the organization he left behind seems willing only to exploit his legacy, not move forward from it.

As is quite evident, Steven Spielberg was to take the basic idea of the Witch Mountain films—a stranded extraterrestrial—and build something on it of which Walt Disney would have been quite proud.

THIS LOOKS LIKE A JOB FOR SUPERMAN

"Everyone...for at least one moment...wants to be Superman."

Truer words were probably never spoken and they were spoken by Ilya Salkind, the producer of what was to become the most expensive undertaking in the history of English-speaking entertainment—*Superman: The Movie.*

The basic legend of Superman is simple. Born on Krypton, Kal-el was the son of scientist Jor-el and Lara. When the planet was in imminent danger of destruction, Jor-el placed his son in a rocket which landed on Earth. Adopted by a farmer and his wife, the boy was christened Clark Kent, but had powers and abilities far beyond those of mortal men. After Pa Kent died, he went to the big city of Metropolis, adopted glasses as a minor disguise and led a double life of a mild-mannered reporter for the *Daily Planet* newspaper and Superman.

The film project started in 1975 at the Café de la Paix in Paris. Salkind had seen the release of *The Three Musketeers* (although filmed as one four-hour film, it was released in two parts in 1973 and 1974), which he had produced. His father, Alexander Salkind, the patriarch of their European filmmaking clan, asked, "What's next?"

Superman was the answer. It took Salkind almost a year to secure permission even to attempt adapting the superhero into a movie character. Once he got the go-ahead from Warner Communications, who held the character's copyright, he

Christopher Lee is levitated by the two alien children in *Return from Witch Mountain.*

George Reeves was the original television *Superman*.
The difference between the two is telling.

humanistic, making the cartoon character into a real person.

In Puzo's work, the bond between Kal-el and Jor-el was all-important. He made the creation of the superhero costume into a maturation rite in which the son is handed down the father's Kryptonian seal—which explained the odd-looking big red "S." Then, Superman decides to become mortal so he can be with the woman he loves.

Things did not work out the way Puzo had planned. The author more or less washed his hands of the project after a post-script conference with Salkind and co-producer Pierre Spengler in which the young Frenchman suggested such things as Superman fighting with a school of sharks and confronting an armored alien who bore an uncomfortable similarity to Darth Vader.

The producers went in search of other famous scripters, settling upon Robert Benton, David Newman, and Leslie Newman, who, apart and together, were responsible for *Bonnie and Clyde* (1967) and *Kramer vs. Kramer* (1980). Their finished work was reportedly juvenile in the extreme. At one point, Superman spotted a bald man during his search for the hairless archcriminal Lex Luthor. When he investigates, it turns out to be Telly Savalas who gives him a lollipop and says "Who loves ya, baby?"

For some reason, most writers equate comic books with campy parodies. What no one seems to understand is that comic-book readers take the format and the characters *very* seriously. The comic-book fan is the least pleased when his hero is held up to spoofy ridicule.

Superman fans had all but lost hope when the news got out that Guy Hamilton was signed to direct and the entire production would be filmed in Italy. Although Hamilton had done good work in the fifties, his later work seemed haphazard and uninteresting. Tax problems prevented the film from being shot in Rome and kept Hamilton from working in England, so the producers essentially offered the project to whichever director was "hot" at the moment—including Francis Ford Coppola and Steven Spielberg.

They found their director after the release and subsequent success of *The Omen*. Richard Donner agreed to helm the project at Pinewood Studios with very little pre-production time if he could bring in his associate, Tom Mankiewicz, for a script rewrite. All was agreed and production got

went in search of the greatest talent money could buy. But in Salkind's case, "the greatest" did not necessarily mean "the best." It simply meant "the best known." To make the movie a going concern, he had to get names the money people (whom he calls the "gnomes in Geneva") recognized.

He lucked out in the case of Mario Puzo, author of *The Godfather.* Intrigued, Puzo wrote a hundred-and-fifty-page script, so they could produce one four-hour movie which they would release as two films a year apart. The original work was glorious; balancing the scrupulously logical with the wonderfully heroic. It was also deeply

Christopher Reeve is the new *Superman*.

under way. It was a long and stormy two-year process.

Donner discovered that little or no research had been done to see if the spectacular feats in the script could be filmed. He wanted Lesley Ann Warren to play Lois Lane, while the producers demanded Margot Kidder. Marlon Brando and Gene Hackman had already been signed to play Jor-el and Lex Luthor at a combined salary of five million dollars. Everyone, however, agreed with the choice to play Superman—a young, relatively inexperienced actor named Christopher Reeve.

Although Salkind had initially wanted a star on the level of Robert Redford or Burt Reynolds to play the role (reportedly also offering or testing Sylvester Stallone and Bruce Jenner) in order to open the Geneva wallets, he decided to make the two other male characters big names and find an unknown for the lead. His strategy worked well. Reeve was really marvelous, but needed several months of intensive training (under the guidance of David Prowse, a.k.a. Darth Vader) to develop the necessary musculature.

Donner settled down with production designer John Barry and a literal army of special-effects people and got to work. The initial budget was thirty million dollars for both movies, but the special-effects experimentation as well as other unforeseen problems pumped the expenditure to over fifty million dollars for the one picture alone. By the end of production, the relationship between director and producers had become so strained

The young Clark Kent (Jeff East) reaches his new home, the Fortress of Solitude.

that Charles Greenlaw, an executive at Warners, and Richard Lester, director of *The Three Musketeers,* were called in as buffers, diplomats, and referees.

The crew pretty much devised tricks as they went along. Cinematographer Geoffrey Unsworth added great visual touches. Derek Meddings did miniatures. Colin Chilvers handled on-set physical effects. And all the while, dozens of technicians were trying to find the perfect way for Superman to fly. It finally came down to a front projection system devised by Zoran Perisic and perfected by Dennys Coop.

The first shot of *Superman: The Movie* was taken on March 28, 1977.

"This is no fantasy," are the first words with which Jor-el (Marlon Brando) sentences three Kryptonian villains to the Phantom Zone. The megalomaniacal General Zod (Terence Stamp) swears vengeance on Jor-el and his family. Jor-el then faces the Kryptonian counsel with news that the planet will be destroyed. They refuse to believe him and, to keep the public from rioting, force Jor-el to swear that neither he nor his wife will leave the planet (in the comic-book version, the escaping rocket was only big enough for the baby).

In the movie version, Jor-el deliberately sets Kal-el on a course for Earth, knowing what changes the planet will work. He includes a glowing green crystal with magical powers. The crystalline ship takes off as Krypton is torn asunder. The following scenes in the young Clark Kent's home town of Smallville (filmed in Calgary, Canada) and his arrival in Metropolis/New York are the best in the picture. Phyllis Thaxter and especially Glenn Ford do a marvelous job as Ma and Pa Kent—Pa Kent's death scene being one of the most simple and affecting moments in the two hour and twenty-three minute running length.

Clark discovers the green crystal "calling" to him; making him walk all the way to the North Pole (having not discovered his flying power yet). There the crystal "grows" the crystalline Fortress of Solitude (built in miniature and full size on the 007 Stage), a Krypton-engineered hideout with the stored holographic images of Jor-el, who can talk to Kent through the miracle of advanced science (and the movies).

Twelve years is condensed in the next few

Marlon Brando plays *Superman*'s father, Jor-el, the man who sends three supervillains into the Phantom Zone. From the left: Terence Stamp, Jack O'Halloran, and Sarah Douglas.

minutes as Jor-el teaches his son all there is to know. At the end of the montage, Superman is revealed full grown and in costume—minus all the fine Puzo concepts. Here he flies for the first time—a disappointing scene which utilized painted-out wires (making him look like a floating Peter Pan). The sequence when he first changes into Superman, to save Lois in a crashed helicopter, is magnificent, however, the best-realized feat of strength and grandeur *Superman: The Movie* was to present.

From there on, the structure goes downhill. Although Gene Hackman does a very good job as Lex Luthor, he was teamed with Otis (Ned Beatty), a retarded buffoon who destroyed all reality the movie had thus far saved up. Because of him, the villain was not threatening, therefore the danger was not real to viewers. Luthor's plot to start a West-Coast-destroying earthquake by planting a nuclear bomb in the San Andreas fault was workable enough, but the filmmakers constantly undercut their movie with slapstick. And while most of the special effects were exceptional, a few done hurriedly and in post-production stuck out like sore thumbs, again damaging suspension of disbelief.

The worst offense was saved for last. In his rush

Superman flies over Metropolis.

to save many lives after patching up the San Andreas fault (another poor effect), Superman is unable to rescue Lois Lane from death as her car is crushed in an earthquake fissure. Grief-stricken, Superman reverses the Earth's orbit, turning time back. Suddenly, it is as if the disaster had not struck. The hero hadn't delayed history, he had half-negated it. Although the earthquake still occurred, according to some Jimmy Olsen dialogue, Superman didn't even have to go back to rescue the car from the fissure. The illogic of the event was mind-boggling, not to mention one of the biggest cop-out cheats in film history.

Strangely enough, when shown on television in an over-three-hour format, several edited scenes were returned to the film, explaining some of the loose ends the theatrical version left hanging. Also of note, the shorter airline version of the film was also superior to the theatrical version, since it clipped out much of the irritating Otis slapstick.

All in all, *Superman: The Movie* was the best it could be considering the trying circumstances under which it was filmed. The music, the performances and sections of the work were absolutely top notch. It is simply a shame that more filmmakers can't seem to tell a super-heroic story without adding ingredients that camp the film up and tear the movie down.

5

1979 THE YEAR OF MONSTERS

MONSTERS NEXT DOOR

SCIENCE-FICTION FILM PRODUCTION was frenzied in 1978, so the number of releases this year was almost double that of 1975. The major studios realized that genre themes could mean big bucks, so they put into production whichever project they thought the public would go for. The independent film producer, in the meantime, could do the same thing faster while caring little for public taste. This resulted in some of the strangest monster movies on record.

Leading the list is *The Watts Monster,* a nasty racial conceit that turned the tables on the usual

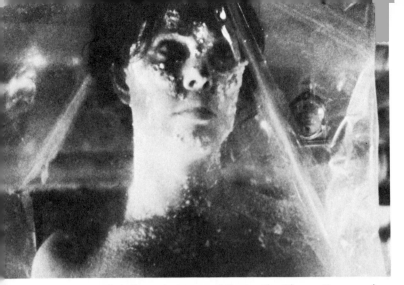

The climactic image of *Parts: The Clonus Horror*, when Timothy Donnelly discovers that he is a clone destined for freezing and vivisection.

Gaze into the face of Misquamacus, the 400-year-old medicine man reborn in *The Manitou*.

bigotry. Instead of a pristine Caucasian hero taking on vile hordes of black villains, this variation of "Dr. Jekyll and Mr. Hyde" had an upstanding black physician becoming an insane white man upon imbibing the infamous elixir.

In fact, the movie was originally titled *Dr. Black and Mr. White*—a somewhat blatant moniker. Realizing that was a bit too much, the distributors toned it down to *Dr. Black/Mr. Hyde,* eliminating

the "and" but not the manifest bigotry. Still, that name was too strong to allow any sale to television, so *The Watts Monster* was born. But under any name, it was a weak realization of the audacious concept.

William Crain, the director of *Blacula* (1972)—the black vampire movie—also helmed this tale from Larry LeBron's script. Bernie Casey starred as the subtly named Dr. Pride, a wonderful ghetto scientist dedicated to the care of the downtrodden. But deep in his heart he longs to fit in with the white middle class. Toward this end he mixes a concoction that turns him into a Caucasian. Only then does he discover that the white man is a natural predator and he goes on a low-budget rampage of destruction.

This film was about as good as 1973's *Black Frankenstein (Blackenstein),* another attempt to adapt classic monsters into the black experience. All concerned should have known that science-fiction beasts have no race, color, or creed. They are for all humanity.

Reaffirming that sentiment was the yellow peril, Godzilla, returning for his latest fight, a rematch against the *Terror of Mecha-Godzilla.* As some woeful kidnapped scientists were to discover, the joy of robot monsters is that they can be rebuilt—which is just what a loony technician wants to do with the disconnected giant machine. With the help of the loony's captives, Mecha-Godzilla is

Oliver Reed tries but fails to kill *The Brood.* They, however, do not fail to kill him.

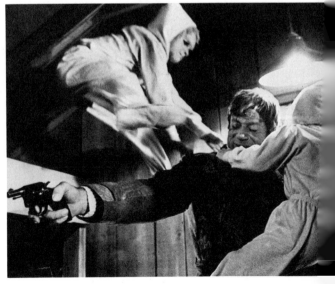

given new life, only to be defeated once again thanks to Godzilla's fancy fisticuffs and the treachery of the mad scientist's aide (Mie Hama, who also was 007's love interest in *You Only Live Twice*).

Cheaper, but with more heart than both previous productions was *Parts: The Clonus Horror*. Here was a low-budget combination of science-fiction and conspiracy themes that could stand proudly alongside things like *Capricorn One* as a political thriller and *Coma* as a medical chiller. Co-producer (with Myrl Schreibman) and director Robert Fiveson did his best with only two hundred and fifty thousand dollars and the increasingly gruesome tale of Richard (Tim Donnelly), a sweet young man who discovers that he and all his friends are actually clones. They were all scientifically developed from the single cell of a mother-born human.

They are controlled and kept in top physical shape, awaiting the day they will be frozen and cut up as transplant parts. Although their intelligence is blunted by drugs, Richard innocently stumbles upon the truth and manages to escape his captors' clutches. Unbeknownst to him, the "Clonus" facility is supported by a powerful politician who sends a team of hitmen out to keep the situation secret. As those around him die, Richard

starts his own search for his original—the person from whom he was created.

Parts is not a subtle or well-made movie, but it is an interesting attempt to be more than just an exploitation picture.

Even stronger stuff could be found in *The Brood*, David Cronenberg's third—and many say his best—horror film. Again produced in Canada for very little money, this was more than just another graphic and violent nightmare. Although still based on the conceit of science gone crazy, the basis for *The Brood* stemmed from an event in Cronenberg's own life: a particularly bitter divorce and custody fight.

The images in this movie are more controlled and stronger for it. Art Hindle stars as Frank Carveth, the divorced husband of psychotic Nola (Samantha Eggar), the vengeful victim of child abuse. He is also the father of their angelic blond child, Candy (Cindy Hinds), who he swears will never be a victim like her mother. The woman is being cared for by Dr. Raglan (Oliver Reed) at the Somafree Institute of Psychoplasmics—an experimenting organization that teaches patients to mentally control their rage.

The doctor is more successful than he'd care to be. His charges are beginning to manifest their

The mutated bear of *Prophecy* strikes!

The zombies as they appeared in *Night of the Living Dead* in 1968.

117

inner anger as sores on their skin. Nola takes it one step further. The mother that beat her as a child is suddenly killed by a child herself. Next to die is Nola's father, also murdered by a tiny figure which dies trying to kill Frank as well. An autopsy reveals that the small, sexless creature died of natural causes—it simply did not have enough energy inside it to kill two people.

Frank realizes that whoever Nola hates is attacked by an avenging child. By then, Candy is kidnapped and her baby-sitting teacher killed by two more pasty-faced kids. The distraught parent tracks them back to the Somafree Institute where Raglan has evacuated everyone but Nola, Candy and The Brood. The doctor explains that the creatures are the children of Nola's rage. Frank himself witnesses another brood birth as Raglan tries to rescue Candy.

The offspring is created in a womb-like sack off Nola's body. She tears open the sack and licks the child clean before Frank's (and the audience's) disgusted eyes. But before Raglan can spirit the little human girl away from the guarding brood, Nola sees through Frank's soothing diversion and gets angry. The Brood instantly attack and kill the doctor as Frank is forced to kill his ex-wife, crushing the new brood baby between their writhing bodies.

Still, Cronenberg cannot resist marring this somewhat happy ending. When Frank collects the stunned Candy from amid the motionless brood (who died the same moment as their mother), the audience can see welts on the little girl's arm—the same sort of bruises that gave rise to her mother's living hate. Even including this cliché ending, *The Brood* was Cronenberg's most accessible, empathetic film to date.

Also *Brood*-like in approach was *The Manitou*, director/scripter William Girdler's movie adaptation of Graham Masterton's novel. The story was an interesting combination of science and the supernatural. Karen Tandy (Susan Strasberg) develops a strange, growing lump on her back. Everything the medical profession does makes the problem worse. Meanwhile, her ex-lover Harry Erskine (Tony Curtis) is being bombarded with occult curses that are distinctly American Indian in flavor.

As the craziness grows, Erskine discovers that the reincarnation of a four-hundred-year-old medicine man, "Misquamacus," is developing in a fleshy sack on Tandy's torso. As the creature's power grows, Erskine tries to fight it with the help of a modern-day medicine man (Michael Ansara). But it is only after they discover that all things have a "manitou"—a powerful spirit whose energy can be harnessed—that they get the upper hand.

Combining the power of love with the manitou of the hospital's powerful computer system allows them to blast Misquamacus into eternity. Girdler does well with a three-million-dollar budget, pulling off the more interesting of the film's effects (such as the monster's birth and its taking over of a surgical laser), but the more spectacular of the concepts (Tandy's hospital floor being encased in ice or transported to outer space) are uniformly wanting.

The Manitou was a minor entertainment, but an interesting one. Sadly, William Girdler was to die in a helicopter crash while scouting locations for his next never completed science-fiction film.

Another sort of brood was on the rampage in theaters. This was director/writer George A. Romero's brood of zombies, the same zombies he introduced in *Night of the Living Dead* a full decade before. Even then, these corpses that rose to devour the living did not just march to the tune

In 1978, these four brave people fight the zombie horde in *Dawn of the Dead*.

118

of an unknown drummer. An alien spore from a returning Venus space probe was causing the dead to turn on the living. And even then, Romero wasn't satisfied to use the plot as simply a means to trot out familiar frights. It was just the start of a grand science-fiction vision of humanity adjusting to the horrific predicament.

That much is clear in *Dawn of the Dead,* the second of a proposed trilogy concerning the "cultural transference" from a capitalistic to a cannibalistic society. The film centers on one four-person team of heavily armed zombie assassins. It starts quietly, with television reports on just how widespread the horror has become. Then the SWAT-like team of a woman, a black man and two other white males start an assault on a housing project where a large group of dead are holed up. The human team are faced with the sickening sight of the zombies lolling about, chewing on various gory limbs.

Although the gathered diners seem somewhat tame, one human opens the wrong door and a horde of raging zombies pile in. For the next few minutes, the sights and sounds are uniformly nauseating. The only way to kill the dead is to blast them in the head, so the opening sequences of frenetic mass slaughter builds from being extremely disgusting to almost a comic-book-like entertainment. The assault team keeps fighting until they barricade themselves in a deserted, but unravaged, indoor shopping mall.

For the remainder of the film's first half, the quartet use the stores' products to create a comfy, almost "normal" home for themselves. For a brief, peaceful respite, they have returned to the relaxed consumers they once were, pre-zombies. In an ironic twist, it is not the unreasoning living dead who destroy their tranquil fantasy, but a human motorcycle gang who decide to trash the unsullied plaza.

For another few scenes, the quartet practically join up with the zombies to kill the cyclists, until they must go back to fighting for their own lives. One of their number is consumed by the starving creatures while another is made one of them. Whoever is left in one piece after a zombie attack, also becomes a living dead. It is this other victim who leads the zombie army to the survivors' hideout—displaying the first sign that the living dead can think and remember.

The surviving duo, played by Ken Foree and

The monster bear rears its mutated head for the final time in *Prophecy.*

Gaylen Ross, do manage to escape in a helicopter, but even that cannot fly them to safety. During the *Dawn of the Dead,* there is no safety. Romero promises that the upcoming *Day of the Dead* will be just as horrific, but will also forward the science-fiction theme of adaptation. Presently set in a Florida retirement home, the third zombie movie will concern the era in which the living and dead have created an eerie, awkward pact. The zombies do the menial work as long as they're kept fed. The question for the living is: who is going to feed them, and who with?

Of all the earth-bound monsters this season, none was dumber than the beast of *Prophecy,* a twelve-million-dollar fiasco produced by a major studio. At first, the picture's appearance came as a surprise. Although other upcoming genre works were being highly touted, this Paramount production utilizing some well-known talents was top secret.

John Frankenheimer directed (as he had for *Seven Days in May,* 1964, and the underrated chiller *Seconds,* 1966) from David Seltzer's script. Seltzer's previous book and script had been *The Omen,* so everyone was expecting another first-class thriller. Instead, *Prophecy* retread some of the hoariest science-fiction clichés in a ludicrous package. The finished film was much like a person with no sense of humor trying to tell a hilarious joke he doesn't know is funny.

Dr. Robert Vern (Robert Foxworth) wants to do something "important," something to help

119

mankind beyond working in the ghetto. He is convinced that packing up his pregnant wife (Talia Shire) and going to Maine to patch up a battle between conservation-oriented American Indians and the owners of a paper mill is important. Upon arrival, he discovers that mill employees are disappearing at an alarming rate while raccoons are going rabid, fish are growing to the size of pelicans, and Masaquoddy Indian babies are being born dead.

It all comes down to the methylmercury the mill had been using for years. It had seeped into the water supply, spawning a variety of maddened woodland mutations; the king of which is a monstrous grizzly bear. Complicating the plot is the Masaquoddy legend of "Katahdin," the guardian spirit of the area who is supposed to eradicate the villains. Well, the giant bear tries to eradicate everyone in sight, whether Indian or mill employee.

From the moment the monster appears, the serious narrative the filmmakers had set up went the way of all flesh. *Prophecy* seems like two movies. The first half was stylish and ominous. The second half was a string of trite chases and shopworn scare tactics. Frankenheimer even goes so far as building the bombastic soundtrack music to a crescendo, having nothing happen, and then letting the bear jump out after the music has died down.

The monster, a much-touted combination of

The Humanoid (Richard Kiel) finds true love with Corinne Clery.

several animals, looked like "The Incredible Melting Bear." It was obviously a man in a hairy suit with a quarter of Chewbacca the Wookie's believability. The monster's first appearance on screen also marked the elimination of any subplot thus far introduced. The Indian/mill conflict was forgotten as was the fact that Vern's wife had partaken of the mutating watersupply, thereby threatening her unborn baby. That threat was never mentioned again.

Finally, *Prophecy* winds up with Vern killing the beast. But that's not all. True to its hackneyed origins, the final shot is of the Verns' plane soaring over the Maine forests, heading back to the city. Just before the screen blacks out, *another* monstrous forest mutation pops into foreground view. This revelation that there were other creatures lurking in the woods only served as a punchline for the joke the producers didn't know was funny.

MONSTERS IN SPACE

Many filmmakers found it too difficult to create another movie in which outer-space aliens are friendly. It was much easier to load the script down with illogical, unsubstantiated special effects and villainous extraterrestrials with unknowable powers. This was the approach of an imported science-fiction shock film.

"We have sought them out with signals in the sky," read their publicity. "If they are fearful beings, it is too late to turn back. They know we are here. . . ." This was the premise of *The Visitor*. The title character was a little bald-headed person (played by a shaved child) who served as spokesman for a race of eyeless, cowled aliens with mind-numbing powers.

The Visitor owes more to *Close Encounters* than its basic plot. It also shares the acting talent of Lance Henriksen, who played Lacombe's second assistant in Steven Spielberg's UFO movie. Here, he shares the screen with Glenn Ford, Shelley Winters, Mel Ferrer and director Sam Peckinpah (*The Wild Bunch*, 1969). All wait in worried anticipation as the aliens display the same sort of powers that kept humans hopping in *The Exorcist*.

Another visitor to this planet was the beast of *The Dark,* an initially interesting attempt to meld the science-fiction format with an urban thriller. Originally, horror director Tobe Hooper (*The Texas Chainsaw Massacre,* 1974) was set to lead the talented cast and crew through Stanford Whit-

As *The Humanoid* grows old, his only friend is "Kip, the Robodog."

After pumping some bullets into the shadowy figure, the police set the thing aflame. After awhile it simply disintegrates, as did the movie's concept. Among the most disappointed was Steve Neill, who had slaved on the alien makeup effects, only to see them misused and barely visible in the finished film. Mercifully, the film was barely seen by anyone.

The Dark's monster wasn't the only humanoid in theaters. There was also *The Humanoid,* a curious European import that featured Richard Kiel as an eight-foot-tall bionic man. The alien Nurek warriors from outer space want to take over a peaceful planet with the help of the humanoid, their ultimate, invincible weapon. But he is shown the error of his ways through the love of a rebel fighter (Corinne Clery), but she is sought by a Nurek princess (Barbara Bach), who needs her for another youth-giving treatment by her doctor (Arthur Kennedy).

It makes for a complex story, with even more subplots concerning an enigmatic oriental boy, a Darth-Vader-like Nurek chief, white-garbed monks who wander the planet's surface, and "Kip the Robodog"—the humanoid's life-long machine friend. The Italian-French co-production was an uncomfortable mixture of some decent ideas and reheated *Star Wars* leftovers.

more's script, but he was replaced with John Bud Cardos by producer Edward L. Montoro after "creative differences."

William Devane starred as Roy, a cop investigating a string of extremely brutal murders. It is only after ninety minutes of gratuitous violence and senseless titillation that the hulking killer is revealed to be a humanoid alien from another world who can punch through doors, rip off heads and send death rays sizzling out of his eyes. It was just another lame excuse to film young people getting massacred—a habit Hollywood was getting into after the success of *Halloween* (1978).

The first publicity catchphrase was suitably ominous. "A word of warning," read the posters just above the title—*Alien*. The second poster made it all the more clear: "In Space No One Can

The spaceship "Nostromo" lands on the desolated planet where they will find the *Alien*.

Hear You Scream." *Alien* was being presented as the first flat-out, modern-day, horror/science-fiction film. Happily, it was a first-class movie that delivered on its promise.

It certainly wasn't alone in the futuristic monster genre. It had its origins in such previous fright films as *It—The Terror from Beyond Space* (1958), and *Planet of the Vampires* (1965), among others. The big difference was that *Alien* was conceived and produced as a major motion picture (rather than an inexpensive exploitation film) by people who loved science fiction.

Heading the list was writer Dan O'Bannon, who conceived the original screenplay, initially called *They Bite.* With the help of Ronald Shusett, the

Inside this derelict ship awaits the *Alien*.

concept of a rampaging space creature was developed further in a second script called *Star Beast*. That was when the duo deliniated the concept of a monster who only killed because it wasn't aware of humanity's basic incompatibility. All it wanted to do was reproduce.

Their idea was arresting, but dangerously sexual in flavor. At that point, Brandywine Productions entered the picture. This movie company consisted of producer Gordon Carroll (*Cool Hand*

Luke, 1967), scripter David Giler (*The Parallax View,* 1974), and writer/director Walter Hill (*48 Hours,* 1982). All three agreed *Star Beast* would make a great film so Hill set about rewriting it to be one of his action-movie vehicles (to follow such previous Hill features as *Hard Times,* 1975, and *The Driver,* 1978). The title was changed a third and final time to *Alien*.

Twentieth Century-Fox Studio bought the script, but Hill stepped out of the project, opting to direct *The Warriors* (1979) instead. While his violent, somewhat futuristic tale of big city street gangs warring for supremacy created controversy because of violence in the theaters where it played, *Alien* created big box-office business. Much of the credit for this belonged to the new director, Ridley Scott.

Although he had only one other film to his credit (*The Duellists,* 1976), he brought together a talented cast and crew who gave atmospheric life to the thriller. He first screened *The Texas Chainsaw Massacre* for everyone—director/writer Tobe Hooper's starkly violent and oppressive exploitation classic. With the proper state of mind infused, he then handed his actors fictional biographical studies of their characters which they could use as background for their performances.

The crew followed this viewing with showings of *2001, Star Wars, Close Encounters* and *Silent Running* (1971) to insure that their outer space paraphernalia looked different from anything preceding it. That much was insured when an art book called *Necronomicon* was brought onto the set. It showed the wondrously perverted work of European artist H.R. Giger, who specialized in painting what he called "biomechanics"—dark images in green and grey of decay, violence, bondage, deformity, and machinery. As soon as Scott saw the images, he knew he wanted Giger as a production designer.

It was Giger's creations and the way that Scott filmed them that made *Alien* the unnerving viewing experience it was.

An Earth-bound space trawler named *The Nostromo* (a name borrowed from the works of Joseph Conrad) is gliding through space, hauling a mile-and-a-half-wide load of ore behind it. The sleeping crew, frozen in suspended animation, is awakened by the ship's master computer—affectionally called "Mother." The ship's easy-going

This is what the derelict ship's entrance looked like on
the set.

This is what it looked like in the finished film.

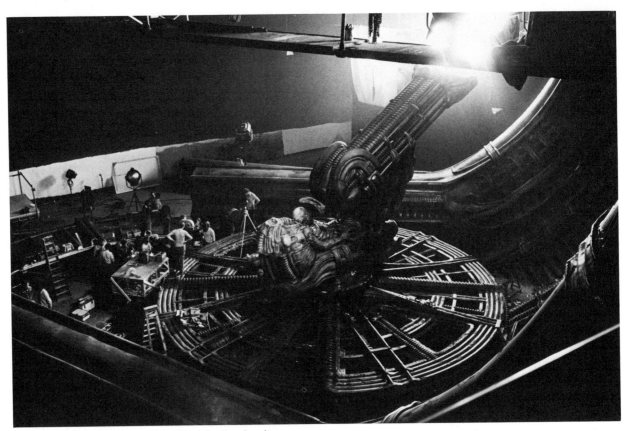

This is what the "Space Jockey" inside the derelict
ship looked like on the set.

Captain, Dallas (Tom Skerritt), and quiet science
officer, Ash (Ian Holm), confer with the machine
while the rest of the group—navigators Lambert
(Veronica Cartwright) and Kane (John Hurt),
engineers Brett (Harry Dean Stanton) and Parker
(Yaphet Kotto), and security officer Ripley
(Sigourney Weaver)—get organized.

This is not the clean cut and capable crew of
previous space movies. These are space truckers;
misfits and rebels who sign on for long mining
missions in return for a percentage of the profit.
So none are too excited when Mother informs
them of an SOS signal emanating from a nearby
planet. Beyond collecting energy sources, the ship's
mission is to make contact with and collect alien
life forms.

So saying, the crew battens down the hatches
and lands on a barren, wind swept planet. Dallas,
Lambert and Kane explore to find a derelict
spaceship—an odd horseshoe-shaped construction
that seems to be half-wreck, half-carcass (the first
appearance of Giger's biomechanic concept). In-

And this is what it looked like in the movie.

side there is the "Space Jockey"—a giant fossilized creature who seems to be part of the ship itself. It appears to have passed on peacefully except for the large hole in its chest.

Kane then discovers that the base part of the ship is covered with what appear to be eggs the size of potato sacks. Much to his fascination, the first one he touches seems to come alive. The surface turns transparent and the top opens. A second later, something leaps out, attaches itself to Kane's helmet, burns through his faceplate, and adheres itself to him. This is "The Face Hugger," another Giger concept. When John Hurt as Kane looked down, special-effects man David Watkins threw a few pounds of liver and an attached sheep stomach at him from under the set.

Dallas and Lambert hustle their friend back to the ship, where Ripley refuses to let them in, fearing contamination. But Ash overrides her, allowing their fallen friend into the "auto-doc"—the *Nostromo*'s automated sickbay. After cutting off his helmet, they find what looks to be a combina-

tion of a crab, spider and snake latched to Kane's visage. It tightens its hold around the astronaut whenever they try to get it off and cutting it with a laser knife only unleashes its acidic blood—which nearly gets them all killed when it almost burns through the hull of the ship.

To everyone's surprise, the Face Hugger dehydrates and falls off Kane of its own accord. He rises, seemingly fine, but needing food. Much relieved, the crew adjourns to the dining room where they sit down to a friendly, much-needed meal. Kane only gets one mouthful before he starts coughing and writhing in pain. The shocked crew get him pinned to the table just as his chest explodes out in a shower of blood and gore. Emerging from his torso is the infamous "Chest Burster"—a Roger Dicken puppet creation—marking the birth of the creature the Face Hugger had planted, then nurtured, inside Kane's body.

To further heighten the horror, director Scott did not inform his cast exactly what would happen. Their looks of surprise and disgust are real as they are splattered with fake blood and guts. The Chest Burster lets off a birth yowl and then skitters off to hide within the massive ship. As shocking as that is, the crew still thinks it has to capture the tiny creature. They do not realize how fast and how large it grows until it is too late.

Brett is the next to go, attacked by the fully matured, eight-foot-tall monster while searching

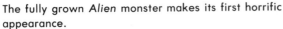

Sigourney Weaver, Yaphet Kotto (center), and Harry Dean Stanton search for the murderous *Alien* inside their ship.

for the ship's mascot—Jones the cat. Much to his credit, Ridley Scott uses Jones the cat as the only shock scare tactic. Whenever the Alien comes on screen, the audience has plenty of time to adjust. The director always shows the monster readying to strike, rather than having it come leaping out of nowhere.

Again, to his credit, Scott knew his movie was gruesome enough without gratuitous gore. So while Brett was originally to die by having his heart ripped out, Scott left the actual death to the audience's imagination. Although he filmed the Alien's bone-like tongue slamming through Brett's skull, he edited the sequence out before the film's release.

Many viewers were dismayed by Brett's seeming stupidity in searching for the cat alone, without a weapon. Harry Dean Stanton, the actor who played Brett, addressed that question. "He just figured that the crew was familiar, on a mundane level, with alien creatures," he said. "We figured that they had been heard of and talked about before. Probably a lot of other crews had found weird things before. That's the only logical way we could have acted the way we did."

Next Dallas tries to corner and kill the thing in the *Nostromo*'s labyrinthian air ducts, only to have the fast, strong creature sneak up on him instead. Totally terrified, the survivors band together for protection. Ripley takes command, only to be attacked by a suddenly beserk Ash. It turns out that the science officer is a robot—built and installed by the mining company to insure the

The fully grown *Alien* monster makes its first horrific appearance.

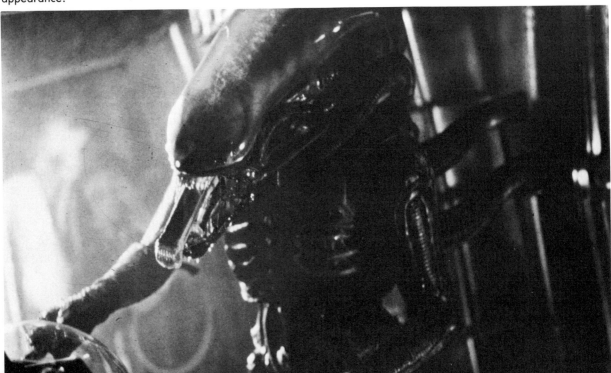

corporation's directives were followed. Parker rips its head off then burns it to a crisp with a flame-throwing rifle.

They all agree on a plan to destroy the *Nostromo* and escape in the *Narcissus*—a small

Scott was forced to jettison both scenes for pacing's sake.

"Originally, you see, the movie was three hours long," H.R. Giger explained. "This cocoon scene slowed the momentum of the climax. It was much

The author, holding the actual *Alien* head used in the film.

In a never-before-seen scene, Captain Dallas (Tom Skerritt) is being slowly turned into an *Alien* egg. Although he begs to die and is killed by the Ripley character, this sequence was edited out of the finished film.

escape vehicle. But before they can collect the necessary oxygen, Lambert is cornered by the thing, and is too scared to get out of the way when Parker tries to fry it. Instead, the Alien kills them both. Much of the film's success must be credited to the screenwriters and director who have the characters die because they care so much for each other. The Alien would not have gotten on the ship had they not wanted Kane to live and Parker would not shoot with Lambert in harm's way.

With everyone else gone, it is Ripley versus the monster. Originally, she was to find the remains of Brett and Dallas. The two were slowly growing into the eggs the original alien was born from. Upon the Captain's anguished plea, she kills them both. Following that she was to come upon the hunched Alien in a passageway. The creature then unfolded itself majestically, giving the audience its first full look at the complete thing. Director

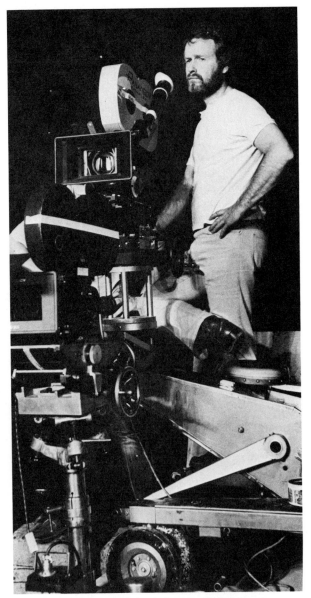

Alien was the fine work of director Ridley Scott.

animation sleep, the Alien reveals itself. It had stowed aboard among the machinery.

Numbed, horrified, Ripley crawls into a space suit and empties the craft of air. When that doesn't suffocate it, she bombards the alien with various gases. When that doesn't slow it down, she opens the air lock, which sucks it outside. The Alien just manages to hold on to the doorway, however, forcing Ripley to shoot it with a harpoon pistol. The airlock door closes on the harpoon cord, creating a leash that drags the monster behind the escape craft. Ripley waits until the still living thing drifts in front of the engines and then turns the power on full.

The Alien is totally destroyed and Ripley is finally allowed some rest. For a split second the soundtrack music becomes ominous at the end, before fading off on a positive, peaceful note. That warning music is all that's left of *Alien*'s original downbeat ending—where one more egg was revealed to the audience, hidden behind the *Narcissus*'s wall of machinery. But once again, Ripley Scott's filmmaking ability was triumphant. After all the preceding action and suspense, the director relieved his audience's tension instead of opting for a cheap, cynical conclusion.

The eight-foot-tall monster confronts its pursuers in *Alien*.

more effective to take it out. Although I asked for this explanation of how the eggs were created to be filmed, I thought the final version looked terrific and I think Ripley is great."

With those sequences gone, there was nothing to deter from the film's exciting finale as Ripley races from the auto-destruct room to the escape vehicle as the ship starts to destroy itself around her. Only after the *Narcissus* blasts off and the *Nostromo* explodes, does she relax. But just after she prepares herself for a renewed suspended

MONSTROUS DISASTERS

Alien may have been a box-office and critical success, but several other films either concerned ecological disasters or were embarrassingly bad in execution and performance. One or two were both. *The Ravagers* was one such movie. It seemed like it was an attempt by producer Saul David to go over the same path his *Logan's Run* trod to see what went wrong. While there was no computer that blew up if one contradicted it, there was Richard Harris as Falk, a survivor of Armageddon. Instead of "Sanctuary" (where over-thirty-year-old runners went in the latter picture), there was the mythical land of "Genesis" where post-holocaust people would be safe. And instead of "sandmen" to track them down, there were the *Ultimate Warrior*-type gang members called "The Ravagers."

They live up to their name by slaughtering Falk's wife in the opening minutes of the feature, then mercilessly stalking the hero across the radiation-scarred world. There are some nice futuristic touches as Falk discovers one strange society after another on his trek, but these concepts are simplistic for the most part and only momentarily satisfying. The best of the lot is Art Carney as a war-mongering sergeant holed up in a heavily armed bunker. The worst of the lot is Genesis itself, a Quaker-like hierarchy led by Rann (Ernest Borgnine), living out of a beached oil tanker filled with all the comforts of home.

Being something of an uneducated slob, Falk leads the Ravagers right to Genesis, making a fight to the finish necessary. While all the killers and Renn are wiped out, so is the oil tanker, leaving the survivors pretty much where they started. Although they decide to rebuild their own sort of Genesis in a different image, it is hard to hold out much hope for this fetid lot. *The Ravagers* was a middling film, easily forgotten once it was over.

The same was not exactly true of *Quintet*. Although boring, awkward, and dreadful for the most part, there are fleeting images and concepts that do resonate in the memory afterwards. Much of that effect was traceable to its director/writer Robert Altman and star Paul Newman. Altman was a "critics' pet" thanks to a string of fascinating movies in the early 1970s, including *M*A*S*H* (1970), *McCabe and Mrs. Miller* (1972), *Thieves Like Us* (1973), and *Nashville* (1975). He was get-

Paul Newman and Brigitte Fossey view the confusing floor plans of an ice-shrouded apartment complex in *Quintet*.

ting so successful that he was beginning to rush even his dreams onto celluloid.

Quintet was one such dream. Co-written with Frank Barhydt, Lionel Chetwynd, and Patricia Resnick, it visualized an Earth frozen by the gradual decay of the sun. The world is completely ice-bound, the few survivors huddled together in cold pain. The planet is slowly dying, taking all its inhabitants with it. But there are still some bestial humans who see this as an opportunity to

Director Robert Altman instructs Paul Newman on how to get through *Quintet*.

gain power over others. The sheer hopelessness of the situation gives rise to the game of "Quintet"—where the rules always seem to change and death is the only way out.

Into this strange environment comes Essex (Newman) and his pregnant companion Vivia (Brigitte Fossey). They find Essex's brother but both he and Vivia are killed in a Quintet-related bomb blast. The only thing Essex can recover from the explosion is a Quintet token, making him part of the game. All he has to do then is discover the identities of the other players and kill them before they kill him.

He has five sections of an ice-capped city in which to look, coming upon and murdering such acting luminaries as Fernando Rey, Bibi Andersson, Vittorio Gassman and Nina Van Pallandt (who gets a skewer right through her head). Once the other players are eliminated, Essex returns from whence he came, trudging back into the woods to brave the wild dog packs rather than the human variety.

Even at a hundred minutes, *Quintet* seemed way too long, thanks to Altman's meandering storytelling. Rarely did the game or plot of *Quintet* convince, and dramatic structure was just as frozen as the locale. Rather than being challenging, the movie was numbingly pretentious.

Meteor was only numbing in that seventeen million dollars was spent over a three-year period to mount one of the most stolid disaster movies on record. Producer Theodore Parvin found the creative cupboard almost bare thanks to the work of Irwin Allen. Instead he looked to a *Saturday Review* article by Isaac Asimov for inspiration.

"We now live with the knowledge that there is a chance that a large meteorite. . .may strike and demolish a city on earth. . .at any moment. . . ," the learned doctor wrote. The filmmaker also discovered the existence of "Project Icarus," a 1968 study worked up at the Massachusetts Institute of Technology which planned for a comet entering Earth's atmosphere.

Although his partner, Arnold Orgolini, was not initially impressed with the dramatic prospects thereof, Parvin convinced him of the project's possibilities. From there, the idea went into the hands of screenwriter Edmund H. North, who had penned the classic *Day the Earth Stood Still* (1951). While that film concerned the first intelligent alien contact with this world, the new script called for international cooperation in the face of an unreasoning threat.

Two comets collide in outer space, sending a five-mile-wide chunk of debris on a collision course with the Earth. Spinning in front of it are "splinters," relatively small hunks of the shattered rock, dotting the planet's surface with disaster. One slams into Siberia, leveling much of the area. Another crashes into the Alps, creating an avalanche of mammoth proportions. A third dives into the China Sea, making a tsunami to end all tsunamis. And the final hits smack dab in the

The cast and crew of *Meteor* pose for a family portrait; including director Ronald Neame (front, seated), Sean Connery, Natalie Wood, and Henry Fonda (far right, front, standing).

A rock "splinter" of the *Meteor* destroys the World Trade Towers in Manhattan.

middle of Central Park—reducing Manhattan to ashes.

Even with all this destruction, the big daddy meteor has yet to hit. Unless the superpowers agree to turn all their orbiting nuclear missile satellites on the rock, Earth will be splashed all over the galaxy. Taking the taut political disaster thriller and turning it into a bombastic, simplistic, over-wrought movie was fairly easy. They tried to do too much and they did it all badly.

The script was rewritten by Stanley Mann, then turned over to *The Poseidon Adventure* director Ronald Neame. What he had was about an hour's worth of tight plotting, which was turned into a hundred and three minutes of drivel by casting stars in almost all the roles and laboriously—sometimes ridiculously—padding out every major scene. Sean Connery starred as ex-NASA scientist Paul Bradley who had conceived Project Hercules in case of meteor attack.

He's called back into service by Karl Malden, playing NASA head Harold Sherwood. Curious-ly, American Express, who utilizes Malden's ser-vices in their commercials, refused to let his visage be used in publicity, except in "special cases" (according to his *Meteor* contract). Car part manufacturer NAPA tried to pull the same thing with their actor/spokesperson Joseph Campanella, who was playing General Easton, father of a Skylab (called "Challenger Two" in the film) astronaut killed by the comet collision.

Natalie Wood co-starred as a Russian translator with Brian Keith as Alexei Dubov, Bradley's opposite in the Kremlin. Martin Landau was featured as Project Hercules's military advisor, a hysterical Russian hater, and Henry Fonda rounded out the cast as the president. The movie got out of hand almost from the very beginning. When the script wasn't trying to supply limp character development with throwaway scenes, it was cutting back to the meteor which was slowly drifting through space.

This cutting from slow drama to slow special

The original cast of *Battlestar Galactica* look intense. From the left, Maren Jensen, Dirk Benedict, Richard Hatch, and Lorne Greene.

Although much of the world lay in ruins, the *Meteor* scientists have prevented the Earth's destruction. From the left, Karl Malden, Sean Connery, Natalie Wood and Brian Keith congratulate each other for surviving a mud slide in a Manhattan subway.

effects cursed the entire production. If it wasn't shots of the meteor, then it was shots of the missiles slowly blasting off from their orbiting satellite berths. And if it wasn't shots of rockets, it was views of Connery and company staring at monitors as the meteor and missiles approached each other. *Meteor* was the best sleep inducer since Nytol.

Another nail in the movie's coffin was its mediocre special effects. None of the effects were brilliantly realized, from matte paintings to miniatures. Although both *Star Wars* and *Alien* were made for about ten million dollars, *Meteor* couldn't get anything right even at almost twice the price. The climax of the movie came, not with the main meteor's destruction, but with the Project Hercules scientists' escape from the dangers the Manhattan splinter wrought.

Somehow or other, the heat of the crashing splinter melted the ground so the subway tunnels filled with mud. And since Project Hercules's HQ was beneath the New York streets, all the actors had to wade through tons of gunk poured into an exact recreation of the Fulton Street subway tunnel. The sight was about as inspiring on screen

The Cylon fighter pilot robots mercilessly track the *Battlestar Galactica*.

The Cylon's imperious Leader (Dick Duroc) plots to wipe out the humans on the *Battlestar Galactica*.

as it reads on paper. But the filmmakers broke the camel's back by continuing to make inflated claims to fans about their movie.

"It is quite likely the most dangerous scene ever filmed," they said of the mud slide. "It lasts all of eight minutes on the screen. . .but it will be one of the most exciting and terrifying eight minutes you'll ever see. . . ." The only thing terrifying about *Meteor* was the amount of time and money spent to produce such labored results.

The best of the otherwise feeble lot was *The China Syndrome,* which managed to be science fiction by just a few days. Originally, Michael Grey's screenplay called *Power* was shunned by almost all the major studios because of its volatile political content. Although intended as a "fictional documentary" which would chronicle the possibilities of a nuclear power plant disaster, producer Michael Douglas decided to make it a multimillion-dollar thriller—a movie which would sugarcoat the frightening real possibilities with action clichés.

Nevertheless, *The China Syndrome* was filled with realistic touches as well as allusions to real-life events. Jack Lemmon was signed to star as a California electric company executive who fervently believes in nuclear power but is swept into the coverup of an accident that nearly filled the atmosphere with deadly radioactive gas. When the liquid cooling the unbelievably hot core of the nuclear reactor is accidently diminished, the power-creating rods are nearly exposed—which could have caused a "meltdown" through the bottom of the reactor ("all the way to China," feebly jokes a character).

Richard Dreyfuss was set to star as a TV reporter who uncovers the truth, but when other commitments forced him to step out, Jane Fonda stepped in. She had been trying in vain to cinematically tell the story of the death of Karen Silkwood, who supposedly was murdered to prevent her testifying against nuclear power execs in court on safety violations. This incident was dramatized in the film as the incredibly evil businessmen set about murdering whomever might threaten their coverup.

This was *The China Syndrome*'s main strength as well as its main failing. While it was able to say more under the guise of fiction, that fiction had far less impact. The Jack Lemmon character, Jack Godell, is brutally murdered by a SWAT team after he barricades himself in the reactor control room to gain media attention. One of the witnesses is the main company exec whose totally unbelievable reaction is to grin evilly at the bloody corpse.

133

Here's a *Battlestar Galactica* nightclub singer who can do her own harmony.

The new cast of *Galactica 1980* featured Robyn Douglas, Kent McCord, a bearded Lorne Greene and Barry Van Dyke.

Director and co-scripter James Bridges is careful to show both sides of the nuclear power question, but makes the power and construction companies the totally black villains. Although the nuclear reactor's safeguard systems do save the day despite corrupt building shortcuts that caused the problem in the first place, the movie's message is clear. Where greed versus public safety is concerned, greed will win out every time.

What made *The China Syndrome* more than just a nuclear rehash of *Capricorn One*'s mass murder conspiracy paranoia was a similar real-life accident at the Three Mile Island nuclear reactor in Harrisburg, Pennsylvania, a few days after the premiere. What made the movie so chilling and powerful in retrospect were the same sort of cover-up machinations that resulted. Although stopping short of murder, the company spokesmen's feeble attempts at downplaying the danger were rendered ludicrous by the existence of the James Bridges/Michael Douglas movie.

Here was one science-fiction film which was truly prophetic.

TELEVISION MOVIES

Producer Glen Larson knew how to double his pleasure and double his fun. In addition to creating, writing, and executive producing two juvenile science-fiction series for television this season, he also saw both made into theatrical versions. This commercial success did not change the fact that both TV programs and subsequent movie versions were derivative and infantile attempts to emulate *Star Wars*.

Battlestar Galactica was the most obvious offender. It's three-hour television premiere episode was edited down into a two-hour motion picture initially set for European and Canadian distribution—then was shown everywhere. The occasion was given even a greater cinematic gloss by adding the gimmick of Sensurround (a low decibel noise that makes the theater vibrate) to the soundtrack. None of this masked its timeworn origins.

Lorne Greene starred as Commander Adama, a high-ranking Earth Federation official who looks upon a peace treaty offered by war-mongering Cylon aliens as the subterfuge that it is. Count Baltar (John Calicos) has already set up a treacherous deal with the Cylons' Imperious

Leader to attack the humans during their peace celebrations. Only a ragtag fleet of survivors escape the devastation, led by Adama. High among his staff are Captain Apollo (Richard Hatch), a straight-shooting, dark-haired, heroic cliché, and Lieutenant Starbuck (Dirk Benedict), a handsome, devil-may-care, cigar-chomping, blond cliché.

These two clichés protect the "Battlestar *Galactica*," the sole remaining aircraft-carrier around which the various other spaceships huddle for protection. They must fight off the vengeful Cylon warships in order to find a mythical planet of safety, "a planet called Earth." Adding enormously to the show's otherwise makeshift style were special effects supplied by co-producer John Dykstra—who fell out of George Lucas' good graces and fought a lawsuit (for *Star Wars* plagiarism) to do it.

Originally the series (and film) suggested that these space wanderers were the ones who originally cultivated this planet, but the on-going television show was to change things. Although the evil Count Baltar was killed by Cylons in the film, he was resurrected by the series to continue being a thorn in Adama's side until a whole new series called *Galactica 1980* was worked up.

In it, only Lorne Greene survived, while Apollo and Starbuck's grown children witnessed the craft's arrival on present-day Earth. That set the stage for supposedly humorous antics as the Galactica's denizens dazzled motorcycle gangs and policemen with their futuristic machines. Although they were supposed to explore Earth before making their presence known, the *Galactica*'s fate was not revealed before the series died of viewer indifference.

Buck Rogers, too, went through some heavy changes. Gil Gerard was the new incarnation of the book, comic strip and movie serial hero who was created in 1928. The story stayed more or less the same, even though the pilot and movie added their own version of relevancy. Although originally named Anthony, the character was updated into a space shuttle pilot named Captain William "Buck" Rogers and then frozen into suspended animation by an outer-space phenomenon. He is awakened in the twenty-fifth century by Princess Ardala (Pamela Hensley), the daughter of galac-

Gil Gerard starred as *Buck Rogers* who got to wear this tight suit. Felix Sila played the tiny robot Twiki and got to wear this suit of armor.

Old meets the new. Buster Crabbe played the original movie *Buck Rogers*, and here he crosses rayguns with Gil Gerard as Erin Grey, the new Wilma Deering, looks on.

Buck Rogers reaches the twenty-fifth century in this winged space shuttle.

Rock Hudson (center) ponders the changes during *The Martian Chronicles*.

Caroline Munro joins Marjoe Gortner for a trip through space in *Starcrash*.

Christopher Plummer plays the Ruler of the Universe,

Wesley Eure puts the final touches on the robot dog, the real star of C.H.O.M.P.S.

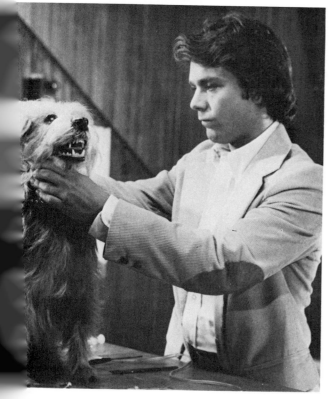

This was the martian landscape before humans arrived to write *The Martian Chronicles*.

The golden-eyed and masked Martians witness the human destruction of their home with pity and sadness during *The Martian Chronicles*.

In the future of *Americathon*, cars become homes since there is no longer any gasoline.

Dennis Dugan is the *Unidentified Flying Oddball*, a space shuttle astronaut who lands in Camelot and falls in love with maiden Shiela White.

tic despot Draco (Joseph Wiseman). She and her henchman, Killer Kane (Henry Silva), think he is a spy for Earth, but the Earth authorities think he is a spy for Draco.

While caught between a rock and a hard place, Rogers tries to adjust to his new environment, depending upon the sympathy of his midget robot companion Twiki (Felix Silla with the voice of Mel Blanc). Offering reluctant love interest is Lieutenant Wilma Deering (Erin Grey) and offering sage scientific advise is Dr. Huer (Tim O'Connor). Buck proves his good intentions by fighting off the Draco minions as they attempt to take over the Earth.

Buck Rogers in the Twenty-fifth Century made for a mediocre movie, but did not suffer undue comparisons to *Star Wars* since it all but admitted being a low-grade cross between the adventures of Han Solo, James Bond, and Burt Reynolds' "The Bandit" (of *Smokey and the Bandit,* 1977, fame). Gil Gerard did his best with the feeble witticisms supplied by writers Glen Larson and Leslie

Stevens, as did director Daniel Haller with the low budget, plastic sets, and trite situations.

When the on-going series began to falter in the ratings, its basic concept was also changed. Suddenly Buck and Wilma were assigned to a space-going ship whose mission and occupants were uncomfortably similar to those of *Star Trek*. But, again, the writing and conception was not even close to that of the success it emulated, so *Buck Rogers* also went down the boob tube.

The preceding two television efforts followed a precedent set by two Marvel comic-book creations which allowed other TV projects to find their way into theaters. *The Amazing Spider-Man* (1977) was extremely similar to its comic-book origins. Milquetoast student Peter Parker (Nicholas Hammond) is bitten by a radioactive spider, thus gaining the arachnid's powers. Unfortunately, low television budgets were hardly equal to the task of properly visualizing the character's high-swinging, powerful-punching, web-shooting adventures. The fact that the scripts and character development was painfully pedestrian also spelled Spider-Man's doom.

To everyone's surprise, *The Incredible Hulk* (1977) did not suffer the same fate, thanks to the sensitive and inventive approach of producer/writer/director Kenneth Johnson. Instead of using the "Dr. Jekyll and Mr. Hyde"-type plot to present scenes of mindless destruction, Johnson used his series as a means to explore the rage within everyone. Bill Bixby played David Bruce Banner, a scientist investigating the roots of strength. When he discovers that Gamma radiation is high on the days incredible feats of strength are performed, he accidentally bombards himself with a massive overdose of the stuff.

Now, whenever he gets angry, he transforms into a green, eight-foot-tall monster—*The Incredible Hulk*. A nosey reporter (Jack Colvin) causes an explosion in which Banner's partner (Susan Sullivan) is killed, an accident which reportedly kills Banner as well. An accident for which the Hulk is blamed. Now Banner is on the run, keeping his identity secret, trying to keep the Hulk inside him, and trying to find a cure for the problem.

The series took it from there, maintaining a sensitive, occasionally experimental approach. Before too long, however, the comic-book aspect of the character outweighed the more serious aspects of

Nancy Morgan and John Ritter, married in real life, also play Mr. and Mrs. President in *Americathon*.

the work, giving *The Incredible Hulk* an identity crisis, from which it succumbed.

A final television subnote must be given to *The Martian Chronicles*, an abominable adaptation of Ray Bradbury's classic literary work. Once again, director Michael Anderson was given the directorship of the project, after having done so poorly with Doc *Savage* and *Logan's Run*. In Bradbury's own words: "The director woke up bored every day and didn't do a thing. The movie was a big dead elephant in the middle of the desert."

BRING ON THE GIRLS

Luigi Cozzi loved science-fiction films. For years he had been trying to produce his script called *The Adventures of Stella Starr*. But after *Star Wars* succeeded, Italian investors gave him a half-million dollars, a hundred technicians, an international cast and almost no time to prepare. Even so, Cozzi wrote and directed *Starcrash*, starring Caroline Munro as Stella. The crew whipped together the sets in two days and it showed, but the film had the antic speed of a mindless oriental entertainment. Munro was packed into a leather bikini for the part and surrounded by eccentric creations.

Marjoe Gortner played her psychic sidekick Akton, who could draw little electric figures in the air with his forefinger and fought with a light-sword just like Luke Skywalker's light-sabre. David Hasselhoff played Prince Simon, who spent most of the movie disguised as a robot so no one would know he was the son of the Emperor of the Universe (Christopher Plummer). Massive, bald Robert Tessier played the evil Thor, the right-hand man of slimey Count Zarth Arn (Joe Spinell).

There were cute mechanical robots, model animated robots, and other adversaries as well, filling the screen with color and light. The plot was simplistic and derivative, utilizing yet another planet-sized killer spaceship and Darth Vader-like antagonists. The special effects were well meaning, but briskly shoddy. Even so, the whole thing was a frolicsome affair, full of vitality and brainless bravado. Cozzi was listed as Lewis Coates in the credits, and while *Starcrash* was universally panned by critics, it made for a good time at the drive-in.

Goldengirl was another matter altogether. Its serious pretentions continually destroyed what enjoyment there could have been in the tale of a super female athlete created specifically to win the Olympics. Susan Anton was being groomed for superstardom much the same way her character was being pumped up with a new hormone by a bunch of businessmen. Curt Jurgens played the "mad scientist" Serafin, who neglects his creation's emotional needs, while James Coburn played the empathetic Dryden, who wants to save the heroine's soul. Also in the fine cast were Robert Culp and Leslie Caron.

Joseph Sargent directed from a script by John Kohn based on a novel by Peter Lear. And while *Goldengirl* was essentially as simple as Sargent's previous science-fiction film, *Colossus: The Forbin Project* (1970), the latter tale of a super computer taking over the Earth was more chilling and believable than this feeble sports story. It climaxes when the girl collapses from too much work and too little love. The film collapses long before the finale, however.

PUNCH LINES

Comedies were beginning to use science-fiction concepts as background. The idea of a robot dog

Harvey Korman plays the drug-addicted host of the *Americathon*, the telethon designed to pay off a 400-billion-dollar national deficit.

Almost everyone in *Americathon* wears a jogging suit and pickets the president.

140

was not unique, having been used in *The Human-oid, Message from Space* and such TV series as *Doctor Who* and *Wonder Woman,* but Hanna-Barbera—the studio responsible for such animated characters as Yogi Bear, Huckleberry Hound, and The Flintstones—thought another might be just the thing to introduce their company to live-action film lovers.

Although existing in the shadow of Walt Disney Productions for some time, the studio saw no reason not to join the Disney people in making whimsical film fantasies. This first effort concerned the Canine Home Protection Systems, otherwise known as CHOMPS. Wesley Eure starred as a young inventory who creates the first robot canine complete with X-ray vision, steel teeth, and rocket paws.

He and his girlfriend (Valerie Bertinelli) get caught between two warring security companies panting for CHOMPS's blueprints. People like Chuck McCann, Red Buttons, and Jim Backus all lent their comedic support, but the result was rather feeble. The movie was too obviously a pale plagiarism of Disney's increasingly wan efforts in the same direction.

As evidence, there was *Unidentified Flying Odd-ball,* a good Disney Productions idea undermined by the studio's callow approach. Don Tait's original screenplay was entitled *A Connecticut Space-man in King Arthur's Court,* then shortened to *The Spaceman and King Arthur.* Both titles were dropped in favor of the dreadful anacronym for UFO.

At first, all seemed idyllic. Producer Ron Miller sent director Russ Mayberry and a good cast on location at two British castles and Pinewood Studios. Dennis Dugan played astronaut Tom Trimble, whose space-shuttle-like craft tumbles through a time warp into Camelot. Kenneth More played King Arthur, who was in the midst of battling the treacherous plots of a now-evil Merlin (Ron Moody) and the villainous knight Sir Mordred (Jim Dale).

Adding medieval color was Rodney Bewes as Clarence, Trimble's medieval manservant, and Sheila White as Alisande, Trimble's love, who spends most of the movie mistakenly thinking that her father had been magically turned into a duck.

141

Merlin and Mordred try to do Trimble in, but his futuristic gadgets save him every time.

Among the science-fiction staples the astronaut calls upon are a NASA laser pistol, a rocket-powered ejection seat, a moon buggy, an inflatable space suit, and an android double. He also uses his wits—shining a suit of armor so that it reflects his laser beam (an impossibility in reality) and magnetizing Mordred's sword so a duel becomes ridiculous. Although otherwise well produced, many special effects were distractingly shabby. The studio's final decision to label it *Unidentified Flying Oddball* only served to keep otherwise interested viewers away.

Even more abominable was *Americathon,* made all the worse because it was supposed to be a mature yet madcap comedy. The science-fiction construct by Peter Bergman and Philip Proctor was rife with comic possibilities: theirs was a 1996 America where public waste had left the nation on the verge of bankruptcy, where people used their cars as homes while walking, bicycling, or skating wherever they had to go. To save the coun-try, the hip president (John Ritter) must pay back a forty-billion-dollar loan to an American Indian manufacturer of jogging suits (Chief Dan George). To do so, the government televises a fund-raising telethon with a drug-addicted star (Harvey Korman) as host.

The humor encircling this basic premise and its subplots was extremely weak. The president has an affair with a Vietnamese "puke rocker" (Zane Buzby) while his wife (Nancy Morgan) settles down with the telethon producer (Peter Riegert). While they fiddle around, the telethon is sabotaged by the United Hebrab Republic (an enormously wealthy nation of coexisting Arabs and Jews) who want to buy America for themselves.

Director Neil Israel and co-scripters Michael Mislove and Monica Johnson fail to present one legitimately funny sequence, rendering the comedian-packed cast (Fred Willard, Richard Schaal, Howard Hesseman, Jay Leno) useless. *Americathon* did not make for good comedy or good science fiction.

The single finest science-fiction moment in any

Graham Chapman survives a UFO crash in pre-Jesus Judea during *Monty Python's Life of Brian*.

This production painting for *H.G. Well's The Shape of Things to Come* was much better than the movie itself.

blasts them with ray gun fire. Irrevocably damaged, they speed back to Earth and crash land precisely where they had picked Brian up. He stumbles away as the chase continues as if never interrupted.

Although his fate is to be crucified among a chorus which sings "Always Look on the Bright Side of Life," Brian's saga is a biting lampoon that not only assails religion's hypocritical precepts, but modern science-fiction film clichés to boot.

comedy this year came in *Monty Python's Life of Brian,* a scathing satire of organized religion's roots, taking place in Judea during Jesus' life. In fact, the movie opens with the Sermon on the Mount, which several people in the back can't hear ("I think he said 'Blessed are the cheesemakers.' ")

Brian (Graham Chapman) has the misfortune of being born next to the manger on December 25, causing a mixup for the Three Wise Men. Religious misfortune continues to stalk the hapless fellow as he teams with the terrorist "People's Front of Judea," a wildly over-organized anti-Roman revolutionary society. To cap it all off, he is then mistaken for the messiah by the hysterical populace ("I say you're the messiah and I should know—I've followed a few.").

Brian is forced to flee from Hebrews and Romans alike, until the chase ends atop an unfinished stairway. Just as it seems he will plummet to his death, a spaceship swoops down and catches him in midair. Two cyclop aliens take Brian on a merry outer-space chase as a larger craft

Malcolm McDowell, playing a young H.G. Wells, is directed by Nicholas Meyer in *Time After Time.*

The Time Machine "Argo" takes H.G. Wells (Malcolm McDowell) to 1979 during *Time After Time*.

In 1979, H.G. Wells (Malcolm McDowell) listens carefully so he will know how to order a "Big Mac" during *Time After Time*.

H.G. WELLS ASSAILED

The father of science fiction did not get off easy this year. A Canadian film used one of his classic stories as an excuse to mount more feeble drivel, while an American production used him as the star character. *The Shape of Things to Come* comes first, an inexpensive remake of the classic 1936 film scripted by Wells, directed by William Cameron Menzies, produced by Alexander Korda and starring Ralph Richardson and Raymond Massey. It was a striking and exciting film that depicted the final fight between the forces of war and peace.

The new version's producers William Davidson and Harry Alan Towers, scripter Martin Lager, director George McCowan, and stars Jack Palance, Carol Lynley, Barry Morse, and Eddie Benton were no way near being in that high-class league. Other than the fact that the leading character is named "Cabal" in both versions, they are not even remotely similar. The new story concerns the peaceful moon settlement of "New Washington" being attacked by the evil robots and spaceships of Omus

David Warner, playing Jack the Ripper, threatens Mary Steenburgen, who plays the bank teller H.G. Wells falls in love with during *Time After Time*.

(Palance), the evil humanoid ruler of the planet Delta III.

Their only hope is the illegal battleship *Starstreak* piloted by Jason Caball (Nicholas Campbell) and crewed by his father, Dr. John Caball (Morse), beautiful Kim Smedley (Benton), and "Sparks," the poetry-quoting wonder robot. They land on Delta III and lead a revolution of captured humans, defeating the insidious Omus inside his own fortress. This movie, which the producers had the gall to title *H.G. Wells' The Shape of Things To Come,* might have been a mildly watchable time-consumer had the filmmakers not decided to exploit the memory of one of the great writers and great films. Instead, this picture is only a lamebrained excuse to show feeble special effects and mediocre writing.

Time After Time was a far superior movie, marking writer Nicholas Meyer's directing debut. After having written *The Seven Percent Solution,* the first of many Sherlock Holmes pastiches, Meyer adapted to film the story of Karl Alexander, who proposed that H.G. Wells not only wrote but also invented the Time Machine itself. It is Wells's bad luck that one of his friends, Dr. John Stevenson, turns out to be Jack the Ripper, who steals his device.

The movie rests on the somewhat shakey premise that once set, the Time Machine cannot be reset. So when the Ripper escapes to 1979, the invention automatically boomerangs back to Wells's study in 1893. Unable to move back a few hours to prevent the theft, Wells is forced to go forward to what he thinks is the Utopia he prophesized in his own works—only to discover that San Francisco of 1979 was not the Eden he thought it would be.

Malcolm McDowell plays the young Wells, David Warner plays the Ripper and Mary Steenburgen is the bank teller the author falls in love with. While some of the movie consists of Wells adjusting to McDonald's and going to the movies to see *Exorcist IV,* much of the film finds him stalking the Ripper, aghast that the late seventies is not Nirvana, but a sordid breeding ground for hundreds like the Ripper. As the villain so chillingly tells him, "I'm home."

Happily, Wells tricks the Ripper into utilizing the Time Machine again to escape, not knowing that the inventor had removed the failsafe device

145

An amazingly realistic miniature built by Derek Meddings for the James Bond movie, *Moonraker*.

Roger Moore makes a face at the giant rubber snake 007 fights during *Moonraker*.

that kept the invention on its 1893 to 1979 track. Jack goes tumbling through time, lost between dimensions, while Herbert George Wells settles down with his modern liberated lady. *Time After Time* was a simple, effective little movie that could delight.

OUTER SPACE BELONGS TO 007

That's what the posters said when James Bond returned to theaters in *Moonraker*. Originally set to make *For Your Eyes Only* after *The Spy Who Loved Me*, producer Albert Broccoli saw the science-fiction possibilities inherent in the third 007 novel. "Moonraker" originally denoted the atomic-warhead-carrying missile megalomaniac Hugo Drax wanted to drop on London. To bring the concept up to date, Broccoli called upon a small army of writers. Even though Christopher Wood got the only on-screen scripting credit, this Bond, as usual, was written by committee—up to and including *Animal House* (1978) director John Landis.

Whoever was responsible, the *Moonraker* screenplay was wall to wall action. *The Spy Who Loved Me* crew was back: director Lewis Gilbert, star Roger Moore, designer Ken Adam, and special-effects director Derek Meddings. The first order of business was to surpass the pre-credit

Roger Moore celebrates his fiftieth birthday on the set of *Moonraker*.

147

sequence thrill created by the previous movie's parachuted ski jump. Incredibly, the group pulled it off with a mid-air freefall fight.

Bond is forced to push an enemy spy out of a plane, only to be pushed after him by Jaws (Richard Kiel). Instead of simply plummeting to his death, 007 catches up with the parachute-wearing enemy spy, battles him for possession of the life-saving sack and then slips the thing on himself—all while in freefall. Even then, his troubles are not over. Jaws comes flying after him. He escapes by pulling the ripcord, leaving the steel-toothed killer to smash into a circus tent.

Before the credits start, the success and failure of *Moonraker* was already evident. While it contained some spectacular sequences, they were always marred by a facile visual joke or completely unbelievable occurrence. While the freefall fight was just too dazzling to let the disjointed, illogical conclusion detract from its enjoyment, it wasn't too long before the continual use of labored jokes ruined the movie. For instance, at the end of this pre-credit sequence, not only does Jaws attempt to "fly" by flapping his arms, but his action is accompanied by goofy soundtrack music.

The film proper starts when a "Moonraker" space shuttle is hijacked off the top of a 747 jumbo jetliner (the first of many exceptional miniature

effects). To find the missing NASA ship, 007 is sent to meet the manufacturer, Hugo Drax (Michael Lonsdale). The billionaire industrialist stole the ship intended for NASA because one of his own fleet had developed problems. He needs six Moonrakers to complete his plan to create a new world in orbit.

Although the identity of the villain is quite clear,

Hugo Drax's Moonraker space station as it appeared on the special-effects set.

A stunt man doubling for Roger Moore takes off on a hang glider from the "Q Craft" motorboat during *Moonraker*.

Bond must follow a wealth of clues all over the world to piece together the plot. First stop, Venice, where a totally unnecessary sequence of events include a knife-wielding assassin hidden in a coffin, a chase on the canals with Bond in a gondola which turns into a high-speed motorboat and then a hovercraft, the discovery of a germ warfare lab, and a fight in a clock tower. The visit ends with a tryst with Holly Goodhead (Lois Chiles), a CIA agent infiltrating Drax's organization.

Next stop, Rio de Janeiro, just in time for the

yearly Mardi Gras. There Jaws returns, now in the employ of Drax, and the antagonists have a fight atop the cable cars off Sugar Loaf mountain. Bond escapes by sliding down the cable just as Jaws succumbs to love at first sight with a pig-tailed beauty (complete with a slow motion embrace while the soundtrack plays "Love Is a Many Splendored Thing"). The killer's amour happens

The evil Hugo Drax (Michael Lonsdale, center left) has a meeting with his corporation in a scene that was edited out of *Moonraker*. This clever table folds invisibly down into the floor.

Roger Moore relaxes with one of the many beautiful girls (wearing a "Premium Bond Girl" T-shirt) hired for *Moonraker*.

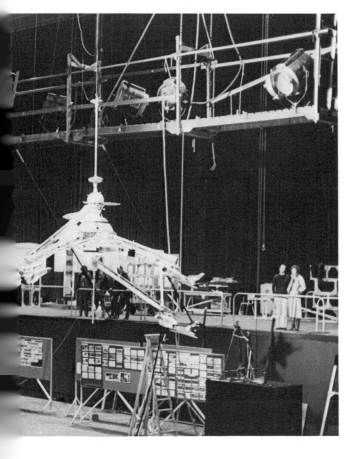

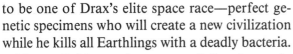

to be one of Drax's elite space race—perfect genetic specimens who will create a new civilization while he kills all Earthlings with a deadly bacteria.

None of this can happen until Bond goes in search of Drax up the Amazon in what is labeled the "Q Craft"—a sleek motorboat equipped with torpedoes, mines, and, ridiculously, an awning that turns into a hang glider when the going gets tough. After a smooth glide, 007 discovers Drax's Mayan Mission Control, where he views the launching of the Space Shuttle fleet. Teaming with Goodhead,

The same space station as it appears close up in
Moonraker.

Bond gains control of one Moonraker and follows the others to Drax's spider-shaped space station in orbit.

There, he sends out a radio message to the "space marines" who blast off in their own Space Shuttle. Then 007 convinces Jaws that Drax's plans have no place for a monstrous freak. All together, they wreak physical and laser havoc on Drax's plans. Bond himself sends the villain into an air lock and then into the vacuum of outer space.

Once more James Bond had saved the world. But at quite a price.

The filmmakers ignored the serious side of their previous success to overdose *Moonraker* with meaningless ingredients. Their concept of humor at the expense of story was painful to see, as was their sense of "action for action's sake." The gimmicks and gadgets in this one didn't even remotely ring true. While it might make a certain fanciful sense to wear a parachute in the Alps or have a

James Bond cuts ott the space station's gravity, making the entire cast of *Moonraker* float.

007 is caught with his pants down by Mission Control at the end of *Moonraker*.

car that could turn into a submarine, the devices in *Moonraker* were almost totally unnatural. The seams also showed in that the sequences were written around the gadgets, rather than the other way around. Scene after scene seemed forced into the plotline simply to spotlight the new 007 toys.

Audiences want to believe in the reality of any science-fiction film, if only for the two hours they are in the theater. But the filmmakers were not taking James Bond or *Moonraker* seriously, so it was impossible for the audience to. Instead of making a worthy successor to *Star Wars* or even *The Spy Who Loved Me*, all they made was a stale, smug satire.

WHERE NO MAN HAS GONE BEFORE

Star Trek—The Motion Picture was a fiasco. Except for a five-minute sequence at the very beginning which detailed the destruction of three alien ships, the film was a collection of mistakes and

Famed science-fiction film producer, writer, and director George Pal (left) joins *Star Trek* producer Gene Roddenberry (center) and director Robert Wise on the set of *Star Trek—The Motion Picture*.

wrong choices. It boasts one of the most inflated budgets (approximately forty million dollars) and labored production histories of any genre movie. Its original genesis is no secret. *Star Trek* lasted two and a half seasons on NBC television from 1966 to 1969. Only after its network failure did it become a spectacular syndicated success, rebroadcasting the same seventy-eight episodes over and over again for the next ten years.

That success led to an animated Saturday morn-

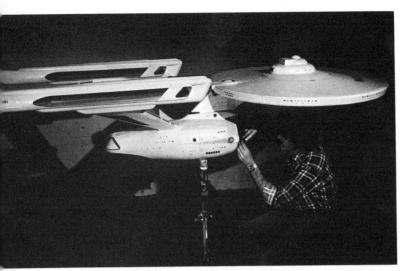

The Starship *Enterprise* of *Star Trek—The Motion Picture* as it appeared in Doug Trumbull's special-effects studio.

And the Starship *Enterprise* as it appeared on-screen in *Star Trek—The Motion Picture*.

ing TV series as well as reams of "spin-off" products—from original paperback books to lunch boxes to toys. Even though its distribution company, Paramount, reaped the lion's share of the rewards, it seemed reluctant to resurrect the series in any live-action form, almost as if that would be like admitting they had made a mistake in stopping production in the first place. The basic attitude seemed to be that they didn't need to spend anything to keep making a lot of money.

Finally, the president of ABC at the time (1976), Fred Silverman, inquired about the possibility of a new *Star Trek* TV movie or mini-series. The series' original producer and creator, Gene Roddenberry, visualized this as a meaningful science-

fiction adventure which would investigate the very nature of humanity. He worked up a script he jokingly called "The Starship Enterprise Meets God." The network was not happy with the controversial script that has the logical half-Vulcan, half-human Mr. Spock say, "This God of yours makes you fall to your stomach every seventh day and worship him—that sounds like a very insecure personality."

In actuality, the producer stated, the network wanted what he called "Flash Gordon Over Easy." When ABC asked for changes, Roddenberry handed the script to Chris Bryant and Allan Scott, who had done the screenplay for *Don't Look Now* (1973). The resulting work was still difficult for

the studio and network to accept, but they were assured enough to ask Roddenberry to find a director for the project. He chose Philip Kaufman.

"We were ready to shoot," Kaufman recalls. "We had artist Ralph McQuarrie working with designer Ken Adam in England. I was ready to move my family to Great Britain when they gave us a definite go-ahead. At first Paramount wanted to do a small, three-million-dollar rip-off, cashing in on the *Star Trek* phenomenon. In the six or eight months that I was involved, it was raised to ten million. Then, one week later, they said, 'Forget it.' "

The end of the initial project was heralded by the premiere of *Star Wars*. Suddenly, the studio

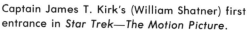

Captain James T. Kirk's (William Shatner) first entrance in *Star Trek—The Motion Picture*.

Mr. Spock (Leonard Nimoy, left, kneeling) faces his Vulcan mentors in an attempt to exorcize his human emotions in the beginning of *Star Trek—The Motion Picture.*

had a much bigger project in mind. They had created "Operation Prime Time," an audacious attempt at instituting a fourth major TV network. In addition to several melodramatic soap opera-like mini-series that were being produced, Paramount thought to also offer *Star Trek-The Television Movie,* followed by a new weekly series.

Trying to make Roddenberry's film script into an inoffensive two-hour pilot were writers R.W. Goodwin and Harold Livingston. The studio promised that production would start in November 1977 for an April 1978 premiere. To show their good faith, they rehired the original cast, except for one holdout. Leonard Nimoy had gone off to do the *Invasion of the Body Snatchers* remake with director Philip Kaufman, leaving the role of Mr. Spock behind. Instead of recasting the part, Roddenberry created a full-blooded Vulcan science officer whose emotionless demeanor made Spock's character seem like Heidi. David Gautreaux was

signed to play the new Vulcan part of Lieutenant Xon.

All was set when the ax fell again. Operation Prime Time was only a limited success and participating syndicated stations balked at *Star Trek's* high price tag. The project was put on hold again, until a new corporate structure took over the studio. Suddenly the green light was given by new production head Michael D. Eisner. A newly revised budget was upscaled to fifteen million dollars and director Robert Wise was signed (he had also helmed the classic science-fiction films *The Day the Earth Stood Still* and *The Andromeda Strain,* 1970). And since his work for Kaufman was at an end and the project was getting the respect he felt it deserved, Leonard Nimoy also came aboard.

From there, the work went right downhill.

Instead of going with such established special-effects talents as Douglas Trumbull, Paramount

The bridge of the Starship *Enterprise* with William Shatner standing to the left, George Takei as Sulu seated in front of him and Walter Koenig as Chekov seated at the far right.

Another unseen *Star Trek—The Motion Picture* ingredient; the wrist communicator and "tricorder" modeled by William Shatner.

gambled on Robert Abel and Associates, a well-respected commercial production house that promised to do all the complex special effects for less than four million dollars. Their decision would haunt them when Abel's budget burgeoned to three times that amount without producing one foot of usable film effects.

By that time it was almost too late. All the live-action footage had been shot—but it too was something of a mess. Walter Koenig, who played the Russian security officer Chekov, remembered it this way. "Our climax must have undergone, very conservatively, thirty or forty revisions. We were getting rewritten script pages not by the day, but at eight a.m., ten-thirty, four p.m., and six-thirty in the evening. It was absolutely insane."

Complications came about because six people had a certain amount of script approval. Whenever anything had to be changed, William Shatner (who played Captain James T. Kirk), Nimoy, pro-

This was another scene that was edited out of *Star Trek—The Motion Picture*: Captain Kirk searches inside an alien being for the missing Mr. Spock.

Just three of the aliens barely glimpsed in *Star Trek—The Motion Picture*, being tended by the makeup crew.

Leonard Nimoy as Mr. Spock and DeForest Kelley as Dr. McCoy restrain William Shatner as Captain Kirk in *Star Trek—The Motion Picture*'s final moments.

ducer Livingston, producer Roddenberry and a new writer, Dennis Lynton Clark, all had a say. The result was filmmaking by committee and chaos. Further problems arose from the director's insistence that almost everything be changed from the TV series.

Wise thought the Starship *Enterprise's* bridge looked like a Holiday Inn, the costumes were too colorful, and the props—like the hand-held communicators—were old-fashioned. In their stead came a cramped, over-staffed bridge, drab, colorless uniforms, and charmless devices—such as a Dick Tracy-like two-way wrist radio that wasn't even glimpsed in the final film. What was all too evident in the movie were the special effects. After Abel was ousted, the producers were forced to seek out Doug Trumbull and all but open the bank for him.

Because he had to do two years' work in the nine months before the film was set to premiere, Trumbull christened his unit the "Star Trek Salvage Division," and got to work. The load was so heavy that John Dykstra was also recruited to realize some sequences. But while they toiled feverishly, Wise and his editors had to wait. The editing process is one of the most important in any film and the *Star Trek* crew was still cutting mere days before Paramount had reserved hundreds of theaters across the nation. The director was so upset by this rushed, haphazard work that he actually sent out a letter of apology to the press for how the film would look.

Wise was correct in that the film had a flat, drab appearance in the non-special-effects sequences. Sadly, so did the script. The basic skeleton of the story Roddenberry had conceived years before was still there, only its teeth, heart and brain were removed, leaving glaring similarities to several *Star Trek* TV episodes, including "The Changeling," "The Immunity Syndrome," and "The Doomsday Machine." Although similar to each, the film was inferior to all.

The galaxy in general and the Earth in particular was being threatened by a massive force which called itself "V'ger." The only ship close enough to do battle was the refurbished *Enterprise,* helmed by Captain Decker (Stephen Collins—originally playing the son of a series character who was killed

The two new *Star Trek—The Motion Picture* stars, Stephen Collins as Captain Decker and Persis Khambatta as Ilia.

in one of the episodes, although that relationship is not mentioned in the film).

Now a Commander, James T. Kirk is sent to take over the *Enterprise's* helm because he is more experienced with the ship. He sends out an order for all his old officers to return, including Dr. "Bones" McCoy (DeForest Kelley). But Mr. Spock is on Vulcan partaking in a ritual which would rid him of his human emotions. It is disrupted by the cosmic force eminating from V'ger (although the Vulcan had told Kirk during the series that "Spock" was just a simple version of his real, unpronounceable name, the other Vulcans clearly call him Spock—a glaring mistake).

Spock returns to the ship to fight the menace in the company of his old comrades; communications officer Uhura (Nichelle Nichols), helmsman Sulu (George Takei), and engineer Scott (James Doohan). Another alien crewmember was also on the bridge. Persis Khambatta played the hairless

Ilia of the planet Delta. As originally conceived by Roddenberry, the Deltans were a race so proficient at love that any liason with an inferior human would render the partner incompetent. But in the film version, that important aspect of her personality is eliminated. And since there was no other character development, her personality was negligible.

Much of the film's two hour and twelve minute running time consisted of boring reaction shots of characters looking at the *Enterprise* or V'ger. And when people weren't staring, they were mouthing extremely banal dialogue. This made for static sequences the likes of which hadn't been experienced by *Star Trek* fans. Even when the series wasn't great, it wasn't boring. *Star Trek—The Motion Picture* both *wasn't* great and *was* boring.

After Ilia is stolen by V'ger and turned into an android, it is revealed that V'ger is actually a Voyager spacecraft, sent on an exploratory mission in the 1970s. It called itself V'ger because the "oya" on its hull had been rubbed off somehow (as Spock would say, "Very illogical." Why would a ship read its own hull?). Instead of planting clues or realistically explaining, the script has Kirk and company guess that it must have landed on a planet of intelligent machines which gave it its present size, strength, and power. Since it was suddenly a sentient being, it wished to return to Earth to meld with its "creator"—that is, find its god.

The ending is pure drivel, as Decker hits upon the idea of melding himself and the android Ilia with V'ger. Naturally his incomprehensible plan results in a fabulous light show out of which the *Enterprise* cruises unscathed, with Kirk, Spock, and McCoy saying something about witnessing the birth of a new life form. That monumental example of the film's failure was all but lost in the unsatisfactory material preceeding it. In the studio's rush to exploit the science-fiction craze, *Star Trek—The Motion Picture* became an albatross instead of a high-flying bird.

6

1980
THE YEAR O
DISASTE

ALMOST ALL THE MAJOR STUDIOS wanted a science-fiction blockbuster now. There had been plenty of time to plan, cast, film, and edit their monumental concepts, each boasting great new advances in special effects. But for one reason or another, almost every high-budget effort presented to the public this year was a failure—in fact, a critical and box office disaster. Each was a film that massively misjudged the tastes of audiences. Each was a movie that, at its base, was condescending to its science-fiction theme.

The Black Hole was aptly named. It was the worst offender and the worst of its kind. It joins

Logan's Run and *Damnation Alley* as one of the most overblown and banal excuses for science fiction ever made. The ultimate tragedy is that it was slated to be the film that would propel Walt Disney Productions into the eighties. It was their first film ever to get a higher rating than "G." It's "PG" rating and the promise of a more adult, literate script thrilled fans. This was, after all, the studio which had produced such charming delights as *The Absent Minded Professor* (1961) and *20,000 Leagues Under the Sea* (1954).

Instead of the movie its producers promised would "surpass the mind's conception of even the most extraodinary of science-fiction extravaganzas," *The Black Hole* was a futuristic *20,000 Leagues* seemingly written by the Absent Minded Professor. The finished film was so derivative of their past triumphs (not to mention *Star Wars*) and so scientifically inaccurate that Walt Disney himself would probably have been aghast. As a matter of fact, *The Black Hole* was a textbook example of almost everything Walt Disney had been against.

The project started as a Jeb Rosebrook-Gerry Day script called *Space Probe*. It was soon rewritten into an adventure called *Space Station One*. It was set for pre-production under producer Winston Hibler before *Star Wars* premiered. But after George Lucas's space opera opened and Hibler passed away, production head Ron Miller saw grander possibilities in the film. He called artist Peter Ellenshaw out of retirement with an offer the man couldn't refuse—the post of Production Designer.

With this new crew came another script. The awesome space phenomenon of a black hole, which was used as a background detail in the original script, became the central device in the new one. Hypothetically, the black holes are collapsed stars with gravitational fields so intense that they can absorb everything—even light and radio waves. Around this concept, Rosebrook, Bob Barash, and Richard Landau attached hunks of Jules Verne's classic sea saga and details traceable to Luke Skywalker's universe. "There is a slight parallel between them," an unidentified produc-

Dr. Hans Reinhardt (Maximilian Schell) confers with his malevolent robot about venturing through *The Black Hole.*

The space ship *Cygnus* of *The Black Hole*.

tion source admitted concerning *20,000 League* plot similarities, "but it's not deliberate."

At first John Hough, the capable director of such atmospheric genre films as *The Legend of Hell House* (1973), was set to direct, but pre-production went on for so long he was forced to honor previous commitments. In his place came Gary Nelson, a man who was better suited to police dramas (his TV Movies *To Kill a Cop*, 1979, and *Murder in Coweta County*, 1983, were both exceptional). Given a strong cast and a twenty-million-dollar budget, Nelson started shooting.

Dr. Hans Reinhardt (Maximilian Schell) confers with his malevolent robot about venturing through *The Black Hole*.

Late in the twenty-second century, the explorer craft *Palomino* heads back to Earth, carrying its space-weary crew. Captain Dan Holland (Robert Forster), First Officer Charles Pizer (Joseph Bottoms), scientist Alex Durant (Anthony Perkins), journalist Harry Booth (Ernest Borgnine), researcher Kate McCrae (Yvette Mimieux, in a part originally set for Jennifer O'Neill), and the Vital Information Necessary Centralized robot, otherwise known as V.I.N.CENT, with which Kate shares a psychic bond.

They spot a mile-long, darkened ship danger-ously close to a black hole, which looks like a floating blue whirlpool (toilet comparisons are almost unavoidable). V.I.N.CENT, a floating ball of machinery with the voice of Roddy McDowall, identifies the craft as the *Cygnus*, the ship of Dr. Hans Reinhardt (Maximilian Schell), which had been lost in space twenty years before.

Upon taking a closer look the power of the black hole grips them. They are only saved by the *Cygnus*, which lights up and extends a landing dock. Soon they are face to face with Reinhardt, a bearded, seemingly civilized madman surrounded by cowled, masked humanoids and guarded by a big red robot named Max—a combination Darth Vader and Cuisinart processor. The *Palomino* crew is given the royal tour—the halls being patrolled by walking sentry robots led by Captain S.T.A.R.

The plot degenerates rapidly. While Booth discovers that the masked humanoids are actually lobotomized humans, Reinhardt reveals to Kate that he is afraid of Max, which kills Durant on a whim. V.I.N.CENT comes upon "Old B.O.B.," a battered robot ball given the voice of Slim Pickens. The two floating machines rescue Holland who saves the tinfoil-swathed McCrae from being made into another masked, cowled automaton. V.I.N.CENT outshoots S.T.A.R., which collapses in a jealous snit, and Reinhardt announces he's going to send the *Cygnus* into the black hole.

Comets go speeding past the ship on their way into the hole, ripping out hunks of the craft in the process. Instead of being sucked out into space and imploding within minutes, Holland and crew continue running and talking as if the vacuum of space was just a minor sleet storm. Booth betrays everyone by taking off in the *Palomino* too soon, but pays the ultimate price when the *Cygnus* blows the escaping ship up. The surviving crew have no choice but to jump into one of the *Cygnus*'s escape vehicles as the mile-long ship is torn asunder by the gravitational pull.

To get to the escape craft, the characters have to run outside the *Cygnus*—a feat they accomplish without spacesuits or any detrimental effect. This time, in fact, they aren't even assailed by sleet, just bathed in red light (supposedly from the heat of the deteriorating *Cygnus*). The only thing in their way is Max, but V.I.N.CENT manages to get in close and disconnect it when Old B.O.B. creates

Joseph Bottoms rides V.I.N.CENT the robot out of harm's way during *The Black Hole*.

a diversion. The battered robot then collapses, drawling out a dying speech as the soundtrack music gets bathetic.

Finally both ships are sucked into the black hole, setting the stage for a Disney Studios idea of a "meaningful" conclusion. Reinhardt wakes up in "hell"—that is, a mountainous landscape filled with fires and wailing victims. The *Palomino* crew flies through "heaven"—that is, a shiny, cathedral-shaped hallway where a floating angel whisks by. Then the *Cygnus* escape craft comes out the other end of the black hole. None the worse for wear, they go soaring off into an unidentified section of space.

The audience was much the worse for wear. Although some of the special effects were good, much of the work ranged from familiar to dreadful and the script was universally horrid. The story was strictly retread and the dialogue unnatural. In almost every scene featuring the floating robots, the wires that held them aloft were clearly visible. Add to that the filmmakers' ignorance of much of nature's law and *The Black Hole* emerged as a film with precious little imagination and not a scrap of verisimilitude.

Plausibility was also in short supply during *Flash Gordon*. Having done over *King Kong*, producer Dino De Laurentiis turned his sights on the character who had inspired George Lucas in the first place. While the young filmmaker hadn't the money to secure the rights to the comic-book hero created in 1934 by Alex Raymond, the Italian entrepreneur did.

Although his presentations sometimes leave a lot to be desired, the producer's original vision can rarely be faulted. At first, he gave the project to screenwriter Michael Allin and director Nicholas Roeg, whose *Walkabout, Don't Look Now*, and *The Man Who Fell to Earth* were all stunning visual achievements. With them in control, the new version of the old hero was bound to be as challenging as it was dazzling.

In retrospect, it wasn't surprising that pre-production stalled with creative differences between director and producer. Soon Roeg and Allin were out and a more pedestrian concept was offered. Michael Hodges was the new director with *King Kong* scripter Lorenzo Semple, Jr., doing the writing honors. What De Laurentiis seemed to be looking for was not an update, but a big-budget remake of the 1930s serials starring Buster Crabbe. This way, the crew didn't have to strive for realistic effects—everything could be high-class camp.

Production, costume, and set designer Danilo Donati was most responsible for any gloss *Flash Gordon* could claim. His designs and their realization were pure *Fantasia*, a light show of art deco glitz—a Las Vegas extravaganza in outer space. Except for the opening minutes at a small American airport, the whole movie was filmed on interior sets built at British studios.

Sam Jones, a muscular blond discovered by De Laurentiis as a contestant on television's *The Dating Game*, starred as New York Jets' football team quarterback Flash Gordon, who shares a fateful plane ride with reporter Dale Arden (although originally cast with Dayle Hadden, her sultry, sleek good looks were too similar to others in the cast, so she was replaced with the "cleaner" Melody Anderson).

They crash land inside Dr. Zarkov's (Chaim Topol) laboratory, who abducts them in his rocket. They crash land again on the planet Mongo, where Ming the Merciless (Max Von Sydow) has been toying with the Earth by creating natural disasters with infernal devices. One glance convinces the dictator that Arden would be a perfect bride. In order to save her, Flash must escape Ming, flee the sexual advances of Ming's daughter, Princess Aura (Ornella Muti, whom Hadden had looked too similar to), and band together the feuding clans of Mongo—led by Prince Barin (Timothy Dalton) and Wing-men leader Prince Vultan (Brian Blessed).

The dialogue and situations are completely camped up, with in-jokes abounding and eccentric doings rampant. Flash finally manages to crash Ming's wedding with a spaceship, upon which he impales the villain. But Ming's magic ring manages to save his life somehow, opening the possiblity of a sequel. Thankfully, none was soon forthcoming, since De Laurentiis' supercilious presentation—his superficial glossing of a

beloved character—was not appreciated by most filmgoers.

The Formula was not whimsical. If anything, the espionage chiller, written and produced by Steve Shagan, was too solemn for its own good. Nevertheless, under John Avildsen's direction, the movie became unintentionally hilarious. George C. Scott starred as policeman Barney Caine, who travels all over the world on the trail of an artificial fuel formula created by the Germans at the end of World War II and repressed by American business interests.

Things get hot in Europe as Caine tracks down one lead after another, each of whom gets brutally murdered *immediately* after talking to him. Although the plot had gotten bombastic early on,

The *Palimino* crew scrambles out of a meteor's way during the climax of *The Black Hole*.

the pomposity deteriorates into slapstick at this point as each character seemingly goes out of his way to die at the hands of the assassins dogging Caine's trail. Naturally Caine himself is never a target, a solution any smart hitman would have hit upon at the very outset.

Instead, Caine returns to the States with all the facts for a confrontation with Marlon Brando, playing oil executive Adam Steiffel (an all-too-obvious version of "stifle"). Brando plays the powerful businessman as a combination of Bugs Bunny and Elmer Fudd, rendering the supposedly serious finale ludicrously funny. When the best line of dialogue in a relevant thriller is, "Care for a Milk Dud?" something is definitely wrong (Steiffel keeps a sterling bowl of the candies in his office).

The movie concludes with Caine trading the formula for the life of his partner (Calvin Jung), figuring that nothing he could do would beat the major corporations anyway. Instead of being frightening, this ending was just a twist of resignation at the close of a story that had lost its audience an hour before.

The Final Countdown was nothing more than an eleven-million-dollar *Twilight Zone* episode padded to a hundred and four minutes. It took four men, David Ambrose, Gerry Davis, Thomas Hunter, and Peter Powell, to come up with the concept of the nuclear powered aircraft carrier *Nimitz* being magically transported back to Pearl Harbor the day before the Japanese attack in 1941.

It took only one man, Rod Serling, to write

An artist's conception of the *Cygnus* entering *The Black Hole*.

"The Seventh Is Made Up of Phantoms" in 1963. That was a real *Twilight Zone* episode in which a tank is sent back to Custer's Last Stand. That story was well maintained over a half hour. Director Don Taylor and a cast which included Kirk Douglas, Katherine Ross, Martin Sheen, Charles Durning, and James Farentino were not so lucky with *Countdown*.

First and foremost, no explanation is given for the "time storm" the *Nimitz* goes through. Sadly, past films have proven that an explanation is needed only if there is no discernible purpose for the occurrence. If there were any oblique reason for the *Nimitz* to be put in such a predicament, then the situation could easily be filed in audiences' minds under "acts of God." Instead, the *Nimitz* crew members take about forty-five mintes discovering what happened, and another half-hour arguing what to do about it.

The only high point in the film comes when two modern jet fighters are spotted by a pair of attacking Jap Zeroes, making it necessary for the enemy witnesses to be swatted out of the sky. The thrill of seeing modern technology decimate our nation's enemy was unparalleled, but the rest of the pedantic film didn't even come close. Just when the crew has to decide whether to lay low or change the course of history, the same time storm politely shows up again, bringing the ship back to 1980.

The only other wrinkle in the film comes at the conclusion, when Cmdr. Richard Owens (James Farentino) shows up as his aged self after having been left behind in 1941. The only other major confusion concern's the movie's title—the meaning of *The Final Countdown* is never addressed or explained. No explanation was needed to address the picture's subsequent failure. It was hollow science fiction, seemingly having been made as a long commercial for the Navy.

LORD LEW'S FOLLY

Lord Lew Grade is a British entertainment impresario who rules ITC (International Television Corporation) Entertainment, the company responsible for such television series as *The Saint* and *The Muppet Show*. One of his few mistakes was to enter the action-film business in a big way with a string of high-budget adventure movies. Although a few were science-fiction related, hardly a one made money. The company's penchant for hiring big names rather than talents specifically suited for the project undercut their possibilities time and again.

Dr. Zarkov (Topol) forces Dale Arden (Melody Anderson) and Flash Gordon (Sam Jones) to join him on a trip to the planet Mongo.

171

Flash Gordon, who wears his heart on his sleeve and his name on his shirt, fights off Ming's minions with football moves as Dale Arden cheers him on.

A sadder story could hardly be found than *Saturn 3*. Originally it was the brainchild of *Star Wars* and *Superman* production designer John Barry—a soft-spoken, immensely talented man. He had written the original story of a love triangle in outer space and was assigned to direct it as well. Famed musical director Stanley Donen was pro-

ducing, but soon started interfering with everything Barry did—constantly second-guessing the director and interrupting the schedule. Two weeks after filming started, Barry was forced to leave the project and Donen took over the directorship himself.

Four months later, John Barry tragically died

of meningitis while working on the *Star Wars* sequel. *Saturn 3* died in sneak preview on November 9, 1979, where it was reported that "the audience was disappointed with the movie which was billed as a horrifying science-fiction film. Many left before the film's end." The picture suffered the same fate when released nationally in 1980. It is hardly surprising, since the story is presented as simplisticly as is *The Final Countdown*.

Both films boast Kirk Douglas as well. Here he plays Adam, who shares the food research base "Saturn 3" with the beautiful Alex (Farrah Fawcett) out on the planet Saturn's third moon. It is a fully automated underground Eden where the duo happily cavort and play away from the Earth which Alex has never seen and Adam describes as a festering pesthole. Into their paradise come two snakes. The human one is the psychotic Captain Benson (Harvey Keitel), who murders a supply ship pilot to bring perverted temptation into Adam and Alex's world.

The inhuman one is "Hector," an eight-foot-tall robot who is the first of the "demigod series"—which is constructed and programmed by Benson to be an insane sexual psychotic. It lusts after Alex and lets nothing stand in its way, not even Benson, who gets his hand and head taken off by Hector with some thirty minutes left in the film. That

Flash Gordon fights the jealous Prince Barin (Timothy Dalton) on a rocking, spike-studded platform.

Prince Vultan the hawkman (Brian Blessed) helps Flash Gordon pilot a spaceship into Ming's palace.

leaves the two lovers to go through all sorts of lame "cat and mouse" machinations before Adam pushes Hector and himself into a convenient acid bath.

Almost nothing makes any real sense in the film and the occasional interesting concepts—such as the twisted laws of the future Earth where drugs

173

and illicit sex are mandatory—are only mentioned and dropped in favor of slow-moving chases and gratuitous fights. This "Adam and Eve" allegory holds no surprises, and even worse, precious few thrills. *Saturn 3* deserves the cinematic oblivion it achieved.

ITC's film company was christened AFD (Associated Film Distributing), and its last stab at success was the twenty-five-million-dollar adaptation of *Raise the Titanic*, based on Clive Cussler's best-selling novel. The writer's work was an engrossing combination of spy and science-fiction saga. In the late 1980s, the American government has devised a laser dome process that would render nuclear war impossible. But to make it work, they need a cache of a mineral called "Byzanium" the only known supply of which was secured in the hold of the sunken *Titanic*.

The Americans want to get it. The Russians want to stop them. The only man for the job is Dirk Pitt, an oceanographic trouble-shooter who rivals James Bond in ability. The techniques he uses to raise the ship from its watery grave are scientifically accurate and the intrigue and action surrounding the endeavor are suitably complex.

It seemed AFD couldn't lose. Adam Kennedy, the author of another AFD failure, *The Domino Principle* (1977, helmed by Stanley Kramer, who was originally set to direct this was well), did the screenplay while Jerry Jameson was given the directorship.

Their first and greatest mistake was casting young, smooth-skinned Richard Jordan as Pitt. He may not have been the worst choice for the role, but he was close. He simply wasn't convincing as a supremely competent, cut-throat operative. And while a lot of money was spent on special effects, they ranged from great to gruesome. At its base, however, the picture was scuttled by a plodding, uninventive script and direction.

The final plot irony is that the Byzanium was not on the *Titanic* after all—it was buried in the grave of the man who was supposed to carry it. The irony of the film version is that by the time the revelation was revealed, the audience was beyond caring. When a production company seems to care more for its special effects than for a tight script, the effects had better be spectacular or they will have no movie at all. *Raise the Titanic* barely made it to the surface in that respect and failed miserably—sinking AFD with it.

An artist's conception of the Hawkmen attacking one of Ming the Merciless's battleships in *Flash Gordon*.

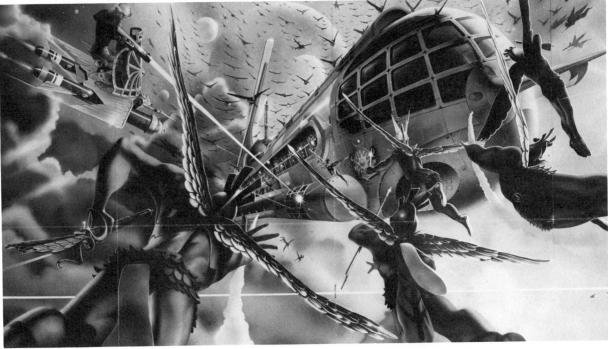

Destroying Farrah Fawcett and Kirk Douglas's idyllic home on *Saturn 3* is Harvey Keitel, playing a psychotic killer, and "Hector," an equally psychotic robot.

CHEAP SHOTS

There were a crop of inexpensive exploitation films this year which were just as bad as their big-budget brethren. *The Day Time Ended* suffered the most, although it started as an intrepid attempt by three young special-effects men to make a mindlessly enjoyable picture which harkened back to the "little films" of the 1950's. The men were Paul Gentry, Wayne Schmidt, and Steve Neill; the latter two had also written the script along with J. Larry Carroll and David Schmoeller.

With the help of model animators Dave Allen and Randy Cook, they told the story of a mid-western family unit who inadvertently build its self-sufficient house on a "time fault line." It isn't too long before outer space aliens and inter-dimensional creatures are traipsing through the place and the house is whisked through all sorts of adventures. Originally titled *Vortex*, the movie had its present exploitative title slapped on when the fin-

ished film appeared to be a well-meaning shambles.

The producers placed most of the blame on their inexperience as well as what they saw as director John Bud Cardos's indifference. A fine cast headed by Dorothy Malone and Jim Davis did their best with stilted dialogue that required them to be dazzled by special effects which would be added after live-action filming ended. Although the finale is a hopeful one, with the family adjusted to flying through time and space, the film was hardly shown in theaters before being sold to videotape.

The previous producer's pain had nothing on what the filmmakers suffered from *Humanoids from the Deep*. Director Barbara Peeters fully intended to make this New World Production into the first feminist monster movie. She cast Ann Turkel as a biologist who runs afoul of a race of

175

sea creatures who look to human girls to serve their watery race sexually. Doug McClure and Vic Morrow were on hand as antagonists who fight over whether the threat should be announced or covered up.

True to its *Jaws* origin, the full-fledged attack of the gill-men—who look like human-sized crosses between the Creature from the Black Lagoon and Godzilla—occurs on the night of a big carnival. The sea beasts go bonzo over the collected girls while the heroes have their hands full shooting the monsters down. Despite its familiar origins and plot, Peeters fully expected her movie to be non-chauvinistic.

Little did she know that studio head Roger Corman assigned director Jimmy T. Murakami to film insert sequences of the humanoids attacking and raping girls in bikinis as well as a climactic sequence in which a gill-baby bursts out of a girl's stomach in an operating room. The director was even more stunned than the audience on premiere night. The irony is that *Humanoids from the Deep* made a tidy profit.

Jimmy T. Murakami was also the director of *Battle Beyond the Stars*, Roger Corman's "big budget" (three million dollars) science-fiction epic. This was another rehash of Akira Kurasowa's classic action/adventure *The Seven Samurai* (1954) by way of *The Magnificent Seven* (1960)—the wild-west version of the tale. In all three films, a warring band of villains descend on a peaceful community, forcing them to hire protecting mercenaries.

In this case, screenwriter John Sayles has the most aggressive young man on the planet, Shad (Richard Thomas), take over a blinded old space salt's computerized ship to seek out hired help. He finds the independent daughter of an armorer (Darlanne Fluegel), a lizard-like alien criminal (Morgan Woodward), an Amazonian warrior who wants to live fast and die beautifully (Sybil Danning), a booze-swigging, harmonica-playing cowboy (George Peppard), an alienated outer-space gunfighter (Robert Vaughn—repeating the role he played in *The Magnificent Seven*), and a team of three-eyed explorers who share the same mind.

They all gang up on the scarred, genetically unintelligent forces of Sador (John Saxon)—a nifty villain who is comprised of his victims' parts. While Sador's army is stupid, it is gigantic, making for a hard-won fight for the hired heroes. But win it they do, although almost everyone dies in the attempt. The final battle pits Shad's suicidal space ship—despondent over the old space salt's death—against Sador's gigantic flying headquar-

Randall Cook model-animates one of the many monsters of *The Day Time Ended.*

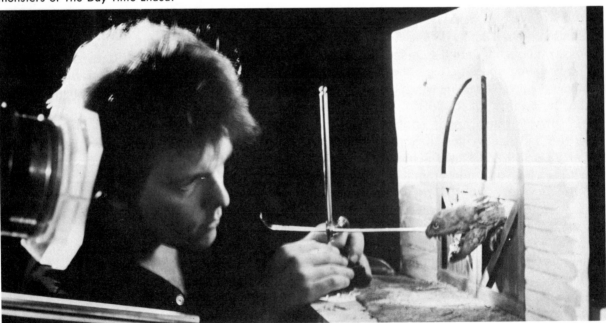

176

A line-up of *The Day Time Ended* creatures.

The Day Time Ended monster as it appeared on screen.

ters. It gives up its computerized life to deal a kamikaze killing blow to Sador's ship.

Battle Beyond the Stars was predictable, hoary, but still fun. Sayles and Murakami incorporate just enough twists and vitality to make the movie an entertaining, well-made and well-acted homage to all the clichés it incorporates.

Without Warning was another kettle of piranha. Producer/director Greydon Clark had also guided *Satan's Cheerleaders*, a hilarious title, but a limp combination of teen-oriented and occult pictures. It took the talents of Lyn Freeman, Daniel Grodnik, Ben Nett, and Steve Mathis to pen this silly saga of an eight-foot-tall, bubble-headed alien who has a collection of tiny round blood-sucking parasites he can throw like frisbees.

The evil alien lives in a forest and is stalked by a demented hunter named Taylor (Jack Palance). The stalker is killed by the creature after wandering teenage innocents Sandy and Greg (Tarah Nutter and Christopher Nelson) get involved. Also fodder for the villain's flying frisbees are such actors as Martin Landau, Cameron Mitchell, Neville Brand, Ralph Meeker, Sue Ann Langdon, and Larry Storch.

Instead of a *Close Encounters of the Third Kind, Without Warning* was a gory encounter of the absurd kind. While there are some neat moments involving the aliens' gruesome appearance, most of the picture is a pedestrian mix of suspense and violence. Except for the nasty parasites, the

turned out to be a pretentious, allegorical joke. Israeli producer and international filmmaker Manachem Golan wrote and directed this affected attempt to mix the totalitarian future with a moralistic fable. Instead of Adam and Eve, there is Alphie (George Gilmour) and Bibi (Catherine Mary

The insidious, scarred villains of *Battle Beyond the Stars* hound peaceful, innocent planets.

alien in the woods might as well have been any one of several dozen human killers glorified in ugly murder movies like *Friday the Thirteenth* (1980).

COSMIC JOKES

More science-fiction humor was trotted out this year with largely negative results. Although conceived and presented as a musical, *The Apple*

Stewart), who wander into the Worldvision Song Contest controlled by billionaire Boogalow (Vladek Sheybal) and his henchman Shake (Ray Shell).

The villains' plan is to further control the masses through song stylists Pandi (Grace Kennedy) and Dandi (Allan Love), who are hypnotizing the audience with their number one hit, "The

178

Jack Palance plays a hunter who captures one of the flying vampire alien disks in *Without Warning*.

Bim." Although thoroughly "Biminized," the syrupy lyrics and tune of Alphie and Bibi's entry, the "Universal Melody," starts to awaken the crowd. In retaliation, Boogalow puts on a tape which drowns out the naïve singers' sweetness with prerecorded derision, then decides to eliminate their dangerous message of nostalgic love.

He works his corrupt temptations on Bibi, who succumbs to the fast life of money and drugs. When Alphie tries to rescue her, he is set upon by bodyguarding "Bulldogs" and sees a demented vision of Boogalow as the devil, Shake as the snake, and all the world's evils in an apple accepted by Bibi. She becomes a Bim superstar while he becomes a bum. He is found the next morning by "The Old Hippy" (Joss Ackland), who brings him to a secret cave where all the outlawed hippies of the 1960's reside.

With a much-needed change of heart, Pandi rescues Bibi and leads her to the cave. Just when it seems they'll all live happily ever after, Boogalow surrounds the place and demands the girl pay for her breach of contract—a cool ten million dollars. Just as all seems lost, the Old Hippy miraculously transforms himself into "Mr. Topps," who has the power to transport all good guys to a wonderful new planet where everything is terrific.

Although one of the few science-fiction musicals (besides *The Rocky Horror Picture Show*, 1975, which was about perverted scientists from the planet Transylvania trying to create a perfect beach boy), *The Apple* betrays its origins by being ludicrous and maudlin—a dreadfully artificial and childish effort that was embarrassing to watch.

Dr. Heckyl and Mr. Hype was better, though also produced by Manachem Golan (and his partner Yoram Globus). This time, Charles B. Griffith wrote and directed another variation on Robert Louis Stevenson's classic tale of the danger in being literally two-faced. Griffith was the man who had written the series of satires for Roger Corman that ended with *Death Race 2000*, so it is not surprising that his new film was also satirical.

Infelicitously, his concept was similar to Jerry Lewis's *The Nutty Professor* (1963). Both featured an ugly Jekyll-type, transformed by the infamous

Maxwell Smart (Don Adams) is stopped by a cop after driving his "Deskmobile" over sixty miles an hour during *The Nude Bomb*.

potion into a handsome rake. In Griffith's case, Oliver Reed played the dual lead—at first a gruesome doctor with makeup by Steve Neill which made him look like an overcooked pizza. After his transformation into the brutishly handsome Hype, Reed becomes a real lady-killer, murdering any beautiful woman who rejects his advances.

Like *The Day Time Ended* before it, *Dr. Heckyl and Mr. Hype* had extremely limited run in movie theaters but a wider distribution on videotape.

organization CONTROL—known to all fans of the television spy spoof *Get Smart*. Lasting a full five seasons on NBC and CBS networks, the intrepid but doltish 86 infuriated his boss—known only as "The Chief" (Edward Platt)—married his female co-spy, known only as "Agent 99" (Barbara Feldon), and became the father of twin boys.

Neither the original Chief nor Smart's family were on view in this new version, replaced instead with a lot of spoken obscenity. Maxwell Smart is

At top, Don Adams as Maxwell Smart assures the United States delegate at the U.N. that there is no such thing as The Nude Bomb. At bottom, he's saying, "Would you believe there's no such thing as Santa Claus?"

The Nude Bomb was the intriguing new title of a comedy originally labeled *The Return of Maxwell Smart*. The latter would have been a more telling title to any television watcher since Maxwell Smart was "Agent 86" of the super secret spy

called out of retirement by the head of the new organization that has replaced CONTROL—PITS (which allows characters to say things like "this is the PITS"). The wit and slapstick was all low grade here, while 86 goes in search of the demented

Herb Kaplowitz was inside this suit, playing Kitty the rock-eating monster in *Galaxina*.

designer of a bomb that can destroy only clothing—and thus it is dubbed the Nude Bomb. The satire was flatfooted as well, just touching upon the 007 milieu as Smart must reproduce himself several times over in a cloning machine to fight his likewise duplicated adversary.

Vittorio Gassman played the villainous Nino Sebastian Sleeve, while Pamela Hensley played agent 36, Andrea Howard played Agent 22, and Sylvia Kristel played Agent 34 (taken together, their numbers make up a beautiful woman's measurements). Eugene Roche was signed to play the PITS Chief, but he was replaced by Dana Elcar at the last minute. Perhaps the former actor was scared off by plot developments which included a mountain with a zippered entrance and a desk that turns into a car. Although *The Nude Bomb* looked pretty good on paper, the movie was a mild diversion at best—ultimately inferior to the fine ensemble playing of the television series.

Many viewers of *Galaxina* wished they had a Nude Bomb on hand, since the star was beautiful Playmate of the Year Dorothy Stratten. Her presence was about the only thing that rendered the otherwise doltish science-fiction satire watchable. Director and writer William Sachs made this cheaply produced exploitation film after finishing *The Incredible Melting Man* and, if anything, this new feature was a step down in style and content.

Galaxina is a humanoid robot—maid, waitress, pilot, cook and companion to the crew of a thirty-first century starship. Avery Schreiber played Captain Butt, a ridiculous, ineffectual leader. The first mates are Buzz (James David Hinton), a drawling space cowboy, and Sergeant Thor (Steven Macht), a handsome, cigar-chomping, womanizing type. Below decks are a black engineer with tiny, useless wings (Lionel Smith) and a wizened oriental who spouts unintelligible aphorisms (Tad Horino). Locked up in the brig is a rock-eating, irritable, foul-mouthed alien named Kitty (Herb Kaplowitz).

During dinner, it is established that Galaxina can't talk and is untouchable. The infatuated Thor risks electrocution to kiss her, frying her no-touch system in the process. Immediately thereafter, the ship is assigned to find the "Blue Star," a giant gem that harnasses the power of the Universe. The men celebrate by going off to an interstellar

Galaxina (Dorothy Stratten) longs to be loved by the suspended animated Sgt. Thor (Stephen Macht).

brothel. For the first time Galaxina feels the pangs of jealousy and gets to work on her own computer program.

Before the crew places itself in suspended animation, the cast goes through a feeble *Alien* satire in which Butt eats an alien egg for no clear reason, does a variety of funny faces, and then spits out a little rubber alien doll which runs off into the ship. It reappears after the men have gone to sleep in their suspended animation coffins, opening the captain's chamber while calling him "Momma."

When the ship enters orbit around the Blue Star planet, Butt discovers that he has grown old and Thor discovers that Galaxina has reprogrammed herself to speak and love. But when the ship crash lands, giving everyone whiplash except the robot, it is she who must brave the world of cannibals to seek out Ordric (Ronald Knight), the half-lizard, half-robot who stole the powerful gem. She discovers he lives over the flesh-serving restaurant owned by the pointy-eared "Mr. Spot" (David Cox).

Wresting the gem from him is only the start of her problems. She is then beset by a gang of toughs who worship the god "Harley Davidson." Thor and Buzz have recovered from their wounds enough to steal the motorcycle the gang prays to and rescue their gorgeous robot. They escape the planet's clutches only to have Kitty eat the Blue Star for desert.

The basic concepts of *Galaxina* were feebly cute, but the presentation was completely staid and lackluster. Scenes were extended as if the actors were making them up as they went along and the director didn't have enough money to film the awkward scenes over again. The set and special effects were equally slipshod and unrealistic.

SMALL IMPORTANT VOICES

Simon put all the previous comedies to shame. Not only was it hilarious, but it was one of the most original, inventive, and thought-provoking science-fiction films of the year. Alan Arkin gives one of his best performances as Simon Mendelssohn, a ridiculous pseudo-intellectual who often misses teaching his college science classes because he is attempting one ill-conceived, under-financed experiment after another. Unbeknownst to him, he becomes the subject of a think-tank's latest experiment—to convince the world that an outer-space alien has been living in their midst for years.

This think-tank has governmental carte blanche and is filled with wildly megalomaniacal geniuses who spend their time seeing how badly they can screw up reality. Led by the prissy, condescending Becker (Austin Pendleton), they have unleashed powerful new sexual diseases, replaced Nixon with a clone, and altered Nielsen ratings so that things like *Donny and Marie* become hits ("We happen to know that only twelve hundred people watch that show," says Hundertwasser as played by actor Max Wright).

A round table discussion of what else they could do to shake up the populace leads them to Simon. They wipe out his memory by putting him in a

Christopher Reeve longs to meet a 1912 love
Somewhere in Time.

sensory deprivation tank for almost two hundred hours and then refill his mind and body with fake evidence. Now all he can remember is being put on Earth by a talking flying saucer with a Jewish accent. And when non-think-tank scientists study his body fluids, they find blood filled with nuts and bolts and sperm with Simon's face.

The think-tank is deliriously happy until Simon is glorified and worshipped as a messiah. He takes the opportunity to pass down dicta from inside a germ-free enclosure. Attacking the "petty annoyances that undermine the American spirit," he calls for the outlawing of Muzak in elevators, paper bands on toilet seats and plastic packets of ketchup. He suggests that lawyers who lose cases should be imprisoned with their clients, and de-

mands fines for anyone caught saying "far out" or "you're invading my space."

Realizing they have created a monster, the scientists try to drug him with a gas that lowers the IQ a hundred points, only to get a whiff of it themselves. The only ones left with intelligence intact are Simon and Becker, who calls upon the military. Saving Simon's skin is his girlfriend Cynthia (Judy Graubart), who convinces him of his human origins then pulls him out from under the noses of General Korey's (Fred Gwynne) troops.

Simon and Cynthia are given haven by a television-worshipping commune, from which Simon continues to declare his philosophy over the airways—using a television-jamming broadcast truck stolen from the think-tank. But all his teachings

Christopher Reeve tries "thinking" himself back *Somewhere in Time*.

Christopher Reeve succeeds in reaching 1912 and a
film crew tries to make the audience believe it.

are for naught. Simon finally realizes that he cannot upgrade the tastes of a nation which loves professional wrestling. He gives himself up to be sent
back into outer space on the Space Shuttle.

At the last moment, however, he switches places
with Becker, tying and gagging the twisted genius
to the driving seat. It is Becker who is blasted into
space while Simon settles down with Cynthia and
writes Nobel-nominated books on the trivial roots
of frustration. Marshall Brickman, who collaborated with Woody Allen on the screenplay of *An-
nie Hall* (1977), which was named "Best Picture
of the Year" over *Star Wars*, wrote and directed
Simon to much less fanfare. Although delightfully
satiric and pointed, the small, inexpensive film
failed to become a box-office success.

Besides *Simon*, there were other small, important voices crying to be heard over the noisy roar
of the big-budget, special-effects-laden movies.
Somewhere in Time was less successful at being
a lush, romantic tear-jerker than *Simon* was at being a satire, but it was still a valiant attempt. Other
than utilizing the concept of time travel, the picture was pure fantasy. Director Jeannot Szwarc
was captured by the thought of mounting this gentle love story, based on the novel *Bid Time Return*,
by Richard Matheson, after having helmed *Jaws
II.*

Matheson himself adapted the book to screenplay form and many top actors were captured by
the lyrical tale as well. Christopher Reeve was cast
as Chicago playwright Richard Collier, who be-

comes obsessed by the photograph of an actress, Elise McKenna (Jane Seymour), dead dozens of years before. But when an old woman (Susan French) approaches him after the opening of his new play and says, "Come back to me," his obsession becomes a hunt.

He hunts down Dr. Gerald Finney (George Voskovec), whose untried theory is that a person could "think" himself backward in time, actually convince his physical body to travel through eras. Totally determined, Collier tries the experiment and succeeds, arriving in the year 1912 to woo his actress love. Trying to prevent the liaison is McKenna's theatrical manager, W.F. Robinson (Christopher Plummer). But try as he might, true love conquers all—except for a 1980 copper penny.

When McKenna finds this coin in Collier's pockets, the spell is broken, wrenching the playwright back to his own time. But soft, love does win out at the end. Szwarc's closing image is of the young Collier and McKenna reunited in death, walking arm and arm through a misty heaven. Everyone in the project was so intent on making this straightforward romance that their integrity showed in the film—rendering an unbelievable concept watchable, although not quite credible.

The production was handsome, costing around six million dollars, but it is unfortunate that a film was not made of the book which inspired Matheson's work in the first place. His "Dr. Finney" was a subtle hommage to fellow author Jack Finney, who not only wrote the book *Invasion of the Body Snatchers*, but *Time and Again*, a monumental work—the ultimate time travel novel—that is on *both* the Mystery Writers of America's and the Science Fiction Writers of America's "Top Five Best Books" list.

Sharing the title "Best of the Year" with *Simon* was *Mad Max*, an Australian movie which many thought to be just another in a long line of "car crash" films inspired by the success of *Smokey and the Bandit*. Instead, it was a superlative, rousing, thunderous science-fiction adventure with more vitality than almost all the movies this year put together. From the opening moments of the action-packed picture, veteran viewers could see they were in for an unusual experience.

The serenity of the sparsely populated Australian outback is split by a mad automobile chase. The eccentric members of the haggard police force are giving chase to a scraggly, earringed gang leader who calles himself the "Night Rider." In a series of frenzied sequences, the Night Rider proves more than a match for his pursuers. That is, until "Mad Max" is called in.

True to the film's mythic approach, Max's face is not immediately shown, but all the accompanying details of his existence are. His high-powered police car engine. His studded leather uniform. His cold, dark eyes. Not even when he plays a game of "chicken" with his quarry is he completely shown. The Night Rider backs down, sobbing. The criminal all but commits suicide, his "edge" gone, his reputation ruined. Mad Max has lived up to his reputation. When he's on the road, nothing can beat him.

But Mad Max is not a crosseyed crazy man. He is one of the most normal-looking people in the film. Mel Gibson plays the role, embodying both Max's humanity as well as his mythic possibilities. It is an auspicious American debut for the actor. Max just happens to be the best officer of a deteriorating police force doing its best to control the rapidly degenerating society of the near future. All the necessities of life are rapidly running out and humans are becoming more bestial and desperate all the time.

While Max tries to eke out a quiet life with his wife (Joanne Samuel) and newborn baby, the gang Night Rider led is thirsting for revenge—led by their new boss Toecutter (Hugh Keays-Byrne). These are no bunch of "Ravagers" or "Ultimate Warrior" ruffians. These characters have a convincing credibility that inspires fear and loathing. They find Max's family first, running them both down with their motorcycles. They don't have to find Max after that—he finds them.

Putting away the "normal" clothes he had been wearing after his decision to quit the force, Mad Max dons his uniform, sick of the society that still protects the "alleged perpetrators" even though the victim count is higher than ever. Max kills gang member after gang member until they lay a trap for him. Even though he is badly wounded, he hounds Toecutter until the man has a head-on collision with a tractor-trailer truck.

Although picturing a bleak, hopeless future, *Mad Max* still managed to be an exhilarating, satisfying film, thanks to producer Byron Kennedy, co-writer James McCausland, and writer/director George Miller. Both producer and director professed disappointment in the finished work because of time and budgetary restrictions, but *Mad Max* stands as a fine accomplishment—one of the best post-apocalypse motion pictures.

BIG IMPORTANT VOICES

Only two major-studio movies managed to make themselves heard above the din of 1980's disasters. In spite of a rocky production history, *Altered States* emerged as a strong, positive cinematic statement concerning the glory of being alive and human. Screenwriter Paddy Chayefsky had established himself as an important film drama writer by penning *Marty* (1955) and *The Americanization of Emily* (1964), among others. But it was with the success of *The Hospital* (1971) and, especially, *Network* (1976) that he attained an influence almost unheard of for a writer.

The contract for the movie version of his first novel, *Altered States*, said that his dialogue could not be changed. This situation put the project's original director, Arthur Penn, in a quandary. He soon left the project, making way for producers Howard Gottfried and Daniel Melnick to choose Ken Russell. Although Russell was unsuited for negotiating with an adamant writer, he was a good choice for handling the film's extreme material.

Russell's works were a study in the extreme. From *The Devils* (1971) through *Tommy* (1975), the director filled his films with macabre, arresting images. With him in control of the movie about science gone insane, the Chayefsky contract was softened to the point that the dialogue could be edited or eliminated, if not changed. The writer responded by taking his well-known byline off the credits to be replaced with "Sidney Aaron"—his first and middle names.

No matter who takes credit, the nimble melding of reality and mutation worked far better as a movie than a book. The novel was slightly pompous while the film was an exciting viewing experience. It was given a scientific anchor, but this was glossed over by Russell's having the actors rattle any technical or metaphysical information out as fast as they could speak. In the Chayefsky scheme of things, the metaphysical technicalities were everything.

He told the tale of Edward Jessup (William Hurt), a young scientist obsessed with discovering the secrets hidden in the ninety percent of the brain humans do not apparently use. This search leads to emotional trouble with his wife, Emily (Blair Brown), his children (Megan Jeffers and Drew Barrymore), and his colleagues, Arthur Rosenberg (Bob Balaban) and Mason Parrish (Charles Haid). The search also leads to existential horror, as Jessup mixes psychedelic drugs with sensory deprivation experiments.

At first he sees only torturing images of his past,

William Hurt (right) tries to tell his assistants Bob Balaban (left) and Charles Haid to take notes of his experiment in *Altered States*.

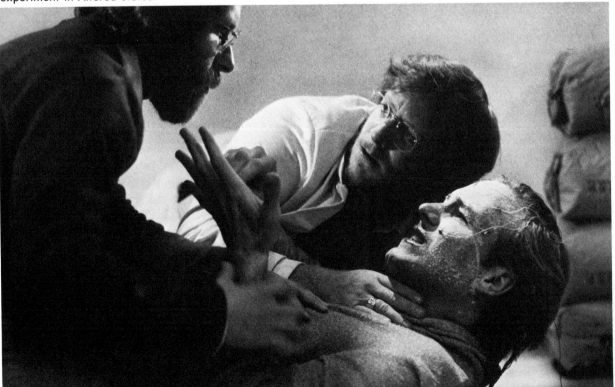

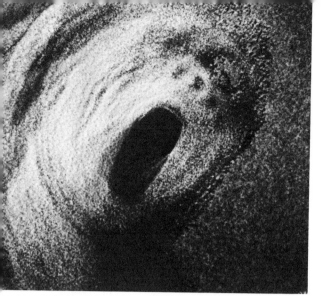

The experiment gets way out of hand in *Altered States*.

present, and future life, but then he starts tapping scenes of all past, present, and future life. As his assistants feared, the experiment gets out of control. One fateful night, Jessup starts changing into what he had glimpsed. Waking from a fitful sleep, he sees his arm begin to ripple and change. He looks into the bathroom mirror to see his brow growing (both exceptional effects by Dick Smith). Soon, he actually regresses into a prehistoric human state, racing about the city at night.

Things go from bad to worse. Even though he places himself under the study of an intrigued Rosenberg and disbelieving Parrish, neither they nor Emily can prevent a cataclysmic evolutionary explosion which brings Jessup to a confrontation with "that ultimate moment of terror that is the beginning of life." He almost becomes a part of the primal source that is life, until Emily braves the form-changing horrors of his lab to literally reach down and drag him back.

But even after that, it may be too late. Although Jessup realizes that the final truth is that there is no final truth (just reality as it appears to be), he may not be able to control the forces he has unleashed. Just as he admits this in his home, those forces attack again, threatening to change him into a blob of protoplasm forever. It is only the love he shares with his wife that prevents that destruction. Its power is enough to stem the flow and turn him back into himself.

The film ends with the two embracing, vowing their love. *Altered States*' plot is almost impossible to impart in a meaningful way without Chayefsky's ornate prose or Russell's exciting visuals.

It is the director's editing and presentation of the writer's concepts that makes the movie accessible and even totally believable. The characters are completely convincing young geniuses, identifiably human in their hopes, dreams and everyday lives. Their realistic actions and reactions make the cosmic events acceptable.

Although not really meaningful above the level of "Life Is What You Make It" or "Love Conquers All," *Altered States* is still a roller coaster of a picture.

Although it is really nothing more than a setup for its own sequel, *Star Wars II: From the Adventures of Luke Skywalker; Chapter Five—The Empire Strikes Back* was also well worth seeing.

Much had happened in the three years between *Star Wars* and its sequel. Firstly, George Lucas revealed that he had a master story line that encompassed nine films—three trilogies. *Star Wars* was the first part of the second trilogy, therefore "Chapter Four" in the *Star Wars* saga. In fact, the re-released *Star Wars* was clearly labeled such on the screen two years after it premiered. The last thing Lucas wanted was for *The Empire Strikes Back* to be known as *Star Wars II*.

The second to last thing he wanted was to write and direct the sequel himself. The hell of making the first film had all but cured him of any direc-

The only thing that saves William Hurt from his form-changing experiments in *Altered States* is the love of Blair Brown.

ting or script-writing desires. His 1977 movie had become the most successful ever made and had spawned a merchandising empire worth millions. Lucas was to hand in his union cards and become a movie maverick, all but owning his own studio. So, he became the *Star Wars* series' executive producer and story writer, leaving details to producer Gary Kurtz.

Kurtz hired five writers to develop plotlines for the new film, then settled on science-fiction author (*The Long Tomorrow*) and screenwriter (*The Big Sleep, 1946*) Leigh Brackett—a combination of the two talents the new picture required. She was to do a thorough story, then the first draft of the screenplay before her untimely death. Lawrence Kasdan was hired to do the final rewrite.

To almost everyone's surprise, Irvin Kershner was signed to direct. An uneven filmmaker who had never handled science fiction before, he was reportedly hired because Lucas appreciated the way he handled the interaction of characters. *Star Wars*, at its base, was less a science-fiction than a fantasy film where the characters made all the plot machinations work. Luke Skywalker, Han Solo, Princess Leia, Darth Vader, and all the others may seem superficial, but it is the audiences' belief in them that really makes the difference.

All the main actors were back (though not without some rumblings of creative discontent) as well as ninety percent of the crew. Conspicuous by his absence was special-effects director John Dykstra, who was somewhat ceremoniously dropped from the fold because of his decision to forsake *Star Wars* for *Battlestar Galactica*. Replacing him was Brian Johnson, a television workhorse who had done *Space: 1999*, among others. In the years since 1977, the sheer volume of special-effects-oriented movies created a pool of dependable technicians who were more interested in good work than fame or power.

Another major change was Lucas's control. With such a great monetary reward possible, the picture's distributor and backer, 20th Century-Fox, did not stint when it came to Lucas's and Kurtz's requests. While production secrets may have been leaked on other blockbuster movies, the only facts about *The Empire Strikes Back* came from Lucasfilm, the *Star Wars* Corporation. The film was made with absolute secrecy. As a result, anticipation was high on premiere date, and, for the most part, the movie didn't disappoint.

The Empire Strikes Back was a clever (some say cunning) combination of the expected and unexpected. Although the pitched spaceship battles and light-sabre fights were well in evidence, so were some interesting plot twists. In retrospect, however, this second Skywalker movie looked even more like a futuristic samurai film than its predecessor. In fact, many feel *Star Wars* was heavily based on Japanese director Akira Kurosawa's *The Hidden Fortress*, starring Toshiro Mifume. Even so, most occidental viewers had not been exposed to the delights of the oriental cinema, so the *Star Wars* experience seemed totally fresh.

The now well-respected Luke Skywalker is exploring a new rebel base on an ice-covered, frozen planet. Within seconds, he is captured by a clawed, fanged Snow Beast who drags him to its cave. Han Solo goes in search of his friend as Leia, Chewbacca, C-3PO, and R2-D2 fear for both their lives. They soon fear for their own lives as Darth Vader and the Imperial fleet catch up with them.

The ghostly image of Obi-Wan Kenobi comes to Luke and tells him to go to the planet of Degoba. Skywalker then discovers that "The Force" can imbure him with telekinetic powers. He retrieves his fallen light-sabre, chops off the Snow Beast's arm and meets up with Solo—none too soon. The Empire troops have unleashed their monstrous "Snow Walkers"—giant animal-shaped machines that walk on four legs, blasting the opposition all the while.

The attack forces the group to split up. Leia and C-3PO go with Solo and Chewbacca while Skywalker takes R2-D2 to Degoba. Complications arise for both. Leia can no longer deny the attraction she feels for the space smuggler, but Solo is being pursued by both Empire forces and mercenaries hired by Jabba the Hut—an alien gambling boss he had cheated. Leading the hunt is a masked killer named Boba Fett (Jeremy Bulloch).

On Degoba, Skywalker sinks his spaceship into a swamp while searching for a Jedi Master—an ancient teacher of the arcane art. Much to his surprise, it turns out to be the diminutive, seemingly addle-brained eight-hundred-year-old alien named Yoda (given life and voice by a team of puppeteers led by Frank Oz). George Lucas originally wanted Kenobi to seem doddering and absent-minded, but Alec Guinness convinced him otherwise. This conceit was put to better use with Yoda.

Solo seeks sanctuary with an old gambling

buddy named Lando Calrissian (Billy Dee Williams). The black man is now a mining boss on a floating city. While they have a temporary respite, Skywalker struggles to accept the amazing levitating powers of "The Force," but he is too occupied with both his imperiled friends and what

walker blasts off in pursuit, Kenobi bemoans that Luke is the last hope of the Jedi. "No," Yoda says mysteriously, "there is another."

Darth Vader captures Solo, Leia, Chewbacca and C-3PO by threatening Calrissian's entire city. Since all the villain wants is Luke, he hands Solo

Part of the wonder of *The Empire Strikes Back* are the "Imperial Walkers," giant battleships that attack rebel outposts.

he thinks is possible. Yoda proves that anything is possible by levitating Skywalker's sunken ship, but Luke still can't accept it.

Things come to a crisis point when the young man's budding telepathy picks up Leia in danger and not even the combined advice of Yoda and Kenobi can make him finish his training. As Sky-

over to Fett, but not before encasing him in a carbonite block for the trip back to Jabba's lair. Just before he is freeze-dried, Leia says she loves him. "I know," he nobly replies. Boba Fett gets away just as Luke arrives.

The light-sabre fight between Vader and Skywalker is extremely impressive for its furious ac-

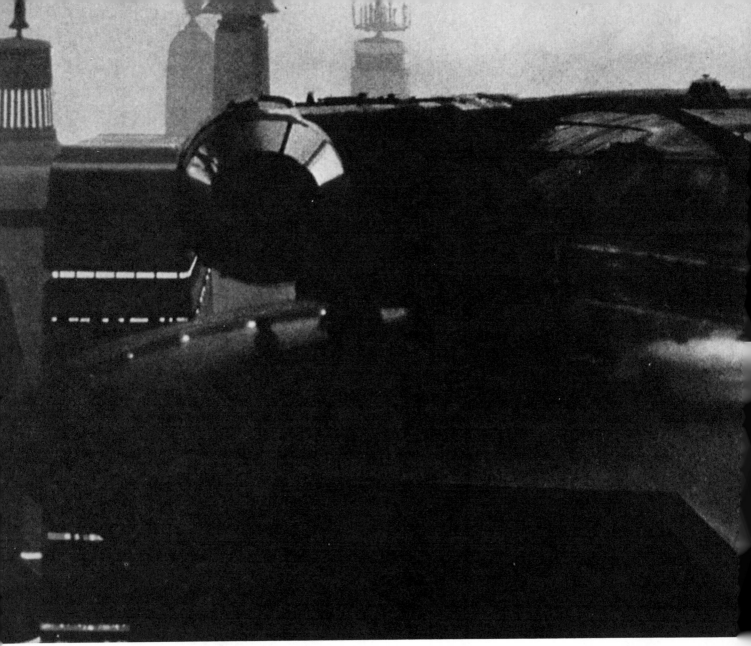

The Millenium Falcon lands in the floating city of Lando Calrissian (Billy Dee Williams) near the conclusion of *The Empire Strikes Back*.

tion. Although Darth always seems about to strike the killing blow, Luke's maturing Force powers allow him to practically fly. Still, it is Vader who has the most experience, forcing Skywalker to the edge of an air duct and then chopping off his right hand.

It is only then that Vader contends that he did not kill Luke's father—as Kenobi and Yoda maintain—but that he *is* Luke's father. He tempts Skywalker with teaming up and usurping the Emperor (Clive Revill). He stresses that the "Dark Side of The Force" is even stronger. Luke just barely staves off the temptation, sending out a telepathic SOS

that Leia picks up. Calrissian had helped them escape in the *Millenium Falcon*, which Chewbacca uses to pick up Luke.

The Empire Strikes Back ends with Luke bitter, but resolute in rescuing Han Solo. He has a new bionic hand, but also twisted memories of Kenobi, Vader, and Yoda.

The movie has a lot of entertainment value in its hundred and twenty-four minutes, and at that length, its plot moves along like a rocket. Strangely, however, every plot twist has its practical side. Interestingly enough, every surprise in *The Em-*

pire Strikes Back could be utilized in its sequel if the male starring actors decided not to return. If Harrison Ford did not sign on, Lando Calrissian—virtually a black mirror image of the Han Solo character—could take over. If Mark Hamill did not play Skywalker, "the other" Yoda spoke of could come to the fore.

Yoda, itself, was a film highlight. Frank Oz is a co-founder of The Muppets, giving voice to Miss Piggy, among others. Unfortunately, the Jedi Master often sound like Fozzie Bear. But if his sounds do not always convince, his combination puppet and hydraulic movements are wonderfully realistic. His character shines while the two robots are almost superfluous in the second *Star Wars* tale. C-3PO's nagging, complaining presence can become especially grating.

These are minor points in the face of the enjoyment the movie can create. All in all, "Chapter Five of the Star Wars Saga from the Adventures of Luke Skywalker" holds up miraculously well. But the reality of the situation is that its true worth can only be measured by how good Chapter Six, *Return of the Jedi*, is. If the finale of the first trilogy were not satisfying, it would render the set-up of *The Empire Strikes Back* irrelevant.

GEORGE LUCAS'S SECOND *Star Wars* epic had just about stretched the genre to its breaking point. His science fantasies were the last word in straight-talking, spaceship-swooping, raygun-shooting breathless adventures. No one else had done it better, so many filmmakers sought to make different kinds of adventures—including Lucas himself. These adventures took place today and tomorrow, on Earth and in outer space, with men and monsters.

HERE AND NOW

Michael Crighton's new film, *Looker*, was a grave disappointment. The plot was clever but the story was meaningless. The plot concerned plastic surgeon Dr. Larry Roberts (Albert Finney), who works on the best and the beautiful. Suddenly the most beautiful women are dying all around him. Upon investigation, he finds that all the dead beauties had worked for the media company run by Jennifer Long (Leigh Taylor-Young) and owned by conglomerate boss John Reston (James Coburn).

It seems as if Reston and company had been replicating these models with the most advanced computer animation devices, creating exact visual duplicates for television commercial work. Once the computer knew how to recreate these girls on screen precisely, the corporation sent out assassins, armed with a light gun which would render the hitmen invisible to their victims, to murder the original subjects.

That was the rub; there was no discernible reason for these women to be murdered, other than the fact that the deaths of beautiful people can be titillating. *Looker* contained the ultimate gratuitous violence—it had its victims killed for reasons that had nothing to do with what was on

Shrinking Man (1957). In that classic movie, the predicament of a constantly shrinking human (Grant Williams) was used to examine humanity's place in the scheme of things. Williams shrinks to less than nothing and becomes one with the Universe. This new version was not the feminist

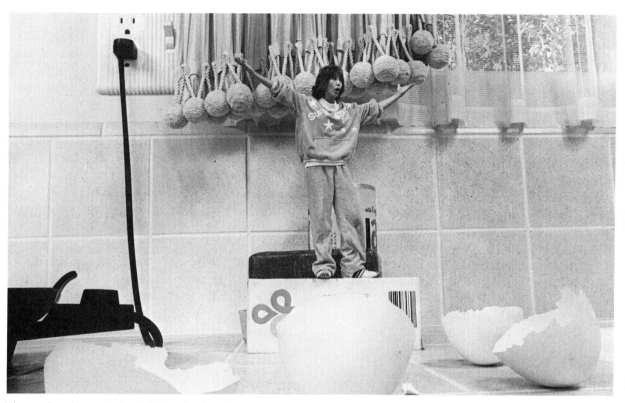

Lily Tomlin plays *The Incredible Shrinking Woman*.

screen. Otherwise, the film was a snappy, well-made thriller. The acting was sharp, the visuals vaguely "new wave" in appearance, and the computer animation was terrific. There was even some commercial television satire that was amusing.

The climax was satisfying taken by itself. The tables are turned when Roberts gains control of the light gun, bringing the murderers to justice. Now if only he could've explained their motive—other than the desire to make money by pandering to the audiences' basest desires—*Looker* might have worked.

Equally confusing was the fate of Pat Kramer: *The Incredible Shrinking Woman*. She owed her existence to the Richard Matheson book and the Jack Arnold-directed movie *The Incredible*

viewpoint on the same subject, but a heavy-handed satire of the consumer society and corporate corruption.

Curiously, it was originally planned in 1976 as a comedy remake of the original tailored for Chevy Chase by scripter Ron Clark. Director John Landis was already deeply into pre-production when the studio rejected his budget of fifteen million dollars. In August 1977, comedian/actress Lily Tomlin and her partner Jane Wagner took over.

Tomlin played the dual roles of initially empty-headed mother and wife Pat Kramer and her socially conscious neighbor Judith Beasley. Wagner rewrote the screenplay to have Kramer, a housewife living in the "Tasty Meadows" housing community, start shrinking from the overuse of useless products. This understandably upsets her husband Vance (Charles Grodin) but throws his boss Dan Beame (Ned Beatty) into a panic since their company manufactures most of those useless products.

At first the family adjusts the best it can. There is some slapstick as Pat attempts to continue her womanly chores, but soon she is forced to set up house in a doll house—setting the stage for even more slapstick. Finally, the ominous big business interests have her kidnapped for study by Dr. Eugene Nortz (Henry Gibson) and Dr. Ruth Ruth (Elizabeth Wilson). She is saved from her fate by lab assistant Rob (Mark Blankfield) and a very intelligent gorilla named Sidney (a wonderfully convincing quarter-million-dollar ape suit built and filled by Rick Baker).

Just as Kramer is about to shrink away into nothingness, she falls into another pile of household items and grows back to her original height. The evil scientists and collaborator Beame are arrested and the reunited Kramer family adopt Sidney as a pet. Just as the movie is about to end, Pat realizes (with a wicked grin) that she has not stopped growing. As the credits roll, one is left with the impression that a sequel would be called *The Amazing Colossal Woman*.

The Incredible Shrinking Woman was fairly funny, but forced. Director Joel Schumacher decided to go with a theatrical, rather than realistic, approach. All the colors are purposefully pastels, all the sets are purposefully unconvincing, rendering the movie's message negligible. If a film's message can't be presented seriously, then it cannot be taken seriously. In that case, why bother having a message at all?

Modern Problems had no real message. Then again, it had no real humor either. The latter was a surprise, considering that the film's director and co-writer (with Tom Sherohman and Arthur Sellers) was Ken Shapiro, the creator of *Groove Tube* (1974), a coarse but funny movie satire of television. Chevy Chase starred in both films, this time playing an air traffic controller who cannot control his jealousy over girlfriend Darcy (Patti D'Arbanville). Things get complicated when he is doused with radioactive liquid, which somehow gives him telekinetic powers. His use of this power—to give rivals nosebleeds and the like —is annoyingly unimaginative and all the plot developments from then on fail to enliven the proceedings. *Modern Problems* turns out to be an unfocused, unfunny movie that is neither effective comedy nor science fiction.

Rescuing *The Incredible Shrinking Woman* from a fate worse than death are Mark Blankfield (right) and Rick Baker, who built and is inside that ape suit.

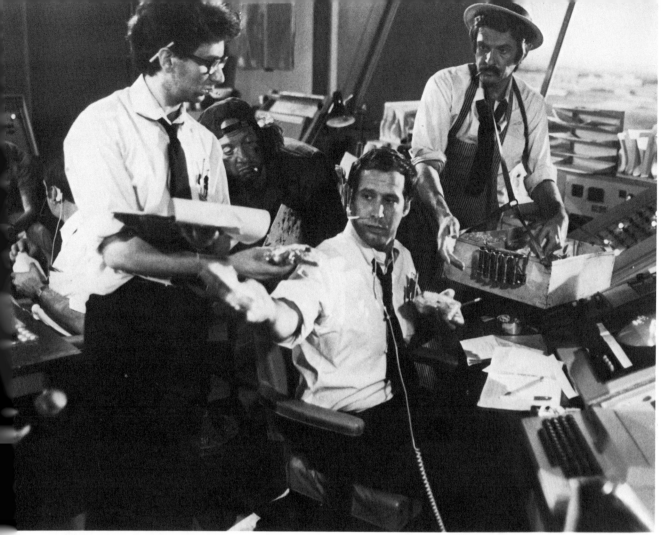

The hapless Chevy Chase (center) has a lot of *Modern Problems* as an insanely jealous air controller.

Condorman did not break the string of Walt Disney Productions' failures. After attempting to jump on the space-adventure bandwagon with *The Black Hole*, they were now trying to jump on the James Bond/Superman express with a story of a mild-mannered cartoonist (Michael Crawford) who becomes his comic-book character "Condorman" to rescue a spy damsel in distress (Barbara Carrera). Although "suggested by" (according to the credits) respected science-fiction author Robert Sheckley's 1965 novel *The Game of X*, Marc Sturdivant's script and Charles Jarrott's direction failed to make the futuristic comedy/adventure palatable. Oliver Reed played Krokov, the bad-guy leader of a fleet of laser speedboats and other fanciful weapons, but *Condorman* displayed even less conviction than the worst of the 007 series. And 007 was first.

The best of this season's modern-day adventures was *Strange Behavior*, an unassuming thriller made in New Zealand. A fine cast and an inventive writer/director slowly built upon a familiar story then threw in a surprise at the end which made the entire exploitation film special.

For some reason, the high school students in a small town start murdering people. Sheriff John Brady (Michael Murphy) is getting nowhere with the investigation because the frenzied murderers kill in private and then revert to their normal, sweet selves.

It is soon revealed that a scientific institute is paying students to be guinea pigs for a brainwashing plot. Fiona Lewis plays Gwen, the late Dr. LaSange's assistant, who is getting revenge on her boss's persecutors. Her greatest triumph will be Pete (Dan Shor), Brady's son. The process starts

197

with an injection into the brain by inserting the needle at the edge of the eye. Fight as he might, Pete cannot prevent himself from becoming a murderer, as had two of his friends before him.

All is revealed at the climax. Brady is tied to a lab chair while Gwen reveals that the doctor is not dead, but disguised as a doddering lab technician (Arthur Digham in a convincing old-age makeup). He had been waiting years to be avenged on Brady, who blames the doctor for his wife's death. LaSange, meantime, blames Brady for wooing the woman—once his trusted assistant—away from him. Although the sheriff is certain that the doctor brought on his wife's fatal bronchial attack, he had no proof.

Now LaSange was set to have Pete knife Brady. "Kill your father," the doctor demands. Pete hesitates. "Kill your father!" LaSange shouts. Pete suddenly plunges the blade into LaSange's own neck. He looks confusedly at the boy. "But you *are* my father," reveals Pete. The police arrive in time to catch Gwen and everything ends happily. *Strange Behavior* was an exploitation movie made with obvious concern and refreshing invention by co-writer (with William Condon) and director Michael Laughlin.

HERE AND TOMORROW

Rollover was a mistake. It was a mistake for star Jane Fonda and it was a mistake for director Alan J. Pakula. Both filmmakers wanted an important film to follow their previous successes. In the actress's case, *The China Syndrome*, and in the director's case, *All the President's Men* (1976). They both thought a story of financial disaster had possiblities. But the task of translating the intricate business of finance and making the super rich empathetic to a mass audience were problems they never overcame.

Fonda plays Lee Winters, the widow of a murdered businessman who had stumbled over an illegal deal going on in his own company. Associate Maxwell Emery (Hume Cronyn) hires corporate trouble-shooter Hub Smith (Kris Kristofferson) to help the woman get her troubled company back on its feet again. That begins a love affair which

mixes business with pleasure. It also leaves the main plot of double-dealing, double-crossing, and murder floundering.

The confusing plot gets murkier as Hub discovers that Emery was using him, and Winters betrays them both by trying to make a secret deal with the Arabs who had instigated the trouble in the first place. Her panicked meddling results in all Arab interests pulling their investments out of American banks, which creates a massive financial collapse, plunging the world into a depression that makes the crash of 1939 look like a minor setback.

Michael Crawford stars as the cartoonist who becomes his own superhero, Condorman, to rescue Barbara Carrera.

Astonishingly, the movie ends with Winters approaching Hub in a darkened stock exchange office, offering condolences and companionship—which the man smilingly accepts. It is as if the filmmakers couldn't bear to admit that Fonda was portraying the person who had plunged the world into ruin. This sort of confusion and hypocrisy marred *Rollover* throughout. It was a film that tried to be both a love story and financial thriller and wound up being no movie at all.

Heartbeeps was also supposed to be a love story. A charming, affectionate love story between two humanoid robots of the future, a love story that was supposed to speak volumes to the human audience. Associate producer John Hill's screenplay was meant to be a celebration of the family unit and the gentle ingredients that make love work. Instead the film was assailed from all sides by production and distribution troubles.

The basic story framework is adorable. Robot butler ValCom-17485 (Andy Kaufman) falls in love with maid robot AquaCom-89045 (Bernadette Peters) at first sight. They escape from the robot factory and run away together, coming upon the junk yard owned by Susan (Melanie Mayron) and Calvin Gort (Christopher Guest). With all the ex-

cess parts there, the machines think they are in heaven and consummate their union by building a "child"—Phil, named for the Philco radio on his chest (the child is a real robot made at a cost of three hundred and fifty thousand dollars).

Meanwhile, the factory workers responsible for the runaway robots (Randy Quaid and Kenneth McMillan) set the malfunctioning CrimeBuster machine on their trail. This police unit is a combination tank and flamethrower which is more

tuary away from meddling humans. CatSkil was originally planned to have Henny Youngman's voice, but Barry Diamond took over, sitting inside CatSkil's trunk and working the machine's mouth like a ventriloquist.

A New World Studio alumnus, Allan Arkush, was signed to direct and he brought with him a few well-known New World actors, like Paul Bartel, Mary Woronov, and Dick Miller. Having directed such features as *Rock 'n' Roll High School*

Lee Majors stars as a rebellious race car driver chased by a corrupt government in *The Last Chase*.

obsessed with catching fugitives than Joe Friday, Steve McGarrett and Dick Tracy put together. It shoots first and asks questions later as it gallops away on spinning treads.

In the meantime, Val's "Uncle CatSkil"—a joke-telling robot seated on a steamer trunk with treads—joins the robot family in search of a sanc-

(1979) in the past, Arkush seemed well suited to the comedic material. The crew was working for a little more than a month when the 1980 actor's strike occurred, delaying production by three months. Once the thespians returned, star Andy Kaufman's eccentric behavior continued to delay filming (by contractual agreement, Kaufman was

200

to have more than an hour's daily "meditation time").

Once the movie was finished filming, its troubles weren't over. It was edited down to less than ninety minutes—much of the slower, "softer" scenes of affection were cut out—leaving the more frenetic slapstick which no longer had much basis. Although Stan Winston's inventive "robot make-ups" for Kaufman and Peters took four hours to apply, they were never really convincing alongside

Hart, the survivor of a viral epidemic that killed his family. The plague couldn't have occurred at a worse time. All gasoline supplies have been depleted and all automobiles have been outlawed—making way for a dictatorial "Safety Commission" to take over the public's lives. Once a racing car driver haunted by guilt for causing a track death, Hart is unable to hand in his Porsche 917-10—opting instead to dismantle and hide it.

Twenty years later, Frank is a spokesman for

It's a Porsche versus a jet in *The Last Chase*.

Phil and CatSkil. After it premiered, the film was universally panned by critics, and audiences did not show up.

Most audiences couldn't even find *The Last Chase*, a Canadian movie featuring two noted American actors. Lee Majors starred as Frank

the "Mass Transit Utility" and the Safety Commission has become an all-powerful agency led by Santana (Diane D'Aquila) and Hawkins (George Touliatos). They harass a teenage electronics genius named Ring McCarthy (Chris Makepeace), who has been jamming their broadcasts. He seeks out Hart and tells him of an underground revolu-

Kurt Russell (right) tries to *Escape from New York* in the company of Ernest Borgnine (left), Harry Dean Stanton, and Adrienne Barbeau.

tion being planned across the country. The two rebuild the Porsche and steal a full tank of gas from the government.

Hart's skill allows them to escape the city. Hawkins calls in Commander J.C. Williams, a crack air force officer who becomes Hart's reluctant pursuer in a Phantom jet. The antagonists play a cat-and-mouse chase across the desert, Hart refusing to give up and Williams refusing to do the car and its occupants in. A brief truce is called when Hart and McCarthy find a Quaker woman (Alexandra Stewart) in a small shelter, but the long-range battle continues as the police move in.

The racing car and the jet play a game of chicken, which Hart wins, exorcizing him of his guilt. But then a laser cannon outpost on the border spots the Porsche and prepares to do what Williams won't. Just before the laser is about to eradicate Hart and McCarthy, Williams crashes

his jet into the cannon—destroying them both. The Porsche makes it to the rebellion headquarters, but Hart returns to the Quaker woman on horseback—leaving the car to McCarthy.

The Last Chase could have been called *Hart's Run* for all the clichés it presented and the facile plot machinations it included. The script by C.R. O'Christopher, Taylor Sutherland, and Martyn Burke was filled with fam   dialogue which director/producer Martyn B   couldn't elevate. The movie made for a mediocre time-filler.

Escape from New York had more inventiveness than the preceding chase picture, but it too became flat in the long run. John Carpenter directed from a script by himself and Nick Castle, hoping the film would be the kind of pulp adventure made famous in story magazines of the forties. In his vision of the future, Manhattan had become a

202

maximum security prison for the worst of the world's scum. The rest of the world was in little better shape, teetering on the brink of war.

The only hope, in Carpenter's simplistic scenario, was a cassette tape held by the president (Donald Pleasance). On his way to the summit meeting which would save or destroy the world, the president's plane crashes in New York and he is taken hostage by the demented denizens within. Security officer Bob Hauk (Lee Van Cleef) sees only one way out—spring hardened criminal Snake Plissken (Kurt Russell) from jail and make him an offer he can't refuse. Either retrieve the president within twenty-four hours or have the explosive surgically implanted in his neck blow his head off.

Plissken angrily accepts the challenge. He lands on the top of the World Trade Center in a glider and starts off on a series of abortive adventures.

He discovers that the "Duke of New York" (Isaac Hayes)—the worst of the worst—has the president. Snake uses the Duke's wimpy assistant, Brain (Harry Dean Stanton), and Brain's moll Maggie (Adrienne Barbeau, in reality the director's wife) to infiltrate the gang.

After beating off much of the scum, Plissken rescues the president and uses an armored taxi driven by "Cabbie" (Ernest Borgnine) to escape. He gets the initially grateful president out of danger and has the explosive taken out of his neck just in time. But then the president reverts to the smug politican he had been before his capture, causing Plissken to pull a switch. *Escape from New York* ends with Snake destroying the cassette which could save the world—just because the president was nasty to him.

Carpenter's relatively low-budget film creaked under the weight of its strong conception. Once

Isaac Hayes played the Duke, who tried to stop Kurt Russell's *Escape from New York*.

Patrick McGoohan (center) leads Stephen Lack (righ
into the weird and violent world of *Scanners*.

establishing the engaging plotline, his story's details did not live up to the basic idea, making the entire experience disappointing. In addition, star Russell did nothing more than an impersonation of Clint Eastwood—down to the walk, the scowl, the expression and the voice. It was a fine impersonation, but it was still an impersonation. It is hard for viewers to believe in a hero who is making believe he is someone else. He was never convincing as Plissken, so the film wound up being hollow at its core. The cynical climax, especially, rang false—coming off as needlessly negative and nihilistic.

Somewhat more successful was *Scanners*, director/scripter David Cronenberg's fourth film. Although less assured than the three gruesome predecessors, it still managed to be his most successful and accessible movie. It starts with a psychic attack in a shopping mall. A derelict named Vale

(Stephen Lack) is unable to control his mental powers, causing a woman to have what appears to be an epileptic fit. Two government operatives hunt him down with a dart gun. The pitiful wretch is handed over to Dr. Ruth (Patrick McGoohan), a high-ranking official of the Consec Corporation.

Consec is trying to organize and control an army of "Scanners," people born with incredible mental powers. The company's trouble begins in earnest at a seminar for those interested in the subject. A low-grade scanner (Louis Del Grande) invites a seminar member to be scanned. In front of everyone, the supposedly powerless volunteer causes the scanner's head to explode. He is revealed to be Revok (Michael Ironside), the psychotic leader of renegade scanners.

Consec wants the psychics as government weapons. Dr. Ruth wants them to be at peace with themselves. Revok wants them to take over the world. His captors try to control him but he men-

Corporation technicians work to create even more powerful *Scanners*.

205

tally forces them to commit suicide. Dr. Ruth trains Vale to control his powers and then sends him out after Revok. Dr. Ruth's associate, Keller (Lawrence Dane), however, has plans of his own. Vale discovers these plans after teaming up with fellow scanner Kim (Jennifer O'Neill).

It seems that Dr. Ruth had invented a pregnancy pill that created scanners years before and tried it on his wife. The result were twins named Vale and Revok. Now Consec is using the drug to create more scanners—scanners who are becoming more powerful all the time. Desperate to maintain his cover-up, Keller kills Dr. Ruth and tries to destroy Vale. Instead, Vale overloads Consec's computer system through a phone, blasting the machine and Keller all over the room.

All that is left is the two scanner brothers' confrontation. When Vale refuses to become part of Revok's revolution, they stage a scanner shootout, causing each other's nervous systems to rupture. Veins grow fat with blood and burst. Eyes cataract over. Flames burst forth. Skin peels off. Finally, Vale's luminous blue eyes explode. All of this memorably stunning sequence was the work of makeup artist Dick Smith, who was hired by Cronenberg in post-production to all but save the otherwise shaky film.

Some time after the psychic fight, Kim enters the office where the battle took place, finding Vale's charred corpse. But Cronenberg's final, and confusing, surprise is that Vale had taken over Revok's mind. "I'm here," Revok says with Vale's voice. "We've won." Although haphazard and illogical, *Scanners* was still a striking vision that was ultimately satisfying.

ADVENTURES IN OUTER SPACE

Outland was the work of writer/director Peter Hyams, whose last science-fiction contribution was *Capricorn One*. Like that paranoid fantasy, this futuristic fable subjugated realism to visual effect. Hyams played fast and loose with scientific accuracy the same way he did with government conspiracy in his prior work. *Outland*'s final curse is that it was woefully unoriginal. Although well-meaning, it has to be marked as the inferior of the two films because it contained much less invention or original thought. It tried to be as action-filled as *Capricorn*, but even the fight sequences are rendered empty because the film-maker's mercenary approach showed through all he did.

The movie was *High Noon* in outer space. No more and much less. Reports have it that that is how Hyams sold the concept to his backers and distributors. In the classic 1952 western, Gary Cooper was a retiring sheriff betrayed by the town when challenged to a last gunfight by a trio of hardened criminals. In this 1981 version, Sean Connery is space marshall O'Neil, assigned to the mining colony of Con-am 27, out by Jupiter.

In this cramped, fetid hell-hole, miners are being driven crazy by a drug that initially ups their production. These men are dying—taking innocent bystanders with them—and O'Neil is sent to stop it. He discovers that mining boss Sheppard (Peter Boyle) is actively smuggling and pushing the drug. Sheppard discovers that O'Neil is onto him so he sends for three hired guns—all out to murder the marshall before he can attain proof.

Naturally O'Neil's deputies and the miners turn their backs on him, forcing a lone confrontation with the killers. The marshall finishes them off, one by one, getting the needed proof in the meantime. He socks Sheppard in the jaw then goes to file his incriminating report. This story just barely holds together from Hyam's ability to create exciting action scenes, but any rational thought reveals holes in the plot a Space Shuttle could fly through. One of the worst is the characters' continued use of shotguns, the last weapon anyone in their right mind would use on a space station where the smallest hole would cause suffocation and implosion.

Galaxy of Terror was crudely better than *Outland* if only because it succeeded in what it set out to do—gross viewers out with the most sickening sights and sounds imaginable. Its original title reveals its intent better: *Planet of Horror*. Space explorers Cabren (Edward Albert), Aluma (Erin Moran), Kore (Ray Walston), Baelon (Zalman King), Quuhod (Sid Haig), and Dameia (Taafe O'Connell), among others, have the misfortune of landing on a world which can make real their greatest fears and worst nightmares. For the next eighty minutes all filmmakers Marc Siegler and Bruce Clark do is establish those fears and then visualize them.

The violence could not exactly be called gratui-

How do I destroy thee? Let me count the ways. First, Michael Ironside sent sparks out of Stephen Lack's head in an unused ending of *Scanners*.

tous—since the movie's main intent is to be pervertedly violent—but the movie could be. The moments of disgust range from a crew member's throwing up to a giant slug's sexually attacking the most beautiful woman explorer. No one escapes unscathed in this vicious, ugly entertainment, but for those who were looking for a pessimistic picture with plenty of gory special effects, *Galaxy of Terror* did not disappoint.

A satire of that very kind of movie could be found in *The Creature Wasn't Nice*, directed, written and starring Bruce Kimmel. Kimmel's previous film had been *The First Nudie Musical* (1976) and his heart seems to lie with sophomoric, scattershot comedy that misses more often than it hits. Here he plays a nebbish on a spaceship commanded by Leslie Nielsen. Once a mean alien gets on board, Kimmel satirical targets include *Alien*,

The over-crowded, drug-ridden mining colony of *Outland*.

Sean Connery plays Marshal O'Neil, who must fight for his life on *Outland*.

Forbidden Planet, The Thing, 2001 and many others. Patrick Macnee plays the scientist intent on maintaining the murderous alien's safety so he can study it, while Cindy Williams and Gerrit Graham are two more daffy crewmembers. Ron Kurowski is the monster who sings and dances after he kills someone. It was a good cast and a good idea, hampered by too small a budget and too unfocused an approach.

Heavy Metal was hampered by a total misconception. A misconception that animation could somehow portray human beings better than live action could. Another minor misconception was that comic strips could be adapted to animation without changing the stilted dialogue and stolid

ideas. *Heavy Metal* first was a comic magazine, the English version of the famous French comic art magazine *Metal Hurlant*. Producer Ivan Reitman decided to take the magazine's concept and several of its continuing comic stories to make a movie.

The magazine's concept was to get a series of "adult" comic strips by exceptional international comic artists and print them beautifully on expensive paper. When that concept was set to be adapted to film, director Gerald Potterton and production designer Michael Gross decided to eschew the "adult animation" approach of things like *Fritz the Cat* (1972)—that is, classic cartoon characters put in risqué situations—opting for a "realistic" science-fantasy conceit. They would

The new leaner, meaner James Bond (Roger Moore) of *For Your Eyes Only*.

animate a series of futuristic adventures with human characters.

Dan Goldberg and Len Blum wrote the screenplay, incorporating stories by Dan O'Bannon, Richard Corben, Angus McKie, Thomas Warkentin, and Bernie Wrightson. To string all six separate sections together, they had a glowing green ball declare it was evil incarnate and show a captive little girl how it worms its way throughout time and space.

It's first tale was of "Harry Canyon," a cab driver in the ultraviolent, overpopulated Manhattan of the next century. Harry gets involved with the beautiful daughter of a scientist who discovered the green globe, as well as the ruffians who want to possess the green ball for themselves. Harry hangs around as the green ball melts whomever touches it. Next up was "Captain Sternn," the only outright "cartoon-like" episode in the bunch. In an outer-space court-martial, the unbelievably corrupt Captain Sternn is saved from execution by having one of his witnesses grow to giant size and destroy the place. The captain rewards the agent of his life-saving diversion by dumping the giant into outer space.

"Gremlins" was next, a *Twilight Zone*-type World War II adventure in which the rotting corpses of dead soldiers gang up on living air force men. "So Deadly and So Beautiful" followed, in which a government official turns out to be a robot who attacks his beautiful red-headed secretary. The girl is then kidnapped by aliens who had built the robot in the first place. She wins these drug-addled extraterrestrials over with her sex appeal. "Den" came after, the story of a nerd sucked into another dimension where he becomes a bald, muscle-bound, naked adventurer.

Finally, there was "Taarna," a fable about a female Amazonian warrior who defeats an evil horde of villains on another planet. In a totally unimaginative twist, the green ball reveals that the little girl he has cornered will grow up to be Taarna—the only one who ever foiled him. She escapes and the house the ball is inside blows up. The film ends with the pubescent Taarna saddling up her pet pterodactyl and flying off.

Heavy Metal was an obtuse, boring movie which forced some of the best animation studios in Canada—where it was produced—to laboriously animate full-scale human beings. Ray DaSilva, a

greatly respected New York animator, was one such artist on the picture. "It was awful," he remembers. "Day after day, animating people. That is the most useless kind of thing to animate. No drawing could ever recreate people. Animation is for interpreting characters, not making mirror images move."

The script was unexciting but, even worse, the occasionally striking animation was nowhere near the quality of the comic art it was adapted from. *Heavy Metal* was a totally uninspiring effort—so bad it was almost a non-movie.

MONSTROUS ADVENTURES

Filmmakers didn't seem satisfied with presenting classic monsters with all their mythos intact anymore. Once, werewolves were accepted by audiences as vicious creatures created by the appearance of the full moon and killable only by silver bullets. Author Whitley Strieber knew better. He proposed a race of wolves with far greater intelligence than man who had claimed the crumbling ruins of the South Bronx as their home. They were known as the *Wolfen*, the title of Strieber's novel and the subsequent film.

When a millionaire industrialist decides to rebuild the South Bronx into a better community, the Wolfen correctly assume their home is to be destroyed. They start stalking those responsible with a vengeance. In the taut, exciting book, a detective and specialist run afoul of the creatures. In the twenty-million-dollar movie, a distracting subplot concerning American Indians is thrown in.

Producers Alan King and Rupert Hitzig hired director Michael Wadleigh to film Strieber's screenplay version of his book. Wadleigh, whose only previous film had been the documentary *Woodstock* (1970), threw out that script to write one of his own with David Eyre. The result was a three-hour film which downplayed the Wolfen in favor of the plight of the American Indian. To make matters worse, the vitally important special effects which showed a "wolfen-eyed view" of the proceedings did not work.

Out went Wadleigh. In came uncredited director John Hancock, who filmed new scenes and oversaw optical-effects artist Robert Blalack's useable "wolfen-eye" material. The final hundred-and-fifteen-minute movie was approximately half-Wadleigh, half-Hancock, as well as half—Wolfen, half-American-Indian. Although unfocused, it still made an interesting ecological statement in addition to being an engrossing chiller.

Albert Finney starred as Dewey Wilson, the policeman who takes it upon himself to solve a series of gruesome murders. He loses a medical examiner (Gregory Hines) and a superior (Dick O'Neill, who gets his head bitten off) before discovering that the Wolfen can feel emotions. If a person poses no threat, they will take no offense. *Wolfen* ends on a stalemate. The South Bronx will not be improved, the American Indian citizens will not be blamed for the murders, and the Wolfen will remain a secret civilization.

The Howling was witty where the *Wolfen* was weird, inventive where the other was pedantic. *Piranha's* director and writer, Joe Dante and John Sayles, returned in the same capacity here, for a clever satire of modern news programs as well as a straightforward monster movie. Dee Wallace plays a pretty TV news anchorwoman named Karen who becomes the fixation of a mass murderer. To secure his capture (as well as big ratings), she agrees to meet the killer at a pornography shop. What she sees there so horrifies her, she blanks the memory out. Police arrive to shoot the man down just in time.

The reporter is so shaken by the experience that

On the set of *For Your Eyes Only* with Carole Bouquet, Roger Moore, and Julian Glover (kneeling). Standing behind Glover is producer Albert Broccoli.

The director of *For Your Eyes Only*, John Glen.

media psychologist Dr. Waggner (Patrick Mac-Nee) suggests she go to his forest retreat upstate in the company of her husband Neill (Christopher Stone, married to Wallace in real life as well). They comply and meet all sorts of unusual people, all residing in the rustic community to quell the "beasts" inside them. Soon, it is revealed that they are all werewolves whom Dr. Waggner is trying to adjust to civilization.

Neill is turned into one during a tryst with a gorgeous resident (Elisabeth Brooks) and Karen only gets wise after her visiting best friend (Belinda Balaski) is murdered. Thankfully the best friend's fiancée and fellow TV news worker, Chris (Dennis Dugan), has been investigating the mass murderer, who seems to have upped and left the morgue. Chris comes to Waggner's retreat, armed with a rifle loaded with silver bullets.

214

And none too soon. All the residents surround Karen and are about to make a midnight meal of her when Chris interrupts. As the man shoots them down, locks them in a barn, and sets it on fire, the monsters realize they will never "fit in" with humans. Chris and Karen escape, but not before Neill manages to bite his wife, transmitting the werewolf germ. To prove their story, Karen turns into a werewolf live on the six o'clock news. Chris is sadly waiting offstage to kill her once the on-camera transformation is complete.

The Howling is a terrific entertainment, not even marred by the cop-out ending which shows the Elisabeth Brooks character alive and well and infecting innocents. Filmmakers Dante and Sayles fill the movie with undistracting in-jokes (from the call letters of the TV station, H.O.W.L., to carefully placed cans of "Wolf" Chili on pantry shelves, to TV sets playing "Big Bad Wolf" cartoons). Their werewolves, built by Rob Bottin and his crew, are also great as well as being different from any other screen werewolf.

This makeup crew was also responsible for a fabulous transformation sequence where the mass murderer's bullet-hole-ridden body turns into an eight-foot-tall monster wolf without optical or editing tricks. It was all done with hydraulic makeup effects. Finally, Dante and Sayles tell their story straight, with believable characters who the audience can care about. *The Howling* has great entertainment value and meaning.

It was a better film than *An American Werewolf in London*, but the latter movie walked off with the Oscar for "Best Makeup Effects." It is only right since Rob Bottin learned everything from Rick Baker, who was responsible for the werewolf transformation in this higher-budgeted movie. Although this is not a science-fiction movie, it deserves mention in comparison with the previous two pictures. John Landis wrote and directed the film starring David Naughton as a hiking tourist who is attacked by a werewolf on the English moors.

Much of the movie is concerned with macabre and comedic complications of the situation. The werewolf's horribly scarred victims live on to haunt him, begging him to take his own life so the killings will cease and they can go on to their final resting place. When Naughton asks if a silver bullet is necessary, one corpse tells him to "get serious."

Therein lies the film's greatest failing. The "get serious" line was a way of making the audience laugh which had no reality within the film. Why would the idea of a silver bullet be so ludicrous when living corpses were walking around and a man could turn into a wolf on nights of the full moon? Throughout the picture, Landis undercuts the narrative's believability with striking but essentially meaningless visual concepts.

Evilspeak was the last of this year's horror/science-fiction combinations. The horror was thanks to an ancient satanist whose spirit still lives in the basement of a military academy. The science fiction came in when a greatly abused student named Coopersmith (Clint Howard) uses a computer to resurrect the evil force. This is a deliciously dumb movie written by Joseph Garofalo and directed by Eric Weston as a straight-faced combination of *Carrie* and *The Muppet Movie* (1979).

When a beautiful secretary incurs the wrath of the satanic spirit, it waits until she has taken off her clothes for a bath, then sends enraged boars breaking out of their pig pen to gore her to death. The sight of these hogs nuzzling the naked actress was a hilarious sight to behold, as was the demonically possessed Coopersmith, floating across the academy's chapel with a broadsword in his hand.

The wronged lad hacks apart his oppressors and then falls into a catatonic state. While he is imprisoned in a home for the homicidally insane, the computer in the basement is promising the evil spirit will return. *Evilspeak* was enormously stupid, but all the more fun for it. It is a gruesome horror movie almost impossible to take seriously, but does boast some fine computer animation effects.

GREAT ADVENTURES

Time Bandits was superior in originality and imagination to any other genre picture this year. Terry Gilliam and Michael Palin, two of the six-man *Monty Python's Flying Circus* team, wrote the film fable—a delightful adventure through time and space made for the child in everyone. Gilliam also directed with an incredible penchant for stretching a dollar and presenting timeworn special effects in a completely refreshing way.

Craig Warnock starred as Kevin, a young English boy whose parents are more interested in keeping up with the Joneses and watching television than they are in him. One night a knight astride a horse leaps out of Kevin's closet and goes galloping off through his wall. When Kevin checks, all is unscathed. Absolutely fascinated, Kevin lies awake the next night to see six eccentrically dressed midgets come out of his closet.

When he confronts them, they instantly panic, then contritely offer him "the map." When they realize he is not who they think he is, they attack him and demand to know "the way out." Completely confused, Kevin stammers until one midget discovers that he can push back one of the bedroom walls. They all start to push when a luminous face appears in mid-air demanding, "Return the map. It will bring you great danger."

Frightened, Kevin helps them push the wall out of the way and falls through time to drop into the era of Napoleon (Ian Holm). He discovers that the half-dozen little people are fugitives from the "Supreme Being's" tree-making division. They discovered the existence of a map charting holes in time—where the six-day job of Creation didn't quite take properly. Now they are all intent on being interdimensional thieves, eager to plunder history's wealth.

Their first victim is Napoleon himself, who is a height-obsessed crazy, a self-professed lover of "little things hitting each other." Naturally he makes the seven small folk generals and drunkenly regales them with accounts of the heights of great men of history until he loses consciousness. They rob him blind and even take the fake gold hand he keeps inside his tunic all the time.

Escaping through another time hole, they emerge in Sherwood Forest, where Robin Hood (John Cleese) turns out to be an upper-class twit who distributes all their ill-gotten booty to the poor. At that point the "Supreme Evil Being" (David Warner) decides that possession of the map will make him ruler of all the cosmos, even though the Supreme Being has made him prisoner in a gigantic castle. He supernaturally starts the crooks

Clark Kent (Christopher Reeve) races to transform into his invulnerable alter-ego at the start of *Superman II*.

216

on a search for "the greatest thing in the world" before the luminous face tracks them down again.

Kevin is forced to choose between two adjoining time holes. The one he uses drops him atop a Greek Warrior, thereby saving King Agamemnon's (Sean Connery) life. In return, the fatherly monarch makes Kevin the heir to his throne. Deliriously happy for the first time in his life, Kevin is reluctantly retrieved by the six others. Angry at their interference, he doesn't realize that they are all now sitting on the *Titanic*.

Upon its destruction, the Evil Being sends the group into a mystical world, where they are captured by an ailing Ogre (Peter Vaughan) and his sweetly murderous wife (Katherine Helmond). The tiny robbers foil the monster's plan to eat them by fixing his aching back and then push both it and its wife overboard. The ship is then revealed as the hat of a giant, who rises out of the ocean and walks abroad, crushing houses in the process. The seven concoct a sleeping potion to knock him out, then continue their search for the greatest thing in the world.

The Evil Being lures them into his castle and wrests the map from them through subterfuge. Luckily Kevin had taken a picture of the six holding the map. They all see that Evil's castle is right over the biggest time hole of all. Kevin and Og (Mike Edmonds) go to retrieve the map while the others go for help. Just as it seems Kevin will be killed by Evil, the others return. Vermin (Tiny Ross) comes back with cowboys. Fidget (Kenny Baker) comes back with Roman gladiators. Strutter (Malcolm Dixon) comes back with Knights of the Round Table. Wally (Jack Purvis) returns in a laser-firing space ship, and Randall (David Rappaport) appears in a World War II tank.

None of these heroes or weapons prove to be a match for Evil. He destroys them all and is just about to eradicate the little people when he himself blows up. Appearing then is the Supreme Being, not as a luminous face, but as a fussy, preoccupied bureaucrat (Ralph Richardson). He explains that Evil was just an experiment, as was letting the six steal the map. Just a way to spend the time. "I had to have some way of testing my handiwork," he says. "I *am* the Supreme Being. I'm not entirely dim."

As punishment, the Supreme Being demotes his workers to the Undergrowth Department with a nineteen percent cut in salary "backdated to the beginning of time." He instructs them to collect the pieces of exploded Evil since "one drop. . . could turn you all into hermit crabs." Kevin is placed back in his bed, but the house is on fire. He is rescued by a fireman who looks just like Agamemnon. He finds all the pictures he had taken during his trip through time, then looks up to see the fireman winking at him.

His parents appear, holding the charred remains of a toaster-oven. Inside is a piece of Evil the little people had missed. Kevin tries to warn them, but his parents touch the piece and immediately disappear in a ball of flame. The camera pulls back from the astonished Kevin, then back from Earth, then back from the galaxy, then back from the universe until the picture becomes the map which is rolled up and taken off screen just as the end credits start.

Time Bandits is a totally manic, nearly slapstick, cockeyed view of history, the world, and everything. It is a charming and captivating film full of deft touches and wonderful details. It is a fairy tale for adults and a ripping yarn for children. It succeeds on so many levels, it deserves to become a film classic.

For Your Eyes Only may not deserve to be a classic, but it is a quantum leap over the last James Bond movie, *Moonraker*. Producer Albert Broccoli did some serious rethinking of their previous buffoon-like approach to the character, reshuffling the production crew to mount a leaner, more believable Bond while still maintaining the spectacular nature of the stories. Primarily responsible for the ease of the transition was new director John Glen. Like Peter Hunt (director of *On Her Majesty's Secret Service*) before him, Glen had been an editor of previous Bond films, so he came to the helmsman's position with much-needed experience.

Glen, more than anything, is a practical filmmaker, with an encyclopedic knowledge of how to make movies move quickly, what the character of James Bond was about, and how to make the star, Roger Moore, look good in the role. This time, the script by Ricahrd Maibum and executive producer Michael Wilson was a string of little movies—each one focusing on a single adventure. First, it was a sea adventure, as a vital British spy ship is sunk by an accidental explosion. If the Russians discover the secrets on board before the British can salvage them, the cold war could get a lot hotter.

The man the British send to save the day is not Bond, but noted oceanographer Havelock (Jack Hedley). He and his wife are killed by a secret rival, right before the shocked eyes of the Havelock's daughter, Melina (Carole Bouquet). Agent 007, in the meantime, has his own hands full. An old enemy (although bald, scarred, and petting a cat, the producers refuse to allow the character to be called Blofeld) has plotted Bond's death in a radio-controlled helicopter. Bond disconnects the auto-pilot and uses the helicopter to chase the bald enemy in return.

Afterwards he is sent on the trail of the Have-locks' killers. He traces it back to an assassin named Locque (Michael Gothard; thankfully, the campy character of "Jaws" is absent from this film), whom he corners the same time as the vengeful Melina does. Momentarily outnumbered, they escape, only to cross paths again at a Swiss ski resort. That sets the stage for the second ma-

jor adventure: a ski chase that climaxes with Bond on skis being chased by a motorcycle, which is, in turn, being chased by a bobsled on a bobsled run.

Again, the principals escape. Agent 007 is forced to team up with a mob boss (Topol) who has a grudge against the international double-dealer Kristatos (Julian Glover), the man who hired Loc-que. Together they track down and attack Locque. Bond kills the man himself in cold blood by kick-ing the hitman's teetering car over a cliff. Melina and Bond join up for the next adventure; going back to the sunken ship in a two-person sub-marine. Lying in wait for them is a man in a super-strong aquatic suit and another man piloting a deadly Mantis sub. Bond fights them both off and gains possession of a computer console contain-ing the vital secrets.

Kristatos ambushes the good guys and retreats to his hideout on top of a European mountain to await the arrival of the Russians. The last adven-ture is then set: a breathtaking assault on the mountain by Bond, who single handedly climbs

Superman flies again, fighting three Phantom Zone villains.

up a sheer cliff wall. Agent 007 arrives in time to foil Kristatos' plot. Each of these *For Your Eyes Only* segments was handsomely directed, and each was superior to similar espionage movies that concentrated on only one adventure.

The only problem that now exists for Bond is that no matter what the writers and directors do, 007 has done it before. Although well produced and exciting, the adventures in this new Bond movie were familiar. Sean Connery had scuba-dived in *Thunderball*. George Lazenby had skied and fought on a bobsled run in *On Her Majesty's Secret Service*. More and more, watching a James Bond movie was tantamount to having a two-hour case of *déjà vu*.

THIS LOOKS LIKE ANOTHER JOB FOR SUPERMAN

Another superhero returned this year. Clark Kent, alias Superman, was back in action again in the long-awaited *Superman II*. Originally planned to be released the summer after the first *Superman* movie premiered, production and per-

sonnel problems delayed the picture. The biggest obstacle was the battle between producer Pierre Spengler and director Richard Donner. When the latter delivered an "either he goes or I go" ultimatum to executive producer Ilya Salkind, Donner was dropped, most of his *Superman II* footage was scrapped and Richard Lester was promoted.

Other hassles plagued the production. Between films, production designer John Barry, cinematographer Geoffry Unsworth, and special-effects man Les Bowie died. Their work was supplemented by Peter Murton, Bob Paynter, and Colin Chilvers, respectively. In addition, Marlon Brando filed a lawsuit against the producers for supposedly not paying his contractual share of the profits. To alleviate any further legal complications, the filmmakers eliminated the character of Jor-el in the second film and had the necessary dialogue delivered by Susannah York, who played Lara, Superman's mother. All the other actors returned to their roles.

Instead of taking place immediately after the previous film ended, some time has gone by, allow-

Clark Kent blows Lois Lane's (Margot Kidder) mind. He kisses her memory away at the end of *Superman II*.

Superman confronts General Zod (Terence Stamp) on the streets of New York City for a climatic battle in *Superman II*.

ing Metropolis to adjust to the Superman in their midst. Superman himself had to adjust to the strange romantic triangle he had put himself in. Clark Kent loved Lois Lane, but Lois loved Superman.

Originally, Lois was scripted to test her theory that Clark was Superman by jumping out of a *Daily Planet* window. Kent was to save her by using his super-breath to blow her onto an awning and then into a fruit stand. Richard Donner had filmed such a scene, in fact, as he had filmed the scene where the three super-villains in the Phantom Zone were freed by the detonation of the nuclear bomb Superman had thrown into outer space at the end of the first film.

In the new *Superman II*, this release was accomplished by having Lois cover a French terrorist group's attempt to level Paris by placing a warhead at the top of the Eiffel Tower. Naturally Superman saves the day, hurling the weapon into outer space. It blows a hole in the Phantom Zone, setting General Zod (Terence Stamp), the brutish mute Non (Jack O'Halloran), and the vicious Ursa (Sarah Douglas) free. Also freed is Lex Luthor, who leaves the retarded Otis behind when his female assistant, Miss Teschmacher (Valerie Perrine), picks him out of jail in a hot air balloon.

The next few scenes are about all that remain of Richard Donner's footage. The three super-villains trash a NASA moon landing crew while Luthor discovers the Fortress of Solitude. He had been tracking Superman's North Pole flights with his advanced radar equipment. Once inside, the holographic computer images of Lara makes no distinction between her son and Lex. Whatever is asked, she answers.

Clark and Lois, in the meantime, are assigned to do an investigative report on exploitive Honeymoon Hotels. It is there where Lois tests her secret identity theory after Superman appears to save a drowning child. She throws herself into a river instead of out a window. Kent uses his super-vision to cut a tree limb down which she uses as a raft. Even though his alias is intact, he trips and places his hand in a working fireplace during the very next sequence; his hand emerges unscathed, tipping Lane off to the truth.

Relieved that his secret is finally known by the woman he loves, Superman flies her up to the Fortress while all the bad guys come down south. The three super-villains take over the country while

Superman discovers from Lara that he will have to become mortal to settle down with Lois. This is accomplished with the infamous green crystal that had created the Fortress in the first movie. As Superman goes into the mortal-making chamber, Lois absent-mindedly misplaces the green crystal.

On their way back to Metropolis, the lovers stop in a diner, where Clark Kent is badly beaten by a bully and sees his own blood for the first time. Immediately afterwards they see a television news report of the super-villains' devastation. Realizing he had made a grave error, Clark Kent vows to *walk* back to the now-deteriorating Fortress to try and find some way to change things. Lex Luthor, in the meantime, contacts the super-villains (Miss Teschmacher completely disappears from the film), who have taken up residence in the White House. He promises to deliver Superman to them if they give him Australia.

Coming to an uncertain agreement, Lex leads them to the *Daily Planet*, where they take Lois Lane hostage. Superman has found the misplaced green crystal by then (the audience is left to assume that he rebuilds the Fortress with it and reverses the mortal process, although it is never shown). What is shown is the re-superpowered hero arriving outside the *Daily Planet* window and saying to Zod, "Care to step outside?"

The battle sequence between the four superpowered characters is occasionally good, but it is badly padded with truly absurd comedy relief and seemingly endless shots of the same special effects over and over again. Superman realizes that he is outnumbered and there are too many bystanders around, so he flies off to the Fortress. The others follow, dragging Luthor and Lois along for the ride.

Another minor scuffle between the antagonists ensues before Ursa threatens to rip Lois's head off if Superman doesn't cooperate. Luthor then reveals the secret of the mortal-making chamber. Zod demands that Superman go through the process again. But the hero had somehow reversed the thing, rendering Zod, Non, and Ursa mortal while maintaining his own powers safe inside the chamber. All he and Lois do then is punch, kick and throw the villains off icy plateaus where they disappear into fog flows never to be seen again.

This climax is extremely unsatisfying, as is the subsequent scene where Superman makes Lois

For such a "family entertainment," *Raiders of the Lost Ark* was filled with violence and rotting corpses. Here, Karen Allen shares a scene with one.

forget everything with a kiss. There was no clues as to any of these plot twists before they occurred, making them even more facile than the "turning-Earth-backwards" trick he pulled in the first picture. The only thing that saves *Superman II* from being a bust is the second to last scene of Clark Kent going back to the northern diner to settle with the bully who had beaten him up earlier. That is the only satisfying climactic sequence.

The final scene has Superman replacing the White House dome, then promising never to let the nation down again (almost as if he realized he had let the audience down this time). *Superman II* had some fine moments, but it looked too much like the patch job it was; an awkward melding of five screenwriters' scripts and two directors' work—all glossed over with uninteresting padding.

Raiders of the Lost Ark is not really a science-fiction film. But this collaboration between execu-

tive producer and co-story-writer George Lucas and director Steven Spielberg should be mentioned in comparison to what both men did before and after. It does have a tenuous hold on the genre, however, by right of its fanciful, mystical plot and the many strange devices that would seem futuristic at the time the movie took place, 1936.

The subject of the film was broached by Lucas to Spielberg in Hawaii a week before *Star Wars* premiered. Lucas himself thought his Luke Skywalker story would be a huge failure. When he was told just how big a hit it was a week later, he went into more detail on *Raiders*. He wanted to make an archeology adventure that harkened back to the thrills and spills of serial days.

Although Spielberg wasn't thrilled by the fifteen chapters of *Don Winslow of the Navy* which Lucas showed him, he was excited by Philip Kaufman's and Lucas's tale of teacher/adventurer Indiana Jones. He agreed to direct the film, but only

223

Marion Ravenwood (Karen Allen) tells Indiana Jones (Harrison Ford) just what she thinks of him in *Raiders of the Lost Ark*.

after he completed his previous committment to direct *1941*. That 1979 Three-Stooges-like comedy failed at the box office, and saddled Spielberg with bad reviews and bad publicity. To prove he could make a lean film without overblown pretentions, he vowed to make *Raiders* on time and on budget.

At first, they cast the leading role with a newcomer named Tom Selleck. But as production continued and Lawrence Kasdan finished the script, Selleck was also signed to star in the *Magnum P.I.* television series. The actor's strike threw off his schedule and a network executive refused to let him break his contract, so Lucas and Spielberg cast Harrison Ford. (Word from the set of Selleck's first movie, *High Road to China*, 1983, is that in a scene where dozens of heads are impaled on spears, the makeup men were all instructed to make the faces resemble that stubborn network executive.)

The American government is worried about German excavating parties in Egypt. They know that Adolf Hitler is obsessed with religious doctrine and occult power. Fearing the worst, they call on archeology trouble-shooter Indiana Jones. Jones has just returned from a fateful exploration of the Temple of the Chachapoyon Warriors. There he had braved a maze filled with deadly booby traps including shooting spears, poisonous darts, armies of tarantulas, and a bottomless pit to retrieve a golden idol's head.

His removal of that piece brought on a torrent of new dangers including a giant stone ball that nearly crushed him. Braving the treachery of his own aides, he was captured by his French archeology nemesis, Belloq (Paul Freeman), who took the idol away and sicced a cannibal tribe on him. He just managed to get away, thanks to his pilot, Jock (Fred Sorenson), but as he scrambled into the getaway plane he found Jock's pet snake Reggie in his seat. The one thing Jones can't stand is snakes.

But a snake has nothing on the venom of his ex-love Marion Ravenwood (Karen Allen), who now runs a bar in Nepal. Jones goes there to retrieve the headpiece to the Staff of Ra which her late father, Abner, had found. It is the key to uncovering the exact location of what everyone is looking for: the Ark of the Covenant, containing the broken tablets of the Ten Commandments, which brings mysterious powers to whoever posseses it.

Marion slugs Jones on the jaw and sends him away. In his place comes Toht (Ronald Lacey), a slimy Nazi who is about to torture Marion for the information. Indiana saves the day, but not without bringing down the bar in flaming ruins. Toht tries to grab the burned headpiece only to fry his hand in its image. Marion then joins Jones on a race to find the Ark before the Nazis do.

Desperate dangers assail them from all sides as Toht teams with Belloq to uncover the Well of Souls where the Ark resides. Using all sorts of subterfuge, Jones and Marion infiltrate the Nazi excavation camp and find the Ark, only to be captured and dumped into an ancient tomb filled with poisonous snakes. Indiana tips over one of the giant statues in the tomb to make a hole in the wall. Both escape in time to see the Nazis load the Ark into a truck and drive away.

Jones hops a horse and takes off in pursuit. There follows a famous truck chase sequence in which the determined hero braves an incredible number of obstacles to wrest the Ark from the Germans. Even when he is thrown under a truck, he crawls along its undercarriage and is dragged behind it on the end of his whip, which he uses to climb back aboard.

With the Ark in the hold of a steamer headed back to England, Indiana and Marion think all is well—until a Nazi submarine cuts them off, taking both Marion and the Ark captive. Jones swims to the diving sub and "hitches" a ride to the Nazi's destination. The movie slightly falters at this point. For some reason, the filmmakers decided not to include the sequence in which Jones lashes himself to the sub's periscope. They also neglect to show the audience that the sub's scope remained above the surface the whole trip, allowing Jones to sur-

vive. In the finished film, the audience is left to assume all that.

Jones has a bazooka trained on the Ark, but Belloq convinces him to give himself up. The oily Frenchman correctly assumes that Jones is just as curious about the Ark as the rest of them are—not to mention the safety of the captive Marion. All Indiana has to do after that is just stand back to back with Marion, lashed to a pole, as Belloq and the Nazis go through a ritual opening of the Ark. From there on, the "Supreme Being" does all the work.

The powers unleashed by the Ark's opening seems to attack only those who look at it, while eminating a powerful attraction to do just that. Most of the Nazis are lanced by lightning bolts but Belloq's skull explodes and Toht's head *melts*. Its power expended, the Ark grows quiet. The next scene takes place back in Washington, as government officials refuse to admit the Ark's possible powers, They bury it back in a military warehouse, seemingly just another box among hundreds of others.

Raiders of the Lost Ark was a wonderfully engaging adventure movie that carried audiences along for a breathless two hours. Besides its uneven conclusion, it is surprisingly graphic in its violence. From people being shot between the eyes in close-up to an amazing number of rotting corpses littering several scenes to the climactic melting, the gory effects were not shied away from. Still, very few deemed to notice them. Almost no one faulted its combination of old-fashioned thrills and modern cinematic vitality. All the outlandish locales and accoutrements only served to make the result spicier and more enjoyable.

Some of the highlights include a treacherous monkey who does a German salute, a "flying wing" plane that serves as a centerpiece for a sequence fraught with cliff-hanging, and a memorable fight scene in which an evil sword-master dazzles Jones with his prowess and then moves in for the kill, only to be immediately shot by Jones in the most off-hand manner (although a long fight was originally filmed between the two, actor Ford was suffering from a cold one day and suggested, "Aw, why don't I just shoot him?").

George Lucas and Steven Spielberg had made lightning strike thrice. Their collaborative effort made for a fitting capper to this year of adventure.

225

8
1982
THE YEAR OF THE EXTRATERRESTRIAL

THIS WAS AN UNFOCUSED YEAR in the genre. Almost every aspect of the science-fiction film had been attempted successfully. Space fantasies, monsters, hard-hitting adventures—there was one classic of every kind during the last few years. There were also tens of inferior works in each sub-genre, all but milking the category dry. Stymied filmmakers went on to other things while a variety of holdouts produced sequels.

THE LAW OF DIMINISHING RETURNS

Three such follow-ups proved that absence might not make the heart grow fonder. The sequels were inferior to the inspiring work preceding them. *Jekyll and Hyde Together Again* was the worst of the three. Following the example of *The Nutty Professor* and *Heckyl and Hype* before it, this "new" variation of the Stevenson classic cast Mark Blankfield as the innocuous doctor.

The casting and the film's very conception probably came about when the producers saw Blankfield on ABC television's satirical variety program *Fridays*. Occasionally Blankfield would play a lunatic pharmacist at a "Drugs 'R' Us" shop. Totally addicted to the pills he sold, Blankfield's character would constantly sweat and hallucinate, alternately screaming and cooing. When he wasn't vibrating spasmodically, he would be pulling at his hair, repeating, "I can handle it. . . .I can handle it. . . !"

That character was overused on the series and *Jekyll and Hyde Together Again* overused it by some sixty minutes. Before transforming, Blankfield plays a nice, naïve fellow. After transforming, he is a "new wave" maniac—a frizzy-haired, fancy-dressing life of the party. Blankfield's performance was suitably intense, but the humor fell consistently flat.

Blankfield's movie was just one of several which attempted to create the "joke-a-minute" approach of *Airplane* (1981), a hilarious satire of disaster and the *Airport* movies (1970, 1975, 1977, and 1979). Only no one could do it as well as Jim Abrahams, David Zucker and Jerry Zucker (*Airplane's* writers and directors), and that includes the makers of *Airplane II: The Sequel*. Instead of going off in directions of their own, the follow-up's producers were content to repeat the original's best jokes *ad infinitum*.

The thing that kept *Airplane II* afloat was its science-fiction plot and the fact that the original jokes were so good. Instead of a jumbo jetliner losing its pilot, the sequel had the first passenger-carrying flight of the Space Shuttle sabotaged. Julie Hagerty returned to her role of dippy Elaine Dickerson; she has been promoted from stewardess to computer officer on the *Mayflower One* (which was also the name of *Close Encounters'* NASA astronaut team).

Robert Hays was also back in the part of Ted Striker, the hapless flier who must always land aircraft that lose their pilots. Also as in the original, the supporting cast is overloaded with television perennials, such as Lloyd Bridges as an obssessive air controller and Peter Graves as a lover of gladiator movies and locker rooms.

Almost everything is repeated here, but the most successful jokes are the well-timed background "throwaway" bits, as when Bridges is trying to remember the name of the hero in his office. "Let's see," he muses, then recalls with a flourish, "Striker!" Naturally a man in the background slugs a secretary, thinking that it was the command "strike her." The film is crammed with jokes of the same calibre, the best weakened by familiarity. The film also has some decent special effects evident in the Shuttle flight and subsequent crash sequences.

But *Airplane II: The Sequel* is just like a joke one has heard before. Since someone likeable is telling it and the timing is occasionally good, it is able to inspire some weak mirth.

Also fashioned as something of a comedy was *Halloween III: Season of the Witch*. After a cunning first *Halloween* movie directed and written by John Carpenter in 1978, then an exploitive and gratuitous sequel in 1981, producers Carpenter and Debra Hill decided to eliminate their original plotline of an unkillable "boogeyman" slayer who murders babysitters and a hospital staff on Halloween night. Instead, they decided to fashion a new concept, based on the traditions and history of Halloween night.

Nigel Kneale, the British creator of the excep-

But as Mr. Hyde, Mark Blankfield has no trouble getting girls or dazzling audiences in *Jekyll and Hyde Together Again*.

tional "Professor Quatermass" films, came up with the original story, which was then rewritten by Tommy Lee Wallace, who was also chosen as director. The concept was chilling as well as campy, but the final film seemed exploitative and diffidently made. Dan O'Herlihy did a good acting job as Cochran, an insidious Halloween mask maker. His company, Silver Shamrock, produces a trio of the best-made, cheapest Halloween masks on record.

He hawks these three masks—a skull, a witch, and a jack o'lantern—with endless television commercials that incorporate an annoying countdown jingle: "Three more days to Halloween, Halloween, three more days to Halloween, Silver Shamrock." As the holiday gets closer, the day count diminishes. And, as the holiday gets nearer, the body count rises.

A toy store owner discovers that all is not well, but he is murdered by callow Silver Shamrock assassins. His daughter (Stacey Nelkin) and his doctor (Tom Atkins) investigate to discover that if there's one thing Cochran hates more than the

Tom Atkins and Stacey Nelkin look at *Halloween III: Season of the Witch's* booby-trapped masks with apprehension.

commercialization of Halloween, it's children. He has devised a plan to get rid of them that incorporates ancient witchcraft with modern technology.

Silver Shamrock had stolen a Stonehenge rock and installed a piece of it along with a computer chip in every mask they made. The ancient occult power of the stone combined with the computer programming would create a horrid result when set off by the Silver Shamrock commercial jingle on Halloween night. The good doctor escapes Cochran's clutches but only manages to convince two out of three networks of the threat.

One network allows the ad to run, triggering thousands of deaths as children all over the country have their brains scrambled. Insects, reptiles and serpents come pouring out of some masks as the kids keel over. *Halloween III's* sick joke did not amuse many audiences. In fact, Nigel Kneale's name was not on the film's credits, perhaps marking his dissatisfaction with the treatment. Although the advance publicity promised: "Witchcraft Enters the Computer Age," this third sequel was an unlikely and sadistic story not very well told.

THE LAW OF INCREASING RETURNS

Two movies this year were rare and special. They were sequels superior to the original work. Both had talents at the helm which took off from the initial work, saw the previous film's failings, corrected them, and then built upon them. They were both exceptional movies.

The Road Warrior was one. Titled *Mad Max II* in Europe and the Far East, it reintroduced Mel Gibson as the now totally alienated Australian auto gladiator. In the time between films, he has lost his wife; his only companion now is a small dog. The police are also no more. All Max has left of that experience is his high-powered car.

Society as we know it has broken down completely. A Third World War wiped out most things, and on the Australian outback only those who could forage fuel survived. Survival was the only thing important to Max at the film's start, but even he didn't know why. "In the roar of an engine," said the prologue, "he lost everything. . .and became a shell of a man."

The Road Warrior was more than just a magnificently exciting action drama, it also chronicled the rebirth of Max's humanity. "It was here," concluded the prologue, "in this blighted place, that he learned to live again." That lesson was hard learned. Although many viewers remember the film as incorporating non-stop action, it was actually composed of moments of sudden, surprising violence interspersed with bleak but lyrical visions.

The movie starts with Max coming upon an ugly car crash. Dressed in leather, carrying a shotgun pistol, Max is only interested in the dripping fuel, not the dying bodies. He has a chance confrontation with a gang of maddened freaks led by a masked muscleman called Humungus (Kjell Nilsson). The leader of the road bandits sends his lieutenant, named Wez (Vernon Wells)—a wild-eyed, red-haired, homicidal freak with a miniature cross-bow attached to his sleeve—out to secure a lone oil refinery held by a band of valiant but frightened people.

The refinery people are led by a troubled visionary named Pappagallo (Mike Preston), who fervently believes in the possibility of beginning a new civilization somewhere away from the brutality of the Wasteland. But first he must find a way to carry all the life-giving gasoline. Max is indifferent to their plight, although attracted by the possibility of unlimited fuel. What changes his mind is another chance meeting, this time with "The Gyro Captain" (Bruce Spence), a "reckless stork of a man," as he is described by publicity.

Circumstances lead Max to gain entry to the refinery, offering those within a deal. He will get a tanker truck big enough to hold all the fuel in exchange for some cans of gas. Max finds an abandoned oil tanker and gets it to the hapless people, braving incredible attacks by Humungus's troops. Although he wants to remain alienated from the desperate refinery folk, he gains the respect of Pappagallo and his lieutenants, particularly the "Warrior Woman" (Virginia Hey). He gets more than respect from the "Feral Kid," an eight-year-old wild child who dresses in animal skins, only grunts, and throws a razor-sharp steel boomerang with deadly accuracy.

Turning his back on the group, who want him to drive the full tanker out as well as in, Max takes his cans of gas and drives off, only to be ambushed by Wez, who blows up his car and kills his dog. It is only because of the appearance of the Gyro Captain on the scene that he survives. The crash has badly damaged Max's left eye, but he has no choice but to pilot the gas tanker now.

Outfitted for battle, the Warrior Woman and others take their places on the truck's roof, the Feral Kid leaps on the running board and Max drives off for a brutal thirteen-minute screen battle with Humungus's forces.

Words cannot express the excitement of this and the film's previous "road wars." Drifting between comic-book-like action and literally breathtaking stunts, *The Road Warrior*'s climactic moments deliver a visceral wallop rarely experienced in English-speaking film. With everyone killed but Max and the Feral Kid, they prepare for the final reckoning of Wez and Humungus.

Max wipes them both out but then crashes the tanker. To everyone's surprise, the truck turns out to have been filled with sand—it had been a diversion to lure Humungus away from the fleet of decrepit vehicles that left the compound some minutes after Max's departure. The Feral Kid rejoins the group, now led by the Gyro Captain. As the concluding narration reveals, the Kid grew to be the group's leader, the man who led them to their Promised Land.

As for Max, he is only remembered as the loner he was at the film's start. The last thing the audience sees is him standing next to his car, framed by a glorious outback sunset. Producer Byron Kennedy, director George Miller, writers Miller, Terry Hayes, Brian Hannant, and stunt director Max Aspin (and all the actors) did an incredible job with *The Road Warrior*. It is the best of its kind.

Star Trek II: The Wrath of Khan surprised almost everyone. Costing approximately a quarter of *Star Trek—The Motion Picture*'s budget, screenwriter Jack Sowards, director Nicholas Meyer, and especially producer Robert Sallin pulled off a minor miracle in restoring *Star Trek*'s original invention and humanity as well as expanding the TV series to motion picture quality.

The crew did a complete tune-up and lube job. New, more cinematic sets were built, costumes and props were redesigned to be more colorful, eye-catching and exciting. A plot was built around three important ingredients: *Star Trek*'s TV history, a valid, intriguing science-fiction premise, and, most importantly, the further growth and maturation of the characters.

The TV history aspect was taken care of by bringing back a character from the series' "Space

Paul Winfield and Walter Koenig explore a desolate planet in *Star Trek II: The Wrath of Khan.*

Seed" episode—that of Khan, a genetically mutated super-villain of the late twentieth century. In the episode he had been put in suspended animation along with his followers, only to be awakened by the unknowing *Enterprise* crew. Captain Kirk defeated his takeover plans and then gave him a choice: rehabilitation in a penal institution or survival on the rugged, deserted planet of Ceti Alpha V. Khan replies by recalling Milton. "Better to rule in Hell than serve in Heaven."

The valid scientific premise was "The Genesis Project"—an explosive device which destroys all life on a planet to completely replace it with lush, new life. The project just so happens to be run by Kirk's ex-lover and the mother of his son. That is just part of the character maturation. Now an admiral, Kirk feels alienated from life, he feels that he's getting old—a situation underlined by the fact he needs glasses to read.

Once again, the original cast is supplemented by a newcomer, in this case Kristie Alley playing Lieutenant Saavik, a half-Vulcan, half-Romulan

who is Spock's protégée. It is she who is sitting in the Captain's chair when the film begins. Apparently, she is caught in a "no-win" situation. The Klingons are blasting the ship unmercifully, killing Dr. McCoy, Sulu, Uhura, and Mr. Spock. Only after their "deaths" does one wall pull away and blinding lights silhouette the form of Admiral Kirk.

It was all a training exercise which is actually a "final exam" for hopeful Federation officers to become captains. It is a famous test which only Kirk has ever successfully passed. All other officers are judged on how well they respond to the no-win scenario. The scene then shifts to the Federation ship *Reliant.* Captain Terrell (Paul Winfield) and First Officer Chekov are scouting barren planets for a final Project Genesis test. They "beam down" (transport through molecular rearrangement) to what they think is Ceti Alpha VI, only to find the remains of the *Botany Bay*—Khan's ship exiled by Captain Kirk years before.

The Federation men are captured by Khan's

group, and Khan himself (Ricardo Montalban, who also played the character on the TV episode) explains that Ceti Alpha VI was destroyed six months after his exile; making Ceti Alpha V a barren wasteland. He takes over Terrell and Checkov's brains with a "Ceti eel," a parasite which burrows in the ear and wraps itself around the cerebral cortex. Soon he has taken over the *Reliant* and is using Chekov to dupe Project Genesis head Dr. Carol Marcus (Bibi Besch).

Although her radio transmissions are being blocked by the *Reliant,* she gets a message through to Kirk, who is on board the *Enterprise* for a training mission. Although the crew is mostly inexperienced, now-Captain Spock feels they are ready for what appears to be a dangerous mission. The

Vulcan is absolutely correct. The *Reliant* blasts the *Enterprise* when it appears, severely damaging the engines and killing Scotty's nephew (Ike Eisenmann; his character's relationship to the engineer was not revealed in the final version of the film— but unlike Ilia's and Decker's in the first movie, this relationship was not necessary to explain).

It is only Kirk's greater experience that saves the ship, establishing the framework of the subsequent battle. Throughout the film, Kirk's experience and cunning will always defeat Khan's revenge-motivated superior intellect. The tortured Terrell leads Khan to the Genesis Device, a missile shaped machine that can destroy planets before rebuilding them (introduced in a lovely computer animated sequence).

Helmsman Sulu (George Takei), Admiral Kirk (William Shatner), communications officer Uhura (Michelle Nichols), and Dr. McCoy (DeForest Kelley) approach the refurbished Starship *Enterprise* in *Star Trek II.*

Although Khan has the upper hand, Kirk taunts him and lures him into a nebula—a mass of celestial gas and dust—which blocks both their sensors. The ships are heavily damaged and both are flying blind; hoping to destroy each other by luck. Again, Kirk's experience leads him to get behind the *Reliant* and blast it to near destruction. But just before he dies, Khan turns on the Genesis Device. The damaged engine of the Starship *Enterprise* can't get the craft out of range in time.

The engine's power source of dilithium crystals needs to be replaced, but that cannot be done by anyone without unavailable means of protection. It seems that all the crew can do is wait for the end. Suddenly Mr. Spock rises and marches down to the engine room. Both the injured Scotty and the attending Dr. McCoy can see what's on his mind. Although Bones tries to stop him, Spock pulls two weapons out of his alien repertory.

First the "Vulcan Nerve Pinch" which renders McCoy unconscious. And then the "Vulcan Mind Meld," in which Spock's only spoken word is "Remember." The question is, "Remember what?" This mystery, as greatly loved as was Yoda's "There is another," will be answered in the sequel. Spock enters the radiation-filled engine compartment and repairs some of the damage. The *Enterprise* streaks out of range just in time.

But Spock dies from his injuries. He is given a hero's funeral and his casket is left on the lush planet created by the Genesis explosion. Kirk, after a touching reunion with his and Marcus's grown son (Merritt Butrick), muses that if Genesis is life from death, Spock may not be gone too long. McCoy says the Vulcan will live in all their memories. And although Spock gave up his life, the adventure has made Kirk feel young again.

Star Trek II was originally to be called *The Undiscovered Country* and then *The Vengeance of Khan.* But when the third *Star Wars* movie was originally to be named *Revenge of the Jedi,* the title was changed to its present *Wrath* form (only to be made unnecessary when fans convinced Lucasfilm that "Revenge" was not part of the Jedi philosophy and it became *Star Wars: Return of the Jedi*). By any name, it is a fine achievement, a taut, involving movie underplayed for all its worth by actors who had been previously known for their bombastic performances.

The film fittingly ends with the famous *Star Trek* television series' narration—the opening lines read by William Shatner to introduce each TV episode. It was slightly changed to encompass the movie series and fittingly read by Leonard Nimoy, since *Star Trek III* has been subtitled *The Search for Spock.* "Space—the final frontier. These are the voyages of the Starship *Enterprise.* Its mission: to explore strange new worlds. To seek out new life and new civilizations. To boldly go where no one has gone before."

If *Star Trek II* is any evidence of their on-going approach, long may they voyage.

Admiral Kirk sees to it that everything is shipshape in the engine room, lorded over by James Doohan as Scotty.

MILITARY MANEUVERS

The United States' military image has been badly tarnished in the last few years. Between the horror of Vietnam and the disastrous attempt to rescue the Iranian hostages, the American military had been portrayed as incompetent in reality. This year, filmmakers sought to either reaffirm or counter that conception.

Endangered Species sought to reestablish the

232

Mr. Spock (Leonard Nimoy) gives up his li[fe] in *Star Trek II: The Wrath of Kha[n]*

kind of paranoia several 1978 films traded in. The CIA was out to get us again in their never-ending quest to make this nation number one in the world. According to this movie, written by Judson Klinger, Richard Woods, John Binder and Alan Rudolph, the insidious intelligence agency was creating and hushing up nerve gas experiments.

Nerve gas experiments were banned by the government in 1968, but the film theorizes that they are still going on and are responsible for the mysterious real-life cattle mutilations occurring in the midwest. Robert Urich stars as jaded, cynical, big-city cop Ruben Castle, who came out to the Colorado "sticks" for some peace and quiet. JoBeth Williams plays Sheriff Harriet (Harry) Purdue, a lawman intent on discovering why and how carved-up cows are dropping from the sky.

Alan Rudolph also directed this moody, murky thriller, livened by interesting characters, good performances and moments of high style. Unfortunately he has chosen to theorize on a true situation without hope of proving anything. While the movie's solution to the mutilation mystery makes for an intriguing set-up, the payoff is forced to be noncommittal and open-ended.

Did the CIA experiment on cattle? Were the bad guys government-sanctioned? Will the secret operatives continue to kill American citizens to keep the secret? Neither Washington nor *Endangered Species* will say, making the movie ultimately unsatisfying.

What *Megaforce* will say is that America is strong, America is good, America is always right. Much to America's detriment, *Megaforce* says it in the stupidest way possible. *Megaforce* started as a good idea: a thunderously patriotic war adventure in which an elite team of soldiers utilize the most advanced weaponry technology can offer in order to make the world safe from despots, dictators, and demented death dealers.

Unfortunately, James Whittaker, Albert S. Ruddy, Andre Morgan, and director Hal Needham wrote one of the most superficial, corny, and stale screenplays imaginable. The badly miscast Barry Bostwick plays Ace Hunter, the head of the puerile

Barry Bostwick leads the *Megaforce* and will not let freedom fighter Persis Khambatta join in.

Megaforce, a bunch of gung-ho soldiers decked out in skin-tight silver suits. Their mission is to stop a South American guerilla named Guerera (Henry Silva) from destroying the peaceful Latin community of Sardoun.

To rescue the helpless citizens, the Megaforce races to their rocket-firing, machine-gun-toting array of motorcycles, jeeps, and armored cars. They take on Guerera's tanks again and again, shooting and exploding things right and left, although not causing a single death—in fact, not one drop of blood is spilled in the entire pitched battle. Even so, Guerera is soundly defeated although personally unscratched. The Megaforce ride off into the sunset with the words; "The good guys always win. Even in the eighties."

As previously mentioned, it was a good idea, done extraordinarily poorly. *Megaforce* was unconvincing in every way and extremely dull.

Firefox has the same message as *Megaforce,* but says it quietly with a certain amount of credibility. That credibility comes mostly from star and director, Clint Eastwood, who had Alex Lasker and Wendell Wellman do a good job adapting Craig Thomas's novel. Eastwood plays Mitchell Gant, a traumatized Vietnam pilot who is called out of self-declared exile to accomplish an impossible mission—infiltrate Russia and steal their technologically advanced jet, the MIG 31. Code name: Firefox. He has the two prerequisites for the job; he can fly anything with wings and he speaks Russian.

Gant spends a suspense-laden hour and thirty-five minutes getting into the USSR and reaching the hangar where one of the two MIGs is housed. He does so by following a network of kamikaze rebels. A system of spies and moles (Soviet citizens sympathetic to freedom) who give up their lives so Gant might get Firefox to America. He accomplishes just that, walking right up to the aircraft, getting in and taking off—all under the Russians' very noses.

For the remaining forty minutes, Gant races the other MIG fighter back to safety. Not only must he refuel along an ice-cap, but he must think in Russian because the ultra-sensitive Firefox controls respond to the pilot's thoughts. Once the second MIG catches up with the first, the race becomes a high-action chase as the two ships try to outfly each other. Although Gant's Vietnam trauma of seeing a child napalmed threatens to return any second, his superior flying skills gain the respect of his Russian pursuer, allowing Gant just enough time to blow him out of the sky.

rected the movie, which he sold as a black comedy in the tradition of *Dr. Strangelove*, Stanley Kubrick's frighteningly funny view of the end of the world. Brooks's film was less apocalyptic and much less humorous. In fact, the humorous aspects of his tale only detract from the otherwise straight story.

The *Megaforce* attacks with their missile-firing motorcycles.

Firefox was not a completely successful film by any means. The combination of espionage drama, patriotic propaganda, and special-effects extravaganza (supplied by John Dykstra and company) did not meld seamlessly, but enough of each ingredient looked right to make it a job well done.

Wrong Is Right was a little less successful for different reasons. Richard Brooks wrote and di-

Sean Connery plays Patrick Hale, a famous TV commentator who is a combination Mike Wallace and Barbara Walters. He runs afoul of an Arab terrorist's (Henry Silva) deal to buy two atom bombs from an arms dealer (Hardy Kruger). When Katherine Ross, a CIA agent disguised as a journalist, is murdered while trying to get this information back to the States, it sets in motion a complex series of political and military events.

The president (George Grizzard) is in the midst of a particularly ugly re-election campaign while being pressured by General Wombat (Robert Conrad) to blow the Arab nation off the map and take control of the oil fields. Another CIA agent (John Saxon) teams with Hale to track down the bombs while the television network chief (Robert Web-

straight, Brooks's attempt to make *Wrong Is Right* funny kills whatever acceptance the movie might have gained.

All the sets look artificial, all the colors exaggerated, and many scenes are over-played, damaging viewers' belief in the story. Instead of a thought-provoking comedy, it is a snide movie, ap-

Clint Eastwood is Mitchell Gant, the man who infiltrates Russia to steal the jet called *Firefox*.

ber) only wants more and more juicy news. But only the canny head of the CIA (G.D. Spradlin) knows what is really going on.

He plants two fake bombs in New York to make it seem the terrorist is threatening the U.S., so the government has the excuse to unleash Wombat and his men. The film ends with Hale joining Wombat in parachuting into the devastated Arab nation. Although somewhat entertaining if taken

parently made by someone who was afraid the audience wouldn't accept a serious statement unless it was masked by feeble jokes.

BIG BIRDS AND OTHER "THINGS"

Science-fiction monsters reared their ugly heads in mass numbers again this season. Various cheap filmmakers hadn't exploited every ounce of *Alien*'s effects yet. *Forbidden World* was New World's

237

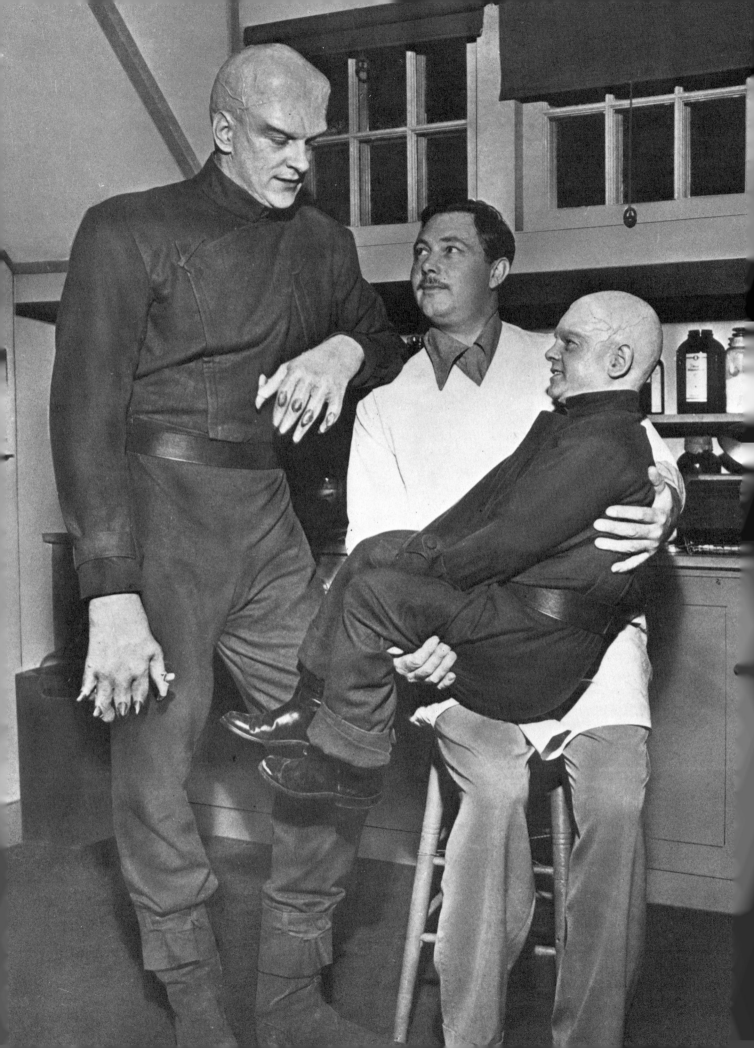

followup to *Galaxy of Terror*, and, if anything, was even more gruesome. A monster invades a space lab and kills most everyone in really awful ways. The truly disgusting climax has a valiant doctor killing the beast by feeding it a cancerous liver.

Alien Contamination wasn't much better, even though it was the latest work of Italian filmmaking fan Luigi Cozzi/Lewis Coates. This was his inexpensive, tacky idea of what would happen if the *Alien* eggs had reached Earth. Just to be even more graphic, the eggs do not contain "Face Huggers" but liquid that makes human internal organs explode.

After these repugnant films, Larry Cohen's *Q* was like a breath of old-fashioned oxygen. Although somewhat bloody at times, it seemed like "The Bobbsey Twins Meet Godzilla" after the repulsive ingredients of the preceding pictures. His is a modern fable, originally called *The Winged Serpent*, about a sleazy, small-time hood (Michael Moriarty) finding the nest of a mythical pterodactyl in Manhattan's Chrysler Building.

David Carradine plays a believing policeman who traces the possibility that this big bird is responsible for a series of highrise murders. He discovers that the remnants of an ancient Aztec sect has brought the creature back to life through skin-peeling rites. Moriarty holds the city for ransom, promising to lead the cops to the nest for a million dollars.

The city reneges on the deal but does corner Quetzlcoatl (pronounced Kewetz-a-quatle) in its lair, finally bringing the giant bird down *King Kong*-style by riddling its hide with bullets. Carradine then saves Moriarty from the angry and vengeful sect, but at the last minute another bird is shown being born in the attic of a New York house.

Q is a quirky, cheaply produced movie with artificial-looking model animation effects by Dave Allen, but it can be enjoyed as a combination homage and lampoon of the "giant monster on the loose" genre.

Silent Rage reintroduced the concept of "Frankenstein's Monster." Scientists brainlessly give amazing regenerative powers and invulnerability to a homicidal maniac named John Kirby (Brian Libby) simply because he's the only guinea pig

around. Kirby thanks them by wiping out much of the small midwestern town he lives in. Only Sheriff Dan Stevens (Chuck Norris), who originally arrested him for killing his own family, stands in his way.

When Kirby isn't stalking and killing people in the best tradition of movies like *Friday the 13th* and *Halloween*, Stevens is beating up motorcycle gang members, romancing town beauty Allison Halman (Toni Kalem), and having his overweight deputy (Stephen Furst) provide comedy relief. The final confrontation between superman Kirby and martial artist Stevens results in the killer being pushed down a well where he will either starve to death or live uselessly forever.

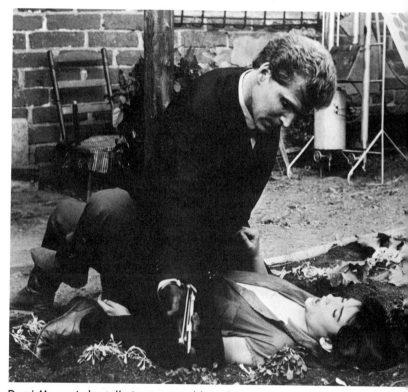

Demi Moore is brutally interrogated by "The Merchant" (James Davidson), a hitman intent on capturing the *Parasite*.

This is a terrible movie, ridiculous and exploitative. It attempts to pander to every audience interest and does so in an obvious, mercenary way.

Parasite was better in the plot department, but worse in its mercenary approach. This, like several films before it, was a motion picture made to see

e original "Thing," James Arness (left), relaxes in
e makeup room along with a technician and the
dget who will make it look as if *The Thing* has
runk.

239

just how grotesque it could be. Besides some clever futuristic touches, all it did was exploit a new dimensional camera. The effort was proclaimed "The First Futuristic Monster Movie in 3-D!"

Alan Adler, Michael Shoob, and Frank Levering wrote the tale of a scientist (Robert Glaudini) running away from the all-powerful Zyrex Corporation with the horrible results of his experiments in a thermos and his own stomach. It takes place in the inflation-gripped world of the near future where gas costs fifty dollars a gallon and paper money is useless. The scientist stumbles into a small town and is captured by a motorcycle gang.

The bikers foolishly open the thermos and unleash a parasite (nicknamed Percy by the film crew) who feeds on human organs until the body is just a skin shell. The scientist wants to save the world from these things, but a corporate assassin (James Davidson) wants to use them for world conquest. This allows the rest of the film to alternate fight scenes between the antagonists with parasite slaughter scenes, in which the parasite explodes out of heads and does other horrid things.

The climax is suitably pessimistic, with the scientist removing a second parasite from his tummy, throwing it on the hitman and then setting both aflame. But he had already established that even the monster's molecules could reproduce, so the flames of the fire are only spreading parasite terror. *Parasite* seemed made for viewers who like their dialogue unnatural and their gore plentiful. The movie didn't make much sense, it just moved quickly along and was shameless in its depiction of violence.

Compared to the other films in this category, *Swamp Thing* looks like Bambi. Producers Michael Uslan and Benjamin Melnicker in addition to writer/director Wes Craven adapted the DC Comics character with care and consideration. Most filmmakers seem to think that the words "comic book" denote bright colors, odd camera angles, and juvenile dialogue. Craven knew that most modern comic books were more sophisticated and poetic.

So the first half of *Swamp Thing* did not talk down to viewers. Ray Wise played Dr. Alec Holland, a man intent on developing food plants that would grow anywhere, turning deserts and, yes, swamps into lush, fertile farmland. He enjoys the life-teeming swamp so much that he has located his secret lab in the midst of one. The government sends agent Alice Cable (Adrienne Barbeau) into the undergrowth to serve as his bodyguard, but she arrives just in time to witness a savage attack by the forces of industrialist Ethan Arcane (Louis Jourdan).

The millionaire wants to control the green, glowing, growing formula himself. He kills Holland's assistant—Holland's sister—and then accidentally splashes the poison on Holland himself. He bursts into flame and runs screaming into the swamp. Rising from his ashes is the Swamp Thing—a crud-encrusted, vaguely humanoid giant embodying Holland's intellect. While Cable tries to escape Arcane's men in the company of a world-wise black boy (Reggie Batts), the Swamp Thing wanders around.

Occasionally he meets up with his enemy's men, but instead of killing them, just throws them around. Only when a sadistic aide chops off his arm and threatens Cable directly does the Swamp Thing crush his skull. Even so, Arcane captures them all and puts them in a dungeon below his mansion. He tests the serum on another one of his aides while Cable discovers that the formula is regenerative—Holland's arm is growing back like a tree limb.

Arcane realizes that the serum, when ingested, turns the ingester into a monstrous version of whatever his human personality is. His assistant becomes a midget rat. Arcane partakes of the potion and turns into a combination of a lion and a ferret. The midget rat releases Cable and Holland and leads them to the swamp. Arcane appears, only to be beaten—apparently to death—by the Swamp Thing.

Although Cable suffers a mortal wound in the fracas, Swamp Thing rubs the injury with some of his body's slime, which also turns out to be regenerative. After bringing Cable back to life, he merely walks back into the swamp, never to be seen again. *Swamp Thing* is enthralling until Holland becomes the monster. After that, the picture becomes meandering and indecisive.

Swamp Thing wasn't the only "thing" in movies this year. Producers David Foster, Lawrence Turman, and Stuart Cohen decided to remake the 1951 classic *The Thing from Another World*, directed by Christian Nyby and produced by Howard Hawks. A better tale of men versus

240

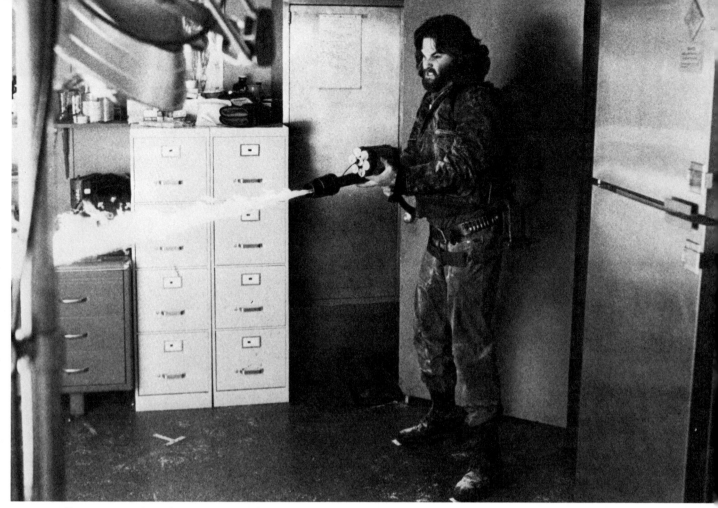

Kurt Russell attempts to fry *John Carpenter's The Thing*.

monster could hardly be done. This story of an Arctic expedition's battle against a beast made of vegetable matter was handled with great realism and great style. All the characters were believable and the humanoid monster (assayed by then-bit-player James Arness) was legitimately mysterious and threatening.

What the 1982 producers were looking for was something closer in tone to the original story by John W. Campbell entitled *"Who Goes There?"* In that award-winning novella, the monster was a chameleon—something that could change its shape, so that identifying it was just as important as killing it. That concept captured the imaginations of the producers as well as director John Carpenter. They hired screenwriter Bill Lancaster and set to work realizing their vision.

The title of the remake was *John Carpenter's The Thing*, so it is the director who must take most of the blame for the grisly, misconceived movie. The basic story remains unchanged. An American Arctic outpost is suddenly invaded by a murderous

creature. But instead of fashioning a strong action film with accurate depictions of intrepid human beings reacting under stress, Carpenter's film spotlighted the mutations of the monster, while failing to present the characters in a believable way.

The height of the absurdity comes when the supposed hero (Kurt Russell) says to a burly black man who wears an earring, "This thing can change its shape. One of us isn't who he appears to be." To which the muscular black man doesn't blink an eye, merely replying, "Then how do we know which one of us is human?" Such instantaneous acceptance of an impossibility has never been so blandly or calmly done. This was but one of the personality oversights the film is rife with.

The special makeup effects were absolutely spectacular, what with teeth-lined torsoes opening up, heads sprouting spider-legs and eye stalks, dog heads ripping open and growing tentacles, and many other nauseating images, but the work was practically for naught since the threatened charac-

241

ters were not convincing or likeable. As a noxious special-effects showcase, *John Carpenter's The Thing* was exceptional. As a movie it was nearly a total bust.

After about an hour of gross goings-on interrupted by misplaced comedy relief, the two survivors (Keith David and Kurt Russell) just sit around waiting to be frozen to death since their outpost had been blown up in an attempt to kill The Thing. The monster's fate is never revealed, making the preceeding adventure all the more useless. *John Carpenter's The Thing* was important in that it shows clearly that a movie can only succeed on its characters and story, no matter how magnificent its special effects are.

I HAVE SEEN THE FUTURE AND IT DOESN'T WORK

The major releases of the year were evenly divided into two categories: pessimistic and optimistic. There were two films in each category. The smallest of all the films in terms of budget and distribution was *Death Watch*. Quartet Films Incorporated released this French-made movie filmed in English. Sensitive French director Bertrand Tavernier also co-wrote the screenplay with David Rayfiel—based on D.G. Compton's novel *The Unsleeping Eye*.

Tavernier's best-known previous film was *The Clockmaker* (1973), concerning a watchmaker who must reexamine his life after his son is arrested for murder. *Death Watch* is directed just as meticulously and contains as much texture and density of emotion as that human drama. In this film's future, all appears exactly as it does today except medicine has won its battle with disease. People die by accident, old age, starvation, or murder but they do not die from illness.

In this slightly off-center society, the most popular television series is "Death Watch." Directed by callow Vincent Ferriman (Harry Dean Stanton) and produced by a man known only as Roddy (Harvey Keitel), the network has "arranged" for a female writer (Romy Schneider) to die of a degenerative disease so the program can record her demise for its audience. At first, the writer, Katherine Mortenhoe, rejects the network's coverage, but when they offer her money to record her death, she accepts—then runs away.

The station was prepared for just such an even-

tuality. Roddy has been equipped with a micro-camera *inside* his head. Everything he sees is recorded on videotape. He is sent after Katherine, assigned to worm his way into her confidence and record her slow expiration. He succeeds all too

Harvey Keitel stars as the producer of the ghoulish television series *Death Watch*, a man who is chronicling the demise of a terminally ill writer played by Romy Schneider.

well, but while she comes to trust him, he comes to love her.

In the end, he cannot continue the deception. Rather than betray her with his eyes, he blinds himself. *Death Watch* is a special film, carefully and morally crafted with a refreshing humanistic approach. It trumpeted the nobility of the human condition rather than degrading it with gratuitous violence or overwhelming it with flashy special effects.

Blade Runner was almost all flash and no substance. It, more than any other science-fiction effort, points up the difference between a "film" and a "movie." "Film" is technical, "movies" are stories. So while *Blade Runner* could be a fabulous film, it was a bad movie. Its technical achievements were marvelous, but its plot did not hold water.

When asked what he wanted to do after helming *Alien*, director Ridley Scott said he wanted to explore the possibilities of doing "a real science-fiction picture." *Blade Runner* was the result. It was based on Philip K. Dick's novel *Do Androids Dream of Electric Sheep* in which a hunter had to track down androids smuggled in from Mars. During his hunt for the illegal imports, the man also discovers that the messiah they are all following may be fake. Translating Dick's existential and dense prose into images seemed to be a greater challenge than anyone was up to.

Robert Jaffe did an initial script, lampooning the original book. David Fancher did two scripts, titled *The Android* and *Dangerous Days*, which were extremely reminiscent of hard-boiled detective novels. When Scott entered the project, David Peoples was brought in for another rewrite which met everyone's approval, even that of Philip K. Dick himself. The sparsely populated world had become the wildly over-populated Los Angeles of the year 2019. The hunter was named Deckard (Harrison Ford), a cynical defeatist who is forced out of retirement for one more job.

He's recruited by his bigoted ex-boss because he's "the best" in the business. His business was being a Blade Runner, a hunter of exact robot duplicates of people. The term "blade runner" is never explained in the film, nor is how Deckard could be "the best" when he appears to be the worst detective imaginable—stolid, cowardly, unimaginative and foolhardy. His only talent seems to be the ability to shoot straight with a nifty explosive-shooting gun.

"Replicants," which was the film's way of saying "androids," had been created by the Tyrell Corporation. Tyrell's (Joe Turkell) four masterpieces, each equipped with an "automatic turn-off" device, had escaped and were desperately searching for a way to prevent their automatic turn-offs. They had lost themselves among the millions of city residents and were leaving a trail of dead bodies in their wake.

Deckard manages to track down and kill one,

Ridley Scott (right) directs Harrison Ford, who plays Deckard, the *Blade Runner*.

Bruce Boxleitner plays *Tron*, the best "disk warrior"
inside a computer.

but is assaulted and badly beaten by another. He
is about to be killed when Tyrell's beautiful and
mysterious assistant, Rachel (Sean Young), saves
his life. Much to her horror and his vacuous
dismay, she turns out to be another perfect replicant. She remains in his apartment while he continues the search. He closes in on the remaining
two replicants as they gain entry to Tyrell's private
home. There, the replicant leader (Rutger Hauer)
kisses and then kills his creator.

Deckard corners and kills the third replicant just
before the leader breaks his trigger finger. The two
have a cat-and-mouse chase through the crumbling
building until they reach the roof. In Scott's future
city, the skyscrapers have become so tall they make
the Empire State Building look like a cottage.
Rather than face the super-strong leader, Deckard
tries jumping to the roof of another building. He
just manages to hang onto the ledge.

The replicant leader leaps to the roof with ease
and sits in the pouring rain silently. Just as Deckard is about to fall, the last replicant suddenly
reaches out and pulls the hunter to safety. Then
he dies. A police hovercraft lands in the next few
seconds (as if it had been watching the whole time)
and the driver, the bigoted boss's assistant (Edward James Olmos), says something strange about

Rachel, like, "too bad the girl has to die." Deckard
returns to his apartment, collects the girl he professes his love to and drives out of the city.

Up until this point, *Blade Runner* was a strong,
endlessly interesting movie to watch. The plot was
pretty weak, but the incredible production and art
design was awe-inspiring. If what the actors said
ranged from pretentious to pseudo-meaningful,
everything on and around them was spectacular.
The costumes, makeup, sets, props, and special
effects were first rate.

But then, suddenly, the movie takes a *Damnation Alley* turn in its last sixty seconds. Just outside the city is the most beautiful acreage this side
of Shangri-La. Rolling hills and lush foilage
abound without pollution in sight. The amazing
stupidity of this finale, where Deckard says that
everybody has to die sooner or later so he could
live with Rachel's automatic termination, negates
all the rich attention to detail that went before.
Blade Runner was a collection of film sets in
search of a movie.

I HAVE SEEN THE FUTURE
AND IT WORKS

Tron is the most important movie Walt Disney
Productions has made since Walt Disney died. It

David Warner plays Sark, the Master Control
Program's evil aide in *Tron*.

is important for two reasons. First, it was made
by outside talent. Rather than depending on their
staff to develop the story, Disney Studios accepted
the work of outside filmmakers. Second, and most
important, *Tron* was the first of its kind. Disney
Productions was not jumping on anybody else's
bandwagon with this movie; this was a unique experiment that was Disney's own.

If any bandwagon-jumping could be charged,
it would be for exploiting the success of video-
games. But even that contention is not exactly true.
While pre-premiere publicity gave the impression
that *Tron* concerned a video game come to life,
it actually told of an adventure inside a computer.
It was an adventure written by Steve Lisberger,
who had directed a winning animated satire of the
Olympics and television sports reporting called
Animalympics (1979).

Lisberger had already conceived and story-
boarded the film when he approached Disney
Studios with it. His audacious concept to com-
bine black-and-white live-action film (that would
be colored by hand) with computer animation intrigued the studio. They financed a test, and were
so encouraged by the results that they went ahead
with the production. Jeff Bridges was cast as
Flynn, a computer programmer who has had the

designs of his "Space Paranoids" video game
stolen by his immediate superior, Dillinger (David
Warner).

Since that time, Flynn has been drummed out
of the company and Dillinger has become the head
of the Encom Corporation—exploiting his noble
workers' achievements for his own advancement.
But he met his match after instituting the Master
Control Program (MCP) in Encom's computer
system. This powerful program was megalomaniacal in its finding and assimilating other programs
from all sorts of computer systems.

Dillinger is warned of this, and of the human
spirit which goes into the making of computer programs, by Walter Gibs (Barnard Hughes), Encom's
oldest employee. His words are prophetic, since
programs are seen in human form inside the computer. The MCP's right-hand man is called Sark
and looks just like Dillinger. The guard of the base
that links programs with their "users"—their pro-
grammers—is Dumont, who looks just like Gibs.

Programs have been fighting the MCP since its
inception, but the MCP is stronger. Those programs it can't use it puts on the "game grid," where
they are "derezzed"—from "deresolution"—for
Sark's amusement. What brings the fight to a head
is Flynn's intent to raid the computer to find in-

245

Tron also features fabulous computer animation, as in this light-cycle sequence.

criminating evidence against Dillinger. He is helped by programmer Alan Bradley (Bruce Boxleitner), who has been trying to write a policing program to control the MCP, and his girlfriend Lora (Cindy Morgan), who has been working in the computer "genesis" department. She and Gibs have just succeeded in actually transferring organic matter into an electronic counterpart inside the computer ("digitalizing it down").

When Flynn sits down to explore the MCP, it retaliates by digitalizing him into the computer. Suddenly he is thrust among the captive programs, where he meets Ram (Dan Shor) and, the best game-grid warrior of them all, Tron (also Box-

leitner). All the actors who performed "inside" the computer were filmed on a sound stage wearing white outfits with black lines drawn on them. Through a camera and animation process, these lines were given color.

For the fights on the game grid, computer animation companies like Information International Incorporated, Bob Abel and Associates, and Digital Effects were asked to deliver more than fifty minutes of computer animation. Up until now this technique was used in only limited capacities in movies like *Futureworld, Looker,* and *Star Trek II.* Now here was a movie that depended upon them.

Sark puts Flynn through the game-grid challenges, but neither he nor the MCP know what powers the human has in the computerized world. When teamed up with Ram and Tron in a "light-cycle" duel, he leads an escape outside the game grid. There he discovers a weird world vaguely similar to Encom. Although Ram loses power and derezzes, Tron finds Lora's electronic alter-ego, Yori, and sets off to destroy the MCP.

Dumont allows Tron to communicate with his user, Alan Bradley, who programs enough power into Tron's "disk"—essentially a powerful fris-bee—to destroy the MCP. Flynn uses his regenerative powers to change the color of his suit (there-

by infiltrating the red-lined MCP troops) and bring Yori back from the dead when her power drains. Finally, to give Tron a chance to slip his disk inside the MCP's defenses, Tron leaps right into the MCP's center.

When the Master Control Program is destroyed, the computer world lights up, Flynn is automatically undigitalized in the real world, and the computer spits out the incriminating evidence against Dillinger. The film ends with Dillinger disgraced and Flynn the new head of Encom.

Tron was a combination of simplicities and complexities. The basic story of two boys and a girl destroying an evil force was simple. Many said their characters were simple. The truth is that their characters were totally dependent on the complexities of computer technicalities. Sad to say, one needed at least a basic understanding of how a computer works to fully enjoy the movie, and there just weren't enough audiences who had that knowledge yet.

The inner meaning of such details as digitalizing, deresolution, programs, bytes, disks, and even the characters' names took some knowledge of computer technology. Everyone agreed that the computer animation was stunning and the occasional sight gag (Pac-Man even appeared at one point) refreshed the effort, but any meaing *Tron* had was hidden in computer jargon.

Although the movie did not do as well as Disney Productions had hoped it would, it will be a film which will grow in stature as the public's knowledge of computers grows. Walt Disney Productions and Steven Lisberger can be proud to know that they made a film which was ahead of its time.

Released late in 1982, *E.T. The Extra-Terrestrial* became the most successful movie of all time by the start of 1983. Story-writer, co-producer and director Steven Spielberg made lightning strike four times. During the filming of *Raiders of the Lost Ark*, Spielberg told the story of a stranded alien to writer Melissa Mathison, who co-wrote *The Black Stallion* script. She was so enthralled by the concept that she slaved until a first draft was produced two months later.

The tale was of an outer-space alien who has the same emotional range as humans, although different abilities. When his exploratory ship is forced to leave without him, he is afraid. It is this fear and human longing that instantly sets E.T. apart from the creatures in other "alien contact" films. Even in Spielberg's own *Close Encounters*, the aliens are pictured as assured and masterful. The other thing that sets the film apart from something like *The Man from Planet X* (1951)— which also concerned a misunderstood extraterrestrial—was the wealth of identifiable reality Spielberg crams into the movie.

His children act the way real children do, not movie kids. Or, at least, his children act the way audiences feel real children do. His comedic situations seem to arise effortlessly, brought on by characters' personalities or identifiable human ex-

perience. One of the best laughs in the picture is brought on by E.T.'s going out on Halloween and following a child dressed like Yoda.

Henry Thomas plays Elliot, the ten-year-old son of a divorced mother, played by Dee Wallace. He has an older brother (Robert MacNaughton) and a younger sister (Drew Barrymore) and they all live in the suburbs. One night he hears some noise out in the tool shed. Upon investigation, he is scared silly by an alien with a tiny body, no legs to speak of, arms as long as his torso, a bulbous head and a neck which can elongate.

Although initially petrified, Elliot becomes intrigued and lures the creature into his room with candy (when M&Ms' manufacturer refused to let their product be used, Spielberg switched to Reese's Pieces). Slowly, but surely, the two learn from one another, establishing a psychic bond, a bond that is celebrated in a magnificent sequence in which E.T. makes Elliot's bicycle fly. The alien also has a healing touch and a luminous red heart.

All the time the two are getting to know each other the alien is stalked by faceless government men, the same men who forced E.T.'s ship to take off prematurely. Soon Elliot's brother and sister know about the extraterrestrial and help him learn English. Using a variety of household items, like a fork, a coffee can, and a record player, E.T. builds a device to "phone home." He wants to contact his ship to pick him up.

But as the government officials close in, the alien's health worsens. Spielberg conceived it as a natural reaction of an alien's biology to Earth's environment. Without a space suit, the creature just can't survive for too long. The government scientists move in on the house just as E.T.'s condition deteriorates. As far as they can tell with all their instruments, E.T. is dead—the psychic bond between it and Elliot is broken.

They put E.T. in a decompression chamber for later study and leave Elliot alone with his friend for a moment. That is just what the alien needed. The decompression chamber renews him like sleep renews humans. Elliot quickly collects his brother and hatches an escape plan. Stealing a government van, they ride to meet his brother's friends and they all outrace police cars on their bicycles. Once more E.T. levitates the bikes and flies all the kids to the rendezvous point.

The alien ship lands. E.T. and Elliot embrace. The extraterrestrial goes home.

There was hardly a dry eye in any theater all over the world. Although the climactic moments could stretch credulity in the cold light of reality, Spielberg's movie clicked. A vast majority of the audience was so enthralled by the time the climax came, they did not care how Spielberg and Mathison did it—they just wanted that alien to live again and get away.

E.T. The Extra-Terrestrial richly deserved its success. It may be a curmudgeon's target, but it is most people's delight. As Spielberg has said, "It's about human values. It's about the understanding people have toward one another. It's about compassion and love."

It is nice that a movie about those subjects became the biggest film success of all time in an age in which callous brutality and ugly titillation are the norm.

And with *E.T.* came the end of an era. An era in which science-fiction films were loved only by science-fiction enthusiasts. Science-fiction movies are no longer a cult secret. The top-grossing film lists are rife with them. The future of the motion picture industry will be dotted with *Star Wars*, James Bond and Indiana Jones; crossed with *Superman, Star Trek*, and *E.T.* 1982 is the end of an era—now science fiction belongs to everyone.

Steven Spielberg directs Henry Thomas in a scene from *E.T. The Extra-Terrestrial*.

9

AFTERWORD
RETURN OF THE JEDI

"I'VE GOT A BAD FEELING ABOUT THIS . . . ."

THE NEW WAVE ERA of science-fiction films comes to a close with the summer of 1983 release of *Return of the Jedi*, the third *Star Wars* movie. Otherwise known as "Episode VI" in the *Star Wars* saga, it ends the trilogy of tales concerning

Luke Skywalker's personal battle with Darth Vader and the Empire. If box office returns are any evidence, it was probably the most eagerly awaited movie in history, not to mention in the genre.

Fan hysteria built to a fever pitch before its premiere. Stories raged in the press concerning the

250

most absurd of topics. Security was so tight on the set that when they had to do on-location work in America, the filmmakers disguised themselves as a production crew for a non existent film called *Blue Harvest*. The necessary deception was played to the hilt, up to and including the wearing of caps and jackets bearing the *Blue Harvest* name and logo.

The height of the stupidity and hysteria came with the change of the movie's title, *Revenge of the Jedi*. For months, rabid fans had been all but screaming that the word "revenge" was not in a Jedi's vocabulary. One particularly ridiculous report denounced producer and storywriter George Lucas for his "greed" because they considered "revenge" a far more exploitive word than "return" (in truth, the film could have been called *Skywalker Has a Sandwich* for all the difference it made). Some people even had the gall to publicly state that they knew more about the *Star Wars* universe than Lucas did.

What none of these people took into consideration was that they were taking words George Lucas had written for Ben Obi-Wan Kenobi for granted. They were assuming that all the things Kenobi said about the Jedis were true. They did not realize that in this third movie, Kenobi would be revealed as, essentially, a liar. They also were not aware of just which Jedi was going to have revenge. It was Darth Vader, not Luke Skywalker, who was to have vengeance.

The Empire has recuperated from its initial setbacks by building a new planet-sized space destroyer, the Death Star II. Personally supervising the completion of the craft is Darth Vader (David Prowse) and the Emperor himself—a wizened, cackling, cowled sorcerer with blanched, wrinkled skin (Ian McDiarmid).

Meanwhile all the main rebel fighters have returned to Luke Skywalker's home planet of Tantooine to rescue Han Solo (Harrison Ford). You'll remember that last time Solo was freeze-dried in a block of carbonite and taken to crimelord Jabba the Hutt by bounty hunter Boba Fett (Jeremy Bulloch). Jabba is revealed to be a gigantic slug-like worm (controlled by puppeteers Toby Philpott, Mike Edmonds, and David Barclay) who keeps a bunch of monsters and captive slave-girls around him at all times.

Luke Skywalker (Mark Hamill) sets his plan in motion by sending robots R2-D2 (Kenny Baker) and C-3PO (Anthony Daniels) to Jabba with a message. Then Princess Leia (Carrie Fisher) shows up disguised as another bounty hunter—named Boussh—who wants to sell Chewbacca the Wookie (Peter Mayhew) to the slimy crime boss. She only gets as far as thawing Solo out before they are both recaptured.

Finally Skywalker himself shows up, promising Jabba death if it doesn't comply with his wishes. Instead, Jabba makes Leia another slave-girl and throws Luke to a man-eating monster called Rancor. Luke defeats the beast (in actuality, a small model animated creation given believable life through the process called "go-motion") by dropping the heavy gate of its own cage on it. Jabba is so irritated by its pet's death that it sentences the three—Han, Luke, and Chewie—to die in a sand creature called a Sarlacc that digests its food over hundreds of years.

Just before he is to walk the plank off a "Sail Barge" (a ship that skims over the surface of Tan-

Supercilious robot C-3PO (Anthony Daniels) considers the various creatures that makeup wizard Stuart Freeborn and Phil Tippett created for "Chapter VI" of the *Star Wars* saga.

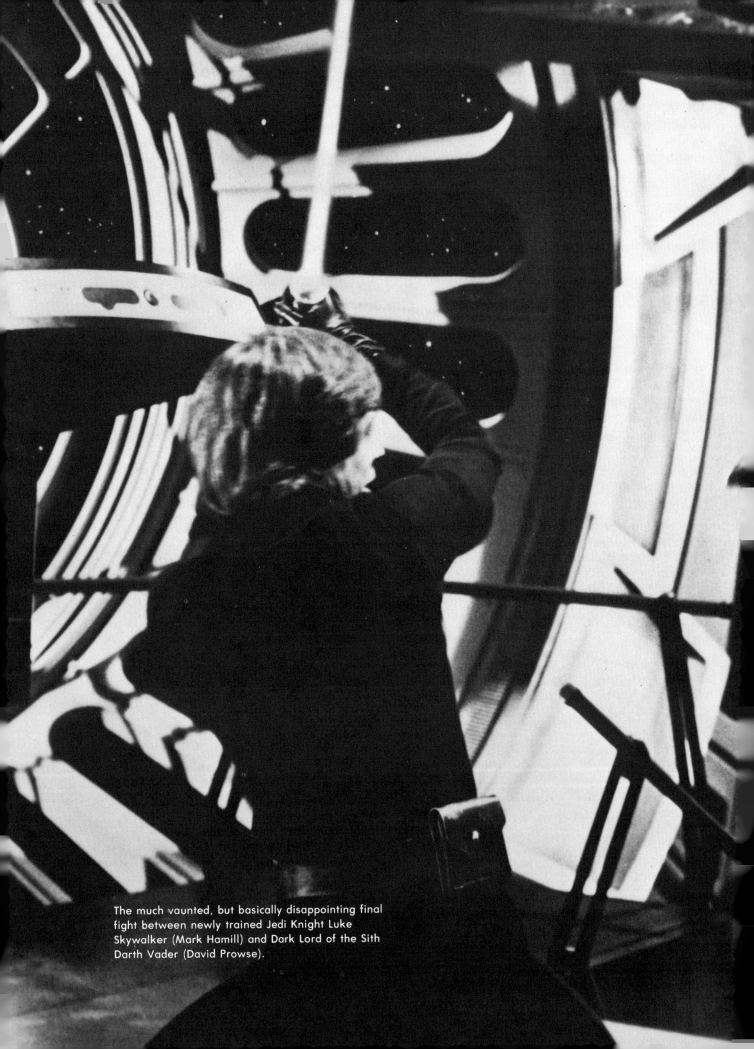

The much vaunted, but basically disappointing final fight between newly trained Jedi Knight Luke Skywalker (Mark Hamill) and Dark Lord of the Sith Darth Vader (David Prowse).

tooine), Luke makes his move. R2-D2 ejects Skywalker's light saber from inside its body, Luke catches it in mid-air and the fight is on. Leia strangles Jabba with the chain that imprisoned her, Solo accidentally sets off Boba Fett's jet pack, which sends the bounty hunter careening off of Jabba's ship and into the sand creature, and Lando Calrissian (Billy Dee Williams) reveals himself from disguise as one of Jabba's guards.

The group gets away and heads for the newly built Death Star, in orbit around the planet Endor. Thanks to some handy secrets that spies have revealed, the Rebel Alliance plans to deal a death blow to the Empire. Han Solo is to lead a group on the moon of Endor to destroy the Death Star's force shield and Calrissian is to lead rebel fighters inside the Death Star to destroy it from within. But before Luke can join them, he has to get some things straightened out on the planet Degobah.

He arrives just in time to see Yoda the Jedi Master die and disappear before his eyes, but not before saying that he must face Darth Vader, his own father, before he can become a complete Jedi. Then Ben Kenobi appears to reveal that Darth is indeed Luke's Dad, that his story of Darth murdering Mr. Skywalker was a bit exaggerated, and that Princess Leia is actually Luke's twin sister.

The main troop is reunited to attack the Endor Moon Empire Outpost. There they discover a tree-covered world crawling with Imperial Biker Scouts —Empire Stormtroopers equipped with air-cycles that can travel through the trees at speeds close to 200 miles per hour. They also discover that it is a "Planet of Killer Teddy Bears." The main inhabitants are "Ewoks"—cuddly little fur-covered creatures bearing an uncomfortable resemblance to the late H. Beam Piper's creations, the "Little Fuzzies."

For no apparent reason, they think C-3PO is a deity and worship him while planning to cook and eat the others. Only after Luke uses some of his Jedi levitating power do they see the light. Luke also sees the light, realizing that Vader can "sense" his presence. Instead of leading Darth to them, Luke goes to confront his evil father, certain that he can lure him back from the Dark Side of the Force.

Captured, and in Vader's company, Luke discovers that the whole setup is a trap to destroy the Rebel Alliance once and for all. He watches

Lando Calrissian (Billy Dee Williams) at the controls of the *Millenium Falcon* in the company of jive-talking co-pilot Nien Numb.

helplessly as the Imperial fleet starts decimating the Alliance's ships, while Han, Leia, Chewie and the others are surrounded on Endor. The Ewoks save the day by attacking the Stormtroopers, while Luke can no longer control his temper. He lashes out at the Emperor with his light saber, prompting a battle between Darth and himself.

The Emperor loves every second of it, knowing that Skywalker's rage and hate will inevitably lead him to the Dark Side. Luke tries to control himself, but when Vader psychically discovers the existence of his twin sister, Luke attacks full force, resulting in Darth's hand being chopped off the way Luke's had been in *The Empire Strikes Back*.

Finally, Solo and company destroy the Force Shield, Lando and company attack the Death Star, and Luke manages to control himself. He vows never to be on the Dark Side. "I am a Jedi," he declares, "like my father before me." The Emperor responds by bathing Luke in lightning bolts that

shoot out of his fingers. Watching his son cringe under the Emperor's death rays proves too much for Darth (not to mention hearing the Emperor admonish Luke to "kill Vader and join me"). He kills the Emperor himself, but not before taking the brunt of the sorcerer's electric power.

As Lando pilots the *Millenium Falcon* inside the Death Star, Luke drags his father to an escape craft. There, Darth asks him to remove the mask that keeps him alive so he can look upon his son with his own eyes. Inside the mask is actor Sebastian Shaw, inexplicably playing Annakin Skywalker, Luke's father, otherwise known as Darth Vader (why they didn't use David Prowse's face has not been explained).

His threat and evil is now totally drained from him, and as Calrissian destroys the Death Star, Luke escapes with his father's body. The movie ends on Endor as the Rebel Alliance celebrates with the Ewoks, complete with fireworks and a funeral pyre for Darth Vader. Luke looks off into the distance, only to see the ghostly apparitions of Yoda, Annakin and Kenobi standing side by side.

More than thirty million dollars were spent and an army of Lucasfilm employees toiled in an effort to bring *Return of the Jedi* to life. The result put most of the 1983 science-fiction films to shame, but sadly, the movie was not all it could have been. Responsibility for that rests at the top—with screenwriters Lawrence Kasdan and George Lucas and especially director Richard Marquand.

Return of the Jedi did not have the vitality of the original *Star Wars*, or the grandeur and style of *The Empire Strikes Back*. The late S-F author Leigh Brackett's contribution to the second film is all the more apparent in comparison to the newest film's script. All the major characters seem to be doing "versions" of themselves, rather than actually existing.

The overuse of lines and images is another example of the makeshift script. Three different characters burp as comedy relief within the first half-hour and the phrase "I've got a bad feeling about this" is used constantly, not to mention "Obi-wan has taught you well." Even worse, all the fascinating plot twists introduced in *Empire* were practically dropped like hot potatoes. The character of Boba Fett and the identity of the "other one" Yoda spoke of are dealt with and eliminated without contributing anything to the story—giving greater credence to the previously mentioned theory that they were safety ploys in case any of the main actors refused to assay their characters a third time.

Especially awkward were the single scenes with Yoda and Kenobi. They are all but cameo walk-ons in the film, simply serving as plot development. Yoda coughs a bit and dies almost immediately, while Kenobi explains away his almost outright lie concerning Darth's betrayal of the Jedi and alleged murder of Luke's father as "depending upon your point of view." Basically he's saying, "So I lied. What are you going to do about it?" In any other film, these cheap ploys would elicit groans. In *Return of the Jedi*, they are frustrating annoyances that keep the film from greatness.

255

These things could easily be forgiven if the live action had crackled with assurance. The battles and intimate scenes lack the strength and clarity they received in the first two films. The things that really sparkle are those that lie outside the domain of director Marquand—namely, the special effects.

Richard Edlund, Dennis Muren, Ken Ralston and their crews outdid themselves in that department, infusing the film with the "guts" it really needed to liven up the audience. All the technicians, in fact, were called on for yeoman duty above and beyond the previous movies. Creature creators Phil Tippett and Stuart Freeborn, sound effects man Ben Burtt, mechanical effects man Kit West, and production designer Norman Reynolds, among hundreds of others, deserve the loudest applause.

Although the majority of critics were lavish with their praise, several echoed similar negative sentiments. Except for the fish-like Admiral Ackbar (Tim Rose), everything oily and bile-drooling was bad and everything cuddly was good. All the Emperor needed was a long mustache and fingernails before his cliched resemblance and manner became identical with *Flash Gordon*'s "Ming the Merciless." The human rebels were mostly pictured as bland, almost zombie-like automotons, throwing the positive future of the galaxy in doubt. And the story just didn't hold together the way the previous films had.

It was hard for me not to long for a more cinematic fight between Luke and Darth, and a final confrontation between the wounded Darth, weakened Luke, and the evil Emperor—resulting in the surprise appearance of the "other one," Leia, to tip the scales. Perhaps this wish was the result of the less than inspired manner in which director Marquand staged the final battle, but whatever my reservations, *Return of the Jedi* still remains the crowning achievement of this new wave in science-fiction films.

It is now time for filmmakers to move on. To fill their films with challenging ideas, engaging characters and riveting stories, not just dazzling special effects and all too easily merchandiseable doll-critters. It is time for films that will so engage our hearts and minds that they will make *Return of the Jedi* seem shallow.

Robot R2-D2 (Kenny Baker) meets an "Ewok" whom most film goers saw as a lovable Teddy bear and most cynics saw as a blatant merchandising ploy.